MW00713229

INTEGRATING QUANTITATIVE AND QUALITATIVE METHODS IN RESEARCH

Third Edition

Edited by
George R. Taylor

University Press of America,® Inc.
Lanham · Boulder · New York · Toronto · Plymouth, UK

Copyright © 2010 by
University Press of America,® Inc.
4501 Forbes Boulevard
Suite 200
Lanham, Maryland 20706
UPA Acquisitions Department (301) 459-3366

Estover Road
Plymouth PL6 7PY
United Kingdom

Library of Congress Control Number: 2010935134
ISBN: 978-0-7618-5360-2 (clothbound : alk. paper)
ISBN: 978-0-7618-5361-9 (paperback : alk. paper)
eISBN: 978-0-7618-5362-6

Table of Contents

Part I
The Research Process

Part II
Quantitative and Qualitative Resource Methods

Part III

Differences Between Quantitative and Qualitative Research

List of Figures

List of Tables

Preface

This book grew out of experience in teaching and conducting statistics seminars to graduate students conducting research in the social sciences at Coppin State University and The Union Institute and University. Based upon students input, questions, and recommendations, the text was revised. Only the essential bases of the subject could be covered due to the time period in which the courses were offered. In teaching these students, it was found that the basic statistical and descriptive concepts could be readily understood when mathematical obstructions were reduced to practical application and non-numerical data were classified and reduced when the most complicated formulas and classification systems could be understood.

Some of the most fearful and dreaded moments of many graduate students are taking courses in statistics and research which are frequently required for advanced graduate degrees. Much of the anxiety experienced can be easily and readily reduced if students would consider both statistics and research as simply tools. They are systematically designed to bring order and logic to the research process. Since most statistical processes have formulas which have been validated and reliability established, the student can simply insert numerical data in the formulas and conduct simple addition, subtraction, multiplication, and division. We attempt to demystify the use of statistics and research by having students to adhere to the basic principles mentioned above.

This book carefully analyzed each quantitative and qualitative method and provides explanations as to when and why a particular method is employed. Attempts have been made to bridge the gap between qualitative and quantitative research. All examples have been selected on the basis of simplicity. The work sessions and problems at the end of each chapter are designed to add to the practical understanding of the material. Additionally, this book is primarily written for graduate consumers of research and statistics. Practical examples and illustrations have been provided to guide the student step-by-step through each quantitative and qualitative method, thus reducing much of the confusion and intimidation surrounding statistics and research.

Changes from the second edition. The essential structure of the book remains the same. All chapters have been updated with the current research in the field. The following new chapters have been added Case Study Methods, Chapter 10, Sampling Methods, Chapter 11, and Introduction Presentation Skills, Chapter 19.

Acknowledgements

The author wishes to express his appreciation to the graduate students at Coppin State University and faculty members at Coppin State University for their advice and suggestions concerning writing an integral book on quantitative and qualitative research methods. The publication of this text could not have been possible without the cooperation of the publishers whose suggestions and recommendations were invaluable in preparing the final draft. The author also wish to extend appreciation to those publishers and authors who gave him permission to reproduce the work.

An appreciation of deep gratitude and thanks to all of the Contributing Authors whose invaluable knowledge and expertise that was provided to create this magnificent textbook. I would like to also personally thank Bernadette Francisco, Ph.D., (deceased), Adjunct Professor of Special Education, Coppin State University, Trina Green, and the editorial staff at the University of Press of America for their generous efforts in editing, and a special thank you to Mrs. Emma "Sisie" Crosby for her dedication in typing this manuscript.

Chapter One
Introduction and Overview of the Research Process
George R. Taylor, Ph.D.
Charity Welch, Ph.D.

OVERVIEW

Research is an integral part of our society. Much of man's actions are based on assumptions and untested hypotheses. Such untested hypotheses are usually accepted on faith or some common belief and no attempt is made to verify them. In contrast, research involves the objective verification of hypotheses. These verifications require the scientific analyses of problems and devising appropriate methodologies for testing hypotheses. Mankind has explored his/her environment since ancient times and has used that knowledge to educate himself/herself as well as to attempt to explain unusual facts or events (Taylor, 2000). Much of this so-called research was based upon trial and error. These beliefs and assumptions guided humankind throughout ancient history and well into the early part of the twentieth century. During this time, man began to systematically and scientifically explore his environment and phenomena affecting it. This process is referred to as the scientific method. The scientific method is designed to discover valid methods of research finding reasons and explanations for controlling natural phenomena which can be replicated.

The Greeks and Romans made significant gains in the field of research through the study of astronomy, medicine, physics, geography, literature, ethics, law, and engineering. They laid the foundation for replacing supernatural events with a systematic way of thinking and investigating problems. Additionally, the Greek and Roman contributions to research enabled mankind to explore the universe and to assist in developing a scientific way for searching for the truth based upon factual information; facts that provided man with more reliable answers to many questions present in his environment.

The research movement was greatly expanded with the work of Galileo's experiments in physics during the beginning of the seventeenth century. Galileo's research sparked research in other fields such as biology, chemistry, and mathematics. It was not until the beginning of the eighteenth century that research in the social sciences began. As indicated, the social sciences were modeled after the physical sciences and attempts were made to make the social sciences as objective as the physical sciences. Thus, around the middle of the twentieth century, qualitative research methods were being explored for use in the social sciences.

Research purposes and the type of information sought vary from study to study, using both *quantitative* and *qualitative* approaches. Psychologists applying experimental methodologies attempt to validate their research by using a multitude of quantitative measures. They are usually expressed as scores and measures which yield numerical data. Deductive principles of control and logic were emphasized. It was readily recognized that all data could not be readily converted to meaningful data using numerical or standard research designs. Experiments with qualitative methods revealed that words (verbal, narrative, and descriptive) could be used as effectively as numbers, and that designs could be flexible rather than using the standard experimental format. Today, qualitative research methods are considered to be valid techniques for conducting research. Data collection and validation consist of in-depth open-ended interviews, direct observation, and written documentation (i.e., questionnaires, personal diaries, and program records). Qualitative evaluation data begins as raw, descriptive information about programs and people in programs (Patton, 1987 & 2002).

Research Defined and Classified

Several types of research will be discussed throughout this text, however, all of the research methods outlined may be classified or used with quantitative or qualitative methods. The basic thrust of all research is to solve problems and to expand knowledge of our universe which necessitates that it is carefully and systematically conducted. Research is needed to find answers to problems in our society, to experiment with the most expeditious way for conducting research to solve societal problems and to validate procedures which can be replicated.

Quantitative and qualitative research share common ground (Glassford, 1987; Pickette & Burrill, 1994). Both are concerned with reliability and study designs, and approaches are similar. The reliability and validity of a research question is determined by whether or not the item or subject elicits the intended information. Research methods are valid if they are successful in eliciting true responses relevant to the information desired. It is essential that the respondent or subject understands and responds to the question as it is understood by those conducting the research if the response is to be valid. Questions posed may be simple or complex in nature. Some systematic approach should be evident in asking questions in order to obtain valid and reliable information. The conceptual framework outlined in Chapter 4 is one recommended approach to aid the researcher in developing a systematic method of inquiry in quantitative and qualitative research. Both quantitative and qualitative research methods are explored in greater depth in Chapters 5 and 6.

Characteristics of Research

According the Leedy, et al (2001) there are seven discrete characteristics of research. They are:

1. *Research begins with a question in the mind of the researcher.* Mankind is in constant search of finding solutions to the many problems facing him in our society. Questions posed with the hope of finding solutions and that research will provide valid and scientific answers.

2. *Research demands the identification of a problem stated in clear, unambiguous terms.* Identification of a problem constitutes one of the most difficult areas in the research process. Researchers tend to over- or under-state the problem. In selecting a research problem, the researcher should select several approaches relevant to how he/she has organized and structured the problem. Intuitive thinking can assist the investigator in structuring the problem providing that he/she has the necessary prerequisites for conducting the study. Experience, competencies and training are necessary components needed in scientific inquiry. Some problems contain too many variables to manage successfully. Other problems include the cost factor, amount of time to conduct the research, experiences, and training, are to name but a few. Problems should be stated in clear and simple terms. Additional information is discussed in greater detail in Chapter 4.

3. *Research requires a plan.* In order to focus and control research, a systematic plan should be developed addressing, integrating, and infusing the various

components. We have attempted to show this integration in the conceptual framework in Chapter 4.

4.   *Research deals with the main problem through appropriate subproblems.* Seldom is the main problem sufficient to conduct a valid research project. There are usually subproblems which emulated from the main or major problem and should be stated in clear and ambiguous terms and address secondary issues associated with the research which cannot be solved without them.

5.   *Research seeks directions through appropriate hypotheses and is based upon obvious assumptions and beliefs.* The researcher must develop hypotheses that either support of do not support the research. Hypotheses guide and direct the research activity.   Methods and procedures, interventions, treatments, instruments and data analyses, are all integrated and connected to the hypotheses. Without hypotheses, there can be no scientific solutions to the problem posed.

Several steps are necessary in testing hypotheses.   They are: (1) formulating null and alternative hypotheses, (2) state the criterion for rejecting Ho, (3) locate the critical value of the Test statistics, (4) obtain the observations, and (5) make a decision.

Formulating Null and Alternative Hypotheses

Once the research hypothesis has been stated, the next step is to translate it into a null hypothesis, followed by an alternative hypothesis. Null hypotheses, unlike research hypotheses, specify a descriptive characteristic of data, assumed conditions about the population, and employs statistics to characterize the population. The hypothesis of no difference, is frequently referred to as the null hypothesis.

6.   *Research deals with facts and their meanings.* The researcher must collect relevant facts and organize them into categories in order for them to be correctly interpreted. The significance of the data depends upon how various researchers organized and interpreted the facts. The philosophy, interest, background, and experiences are all considered when researchers interpret data. To avoid the aforementioned pitfalls, researchers should be as objective as possible and base their interpretations on the factual data rather than their individual beliefs and philosophies.

7.   *Research is circular.* Chapter 4 will show the conceptual framework of the circular nature of research. All of the major parts of the research process have been infused into a model.[1]

These characteristics provided the foundation for constructing the "Conceptual Model for Conducting Research" as outlined in Chapter 4.   The model is premised upon the scientific method and may be employed with both qualitative and quantitative research methods. Some modifications and adaptations are usually required when using qualitative research methods by removing the experimental conditions.

The scientific method is currently employed as the major research mechanism in both quantitative and qualitative research methods. Quantitative research methods adhere most closely to the scientific method than qualitative research. In quantitative research more control and objectivity can be exercised, thus following the scientific method more closely. Both methods seek to discover the truth. Major similarities and differences between the two methods will be addressed in Chapter 14. At this point, it will suffice to say that both methods are orderly systems which may be classified as research, and both methods have led to great

---

1. For specific descriptions of characteristics of research refer to: Paul D. Leedy, 2001. *Practical Research:* Planning and Design. Macmillan Publishing Company.

discoveries and inventions which have aided mankind immeasurably. We have summarized the scientific method in Chapter 4.

Goals of Statistics

The major goal of statistics is to solve questions about behavior, both human and non-human phenomena. Other goals will include describing both human and non-human behaviors through employing sets of numbers in order to make inferences and predictions concerning these behaviors using various types of statistical procedures (Harris, 1995, Kirk, 1990).

Statistical procedures are used in many segments of our society, as indicated throughout this chapter and text, in order to reach conclusions about observations. Without the assistance of statistical procedures, there is a danger of reporting inaccurate findings.

Characteristics of Statistics

Statistics is a brand of mathematics (Elmore & Woehlke, 1997). It was firmly established during the nineteenth century and has permeated all aspects of society. Mathematics shows the naked truth; statistics dresses it and relates it to the realities of experience. Statistics enable us to accumulate, describe, classify and evaluate experiences and phenomena in an objective manner. Statistics provides the researcher with the tools for extracting from a mass of data the truth.

Statistics has already done much to give individuals control over themselves. We are all familiar with the important roles that statistics play in society. For an example, the Department of Labor publishes yearly data on employment by race, gender, occupation, geographic regions, education levels, and salaries. This report keeping and computing of vital statistics is a requirement of government. Other governmental agencies such as the Department of Health and Welfare play a large role in the protection of the health of our communities. Insurance would be sheer gambling if it were not for accurate statistics of mortality and morbidity which enable actuaries to set premiums that are both fair and profitable. Consumer research, the foundation of modern merchandising, and many of its subsidiary activities, i.e., advertising and, production and inventory control, are dependent upon one form or another of statistics. Politics would be adversely affected if statistical research did not suggest where to place money and manpower so as to win votes an elections. Modern warfare uses statistics to discover how best to utilize available military material and personnel. The stock market carefully uses statistics in its daily operations to fashion indices and trends to guide researchers. Some other uses of statistics include:

1. Diagnosing and tracking ailments in hospitals and clinics;
2. Conducting surveys in industry and science;
3. Statistical inquiry for study the behavior of both the nuclear components of the atom and the nuclear mitosis;
4. Creating standards for hiring personnel in industry;
5. Diagnosing ailments in host cancer cells;
6. Constructing and evaluating psychological tests;
7. Grading the progress of pupils in learning;
8. Conducting surveys in sociology and;
9. Estimating the age of ancient relics, are to name but a few uses of statistical data.

Statistical data have significantly influenced our lives by assisting us in conceptualizing and visualizing facts in our society.

First, statistics aid the researcher by setting up procedures for assembling data, recording it properly, and classifying it so that individual facts may be integrated into like-characterized masses. It also helps researchers to order masses and extract whatever knowledge, generalizations, and conclusions may justifiably be drawn from them. Statistics is used to describe when we wish to portray a large body of data in terms of its essential inherent characteristics. Three main functions of statistics are: description, generalization, and measurement of relationships.

Second, we use statistics to generalize when we base knowledge about a large population upon limited observations of a small portion of it. Statistical generalizations are made in almost all research work. Statistics help us to determine when generalizations are sound and how far it is permissible to interpret them.

Third, we use statistics to determine whether there is any relationship between two or more factors which are present in a situation and, if there is, how large the relationship is. This is perhaps the most fruitful realm of statistics, and it has made a great contribution both to our knowledge and to our power to manipulate the forces in our environment. Statistical interpretations and uses are limitless, which frequently gives rise for error and misuse. Thus, it is of prime importance that consumers of statistics be well versed in the use and interpretation of statistics, knowing what to accept and what to reject. Statistics can play a vital role in our society, providing that both producers and consumers are competent and knowledgeable of its many functions (Evans, 1996; Thorndike & Dinnel, 2001).

Uses of Statistics

Students who view statistics as unpleasant medicine to take have not fully understood the systematic methods employed in conducting research. Both statistical manipulations and research design are merely simple tools which are used to support the assumptions and judgments we make day to day. The following stages are recommended to use in the process of statistical decision making:

1.   *Suspicion.* Based upon observations you suspect that differences occur if various treatments are employed. An example might be that you suspect parental involvement will improve the academic achievement of pupils.

2.   *Assumption.* You begin with the assumption that there will be no difference in achievement of pupils whose parents are involved vs those that are not involved. From those assumptions, hypothesis will be developed.

3.   *Data Source.* Some type of instrument or technique must be developed to collect data to support your assumptions. Both pre-and post-achievement scores must be collected on pupils and specific types of parental involvement techniques must be employed over a period of time. A comparison of pre-and post-measures will be taken after intervention to determine if assumptions are supported. Data may be discrete or continuous.

4.   *Statistical test.* An appropriate statistical test should be selected and used to determine if pure change accounted for the differences between the groups. Refer to Chapter 11 for procedures to use in selecting appropriate statistical tests.

5.   *Analysis.* Analysis of data using the appropriate statistical procedure to support your basic hypothesis stated in step 2 will be tested to determine the affects of parental involvement on achievement.

Statistics may be used to compare results between one, two, or multiple groups. Using the example earlier in Chapter 1, concerning parental involvement. In a one-group design two variables should be measured, number, and type of parental involvements and increase in achievement scores of pupils for one single group or class.

Using the same above example, assuming that you want to include a second group or sample using two classes or schools. This is an example of a two-group design. In this type of design you will be comparing the results between the groups. A multi-group design would be to employ the same example, give three or more groups. Those groups may be in the same location or in multiple locations through the school district, the state, or the nation.

With one group of parents, many measures could be obtained. The sex, race, income, and education may be used. On the other hand, if the differences between two sets of parent groups were sought, a two-group measure design would be used. In each of the above cases, the research may expose the group to some type of treatment between two measures. A pre measure will be conducted before the treatment and after the treatment to determine if any changes occurred as a result of the treatment.

Types of Statistics

The type of statistic chosen by the researcher will greatly depend upon the type of analyses to be performed. The following general types of quantitative analysis are discussed below.

Decide on Correlational or Experimental Analysis

I.   Correlational Analysis – to measure the degree of SIMILARITY between or among two or more related variables.

   A.   Two variable analysis – Pearson Product-moment Correlation Coefficient should be applied when there are two variables and when four assumptions are fulfilled.

      1.   Linearity can be tested by plotting and inspecting data. It exists when a straight line describes data better than a curved line. If curvilinear line best describes the data, the correlation ratio must be applied instead of Pearson.

      2.   Homoscedasticity can be tested by plotting, circumscribing, and inspecting the data. Homoscedasticity exists when the circumscribing line forms an ellipse. If homoscedasticity is not present, Pearson can still be computed but it cannot be tested for significance.

      3.   Interval scaled data – data on both variables should at least approach being interval scaled. If the data is obviously only ordinal scaled, Spearman Rank – difference Correlation Coefficient, Kendall's tau, or Kendall's Coefficient of Concordance must be used. If the data is only nominal scaled data, the coefficient of Contingency must be used.

      4.   Data should be continuous, not dichotomous. DICHOTOMY Data is dichotomous when it forms two groups (equal or unequal in size), e.g., the continuous variable age might be split into two groups "39 and younger" and "40 and older."

If one variable is CONTINOUS and the other is a DICHOTOMY, point-biserial r should be used. If BOTH variables are DICHOTOMIES, Phi or Fourfold Coefficient must be used. N.B.: There are other assumptions which must be fulfilled before these correlation coefficients can be computer (Kirk, 1995).

Quantitative statistics may be used:

   1.   To indicate the central point for which data revolves;
   2.   To indicate how wide the data spreads;
   3.   To indicate the amount of deviation spread from the mean;
   4.   To show the relationship between variables;
   5.   To test hypotheses (Leedy, 2001).

In qualitative research, data are usually expressed in words. However, in some instances, hypotheses may be used. Descriptive statistics are frequently used to display some data, such as graphs, charts, percentiles, and measures of central tendency. Most qualitative data are classified and then categorized and extensive narrations are written describing the phenomena in great detail.

Most recently, some researchers have combined the two research methods (Dennis, 1994; Steckler, 1992; Taylor, 2000). Both narrative descriptions and statistics have been used. Narrative data have been used to support numerical data, and vice versa. The process is frequently called triangulation. Refer to Chapter 11 for additional details and strategies for using statistics with qualitative research methods.

Based upon his/her interests and training, the researcher may decide to select either the quantitative or qualitative method for conducting his/her research. Special characteristics and uses of both methods are discussed in detail in Chapters 5 and 6. At this point, it is sufficient to say that the type or method chosen will depend upon the training and experience of the researcher, as well as the nature and type of research to be investigated.

If the data are narrative and descriptive and the research is trained   in   the   use   of qualitative research methods. This approach would be the recommended one to employ. Various types of descriptive strategies may be used to analyze the data (Taylor, 2000; Patton, 2002).

Harris (1995) wrote that if the score on a variable comes in whole units, the variable is discrete. Examples given included family size, number of cars one owns, and number of students in classrooms.

Continuous variables cannot be measured precisely and do not come packaged in units, instead, measures on a continuous variable represent arbitrary degrees of precision. Personality and ability variables, height and weight, and temperature are examples of continuous variables (pp. 12-13).

Research Designs

Statistics may be employed in both quantitative and qualitative research designs. We have given detailed explanation to the two designs in Chapters 13 and 14, and strategies for developing a multi-faced design in Chapter 15.

Research designs are attempts by researchers to set up systematic procedures to solve problems. Most research designs in the social sciences follow the scientific method. We have summarized the components of the scientific methods in Chapter 4, as they apply to a conceptual framework for conducting quantitative scientific research.

Quantitative and Qualitative Designs

Some research designs emphasize the gathering of numerical data and focus on numbers; they are typically called quantitative approaches. Other research designs emphasize the analysis of complex data in terms of its content or narrative interpretation of the data. These designs are referred to as qualitative research designs. Descriptions and characteristics of both designs are elaborated   upon in Chapters 5 and 6. In both methods the issue of ethical practices must be addressed.

Ethical Issues in Conducting Research

Historically, issues related to subjects have constituted the greatest concern to society as reflected above in the violating of human rights during the early part of this century. Specific guidelines will be developed for researchers to follow under the following areas:
1. Consent
2. Harm
3. Privacy
4. Deception

Consent:

Subjects must be given a choice to determine whether or not they wish to participate in the study. Subjects must be both mentally and physically able to make the choice or someone must be designated to act on their behalf. Assessment should also be made of the legal qualifications of the subjects. Subjects under the age of 18 years should not be permitted to participate in the study unless a parent or guardian gives written permission (Kimmel, 1996).

Guidelines
1. *Type of intervention or treatment to be conducted.* Specific procedures for conducting the research should be clearly articulated. Length of time to conduct the research as well as human and physical resources needed to conduct the research.

2.   *Impact upon the normal activities of subjects.* The researcher should address to what extent the research will affect the normal activities of the subjects. There should be strategies to restore subjects to the normal routines of the inclusion of the research.

3.   *Informed consent.* It is incumbent upon the researcher to inform the subjects what is expected of them and what they will be expected to do. This is usually accomplished by consent forms (Refer to Appendices A and B).

4.   *Right of withdrawal.* Subjects should be told and given the right to withdraw from the research at any time. A statement should be developed outlining procedures.

Harm:

Subjects participating in research should be assured that no harm will come to them as a result of their participation. Harm covers physical and psychological factors which may adversely affect the functioning or the well-being of the subjects. The extent and possible harm that subjects may experience should be clearly articulated in the questionnaire or survey completed by subjects. Treatment should not leave the subjects more psychologically depressed or physically incapacitated than they were before the treatment began (Robinson, 1992).

Guidelines

1.   *Safeguarding subjects from harm.* The researcher should ensure the subjects that no physical or psychological harm will come to them as a result of participating in the research. They should inform subjects concerning any possible risks associated with the research.

2.   *High risk subjects.* Researchers should consider the characteristics of the subjects involved in the experiment such as age, physical or mental disabilities. These subjects may be unable to make realistic decisions on their own, thus placing them "in harm's way" for certain types of experiments.

3.   *Assurance to subjects.* It is incumbent upon the researcher that subjects be returned to their original physical and psychological conditions before the treatment.

4.   *Results of other experiments.* The researchers should provide subjects with how other studies safeguarded subjects on how the lack of safeguards brought harm to subjects, and relate how his/her study will avoid some of the pitfalls.

Privacy:

Our privacy in this country is considered to be a valued right as reflected in local, state, and federal mandates. Subjects participating in research should have the right to have some sensitive data collected through the research process to be confidential. Researchers should assure subjects that sensitive data will be held in the strictest confidence in order to protect their anonymity (Kurtines, 1992).

Guidelines

1.   *Selection of the site.* The rationale for choosing the Site should be outlined and clearly articulated. The researcher should consider the setting in which the study is to be conducted.

Settings in public places are not generally considered conductive for assuring privacy. Other factors which should be considered are:

      a.   The reputation and competencies of the staff;

      b.   Safeguarding of information;

      c.   Protecting information from individuals not involved in the research.

  2.   *Making results of the research available.*
Subjects should have an opportunity to review a draft copy of the report in order to determine invasion of privacy. This is especially true when some of the data may be damaging to the institution or subject. Feedback should be incorporated into the final report providing that the hypotheses and findings are not altered.

  3.   *Feedback.* Researchers should assure subjects that they will provide an opportunity for them to obtain accurate information relevant to the research, and that they will respond to all participants' concerns.

  4.   *Confidentiality.* Confidentiality should be maintained at all times. The proposal should indicate that names will not be used or revealed with the data.

Deception:
    Misleading subjects, under or over representing facts are forms of deception. There should be no hidden agenda relevant to the treatment process. Any deception which is an integral part of the research must be explained to the subjects as soon as feasible (Jensen, 1985, 1992).
Guidelines:

  1.   *Limitations.* Factors such as finances, time, resources, and data sources, should not be a standard for using deception.

  2.   *Consent.* Subjects should be given an accurate description of what tasks they will be required to perform.

  3.   *Justification.* Any deception employed should be clearly justified by the researcher and clearly explained to the subjects.

The researcher should indicate what the subjects will gain from the research in the areas of improved treatment, innovative methods, in-service training needs, and the need for additional physical or human resources (Marshall & Rossman, 1989; Bogdan & Biklen, 1992).

It should be incumbent upon the researcher to safeguard all subjects involved in experiments. Certain ethical concerns should be considered. These considerations may involve submitting a research proposal to an ethics committee for approval. In some cases, an oral presentation may be required.

Preview of Chapters Two through Thirteen

Both quantitative and qualitative research follows an orderly and systematical plan and format. A research design enables the researchers to accomplish this goal. In the absence of a well-developed research design or paradigms, the researcher has no systematic plan for scientifically conducting his/her research. This book is designed to provide a framework to guide the researcher through the research maze.

Chapter 2 describes how to effectively use the library. Chapter 3 gives an overview of the use of data-based computer searching when conducting research. Chapter 4 provides a conceptual framework for conducting both quantitative and qualitative methods of research. The model incorporates using both methods. Chapters 5 and 6 report on the various types of quantitative and qualitative research methods. Chapter 7 gives an overview of the use of computers in conducting research. Chapter 8 deals with using descriptive statistics in research. Chapter 9 deals with indicators of relative positions in a distribution. Chapter 10 summarizes some inferential statistical tools used in research. Chapter 11 reviews commonly used parametric statistics in the social sciences. Chapter 12 summarizes the use of non-parametric statistics in research. Chapter 13 is designed to relate how practical research paradigms can be developed in both quantitative and qualitative research methods. Chapter 14 summarizes the similarities and differences between quantitative and qualitative approaches. Chapter 15 provides a format for developing a multifaceted design using both quantitative and qualitative approaches. Chapter 16 reviews guidelines to implement in order to avoid some of the pitfalls of conducting research. Chapter 17 deals with making some concluding remarks relevant to conducting research.

References

Bogdan, R. C., & Biklen, S. K. (1992). *Qualitative research for education: An introduction to theory and methods.* Boston: Allyn & Bacon.

Dennis, M. L. (1994). *Integrating qualitative and quantitative methods in substance abuse research.* ERIC Ej 500515.

Evans, J. D. (1996). *Straight forward statistics.* Pacific Grove, CA: Brooks Cole Publishing Company.

Glassford, R. G. (1987). Methodological reconsideration: The shifting paradigms. *Quest, 39,* 295-312.

Harris, M. B. (1995). Basic *statistics for behavioral science research.* Needhamd Height, MA: Allyn & Bacon.

Jensen, R. E. (1985). *Ethical issues in clinical psychology.* Lanham, MD: University Press of America.

Jensen, R. E. (1992*). Standards and ethics in clinical psychology.* Lanham, MD: University Press of America.

Kimmel, A. J. (1996). *Ethical issues in behavioral research.* Cambridge, MA: Blackwell Publishers.

Kirk, R. E. (1990). *Statistics: An introduction* (3rd ed.). New York: Rinehart & Winston.

Kirk, R. E. (1995). *Experimental design: Procedures for the behavioral sciences* (3rd ed.). Pacific Grove, CA: Brooks/Cole.

Kurtines, M. (1992),. *The role of values in psychology and human development.* New York,: Macmillan Publishers.

Leedy, P. D., Newby, T., & Ertmer, P.A. (2001). *Practical research: Planning and design* (7th ed.). New York: Prentice Hall.

Marshall, C., & Rossman, G. B. (1989). *Designing qualitative research.* Newbury Park, CA: SAGE.

Patton, M. Q. (1987). *How to use qualitative methods in evaluation.* Newbury Park, CA: SAGE.

Patton, M. Q. (2002). *Qualitative research and evaluation methods* (3rd ed.). Newbury Park, CA: SAGE.

Pickett, W., & Burrill, D. F. (1994). The use of quantitative evidence in research: A comparative study of two literatures. *Educational Research, 23* (6), 18-21.

Robinson, D. N. (1992). *Social discourse and moral judgement.* San Diego, CA: Academic Press.

Steckler, A. (1992). Toward integrating qualitative and quantitative methods: An introduction. *Health Education Quarterly,* 19, 1-8.

Taylor, G. R. (2000). *Integrating quantitative and qualitative methods in research.* Lanham, MD: University Press of America.

Thorndike, R. M., & Dinnel, D. L. (2001). *Basic statistics for the behavioral sciences.* Upper Saddle River, NJ: Prentice Hall, Inc.

Chapter Two
Library Resources
George R. Taylor, Ph.D.
Kriesta Watson, Ph.D.

INTRODUCTION

In seeking trust, the researcher must be acquainted with many sources from which to gather information concerning the problem as well as related knowledge. A knowledge of the tools of research is both necessary and beneficial for the researcher and the research being conducted. The broader the knowledge-base, the less the opportunity for error and bias in the study. A contemporary researchers should possess a knowledge of the tools of research such as:
1. Library tools;
2. Statistical tools;
3. The use of the computer;
4. Measurement tools;
5. The use of research language.

This chapter will discuss library tools. Frequently used /measurement and statistical tools of researchers are highlighted and summarized in Chapters 8 and 10. The use of research language is projected throughout the text.

Extensive use of the library is essential in summarizing the review of the literature. It is essential for the researcher to judge the quality of their research. We have addressed the importance of the review of the literature in Chapter 4. This review will:
1. Enable the researcher to discover past events and methods which have been proven successful by others;
2. Provide information which may stimulate interest and new ideas for exploration and investigation;
3. Assist in refining the research problem;
4. Assist in locating primary and secondary resources;
5. Enable the research to identify periodical indexes;
6. Avoid fruitless approaches by identifying lines of inquiry not related to the area under investigation;
7. Provide the researchers with the status of the research in his/her field;
8. Indicate to the researcher what methods strategies, and techniques have been successfully used as well as those that have not, such as developing hypotheses, defining terms, and organizing the review;
9. Seek support for ground theory. According to Glaser (1978) the review should be conducted after the study. Refer to Chapter 6 for additional information.

Recommended Steps in Evaluating the Review of Literature

The following steps are recommended in reviewing the literature:

1. Comprehensively cover previously research topics. Make sure that major topics, trends, principles, and authors' works are objectively reviewed, analyzed, and summarized.

2. Review the most recent studies completed. In the social science field, many older studies are no longer relevant. Research in the field is constantly changing. Information published in the 1960-1980 may not be relevant to the topic under study today.

3. Arrange results by topics, categories, or years that studies were completed. This approach will assist in integrating and infusing information.

4. Some association should be made between the review and the methods and procedures articulated in the research project.

5. The review of literature should provide a clear theoretical framework for conducting the study. Refer to Appendix B for specific strategies and techniques to use in quantitative and qualitative research methods.

The purpose of this chapter is to provide information that will enhance the researchers' knowledge and skills in accessing information sources in printed and electronic forms. Most of the necessary tools can be found or accessed in local and school libraries, and many of the electronic sources can also be accessed from home if you have the required programs and linkages. Therefore, this chapter is designed to summarize some of the commonly used library tools by researchers. There are ample texts which provide specific details on the use of library resources. In addition, the library contains an array of article reviews, summaries, and hard copy references for all fields of interest. Further, for foundation information and data, your library becomes your best source of information because housed on the shelves is documentation of what is known, what has been investigated, and the success of or lack of success of these previous investigations (Taylor, 2000).

The local and school libraries are primary sources of information; however, they can become primary sources of frustration if one is not familiar with the process of utilizing the available resources to locate or retrieve the desired information. Thus, learning to use the local or college library to find information is an important part of any research endeavor. Further, it might be helpful for the researcher to utilize the following four sequence suggestions in preparation for a research project:

1. Do not select a topic that is too broad, set limits. Review a variety of literatures on a selected topic to determine if sufficient data are present to conduct the study, as well as, determining whether or not you have the necessary human and physical resources to conduct the study.

2. Consult a periodical index to locate recent articles on a selected topic. Choose a periodical in your area of interest; choose only the most recent articles. These articles will provide an overview of the most recent advancements in the field.

3. From each relevant source, review the cited bibliography for additional and more in-depth information in order to know the controversies in the field, as well as to take a position on the subject.

4. Review the current yearly publications of *Review of Research in Education, Encyclopedia of Educational Research, Resources in Education, Education Index, Digest of Educational Statistics,* abstracts in the discipline being investigated, and dissertation abstracts just to name a few. These valuable sources may be found at the reference desk in most libraries. Proper use of these sources will save the researcher countless hours in conducting his/her research. It is recommended that only the most recent volumes be used, unless the investigation under study is historical in nature.

The Dewey Decimal System

Knowledge of the use of this system can also expedite the researchers' time in the library. Within each one of the ten broad categories of the Dewey Decimal System (DD), are ten divisions thus totaling 100 sub-division groups.

00-99	General Works (books about books, magazines, newspapers)
100-199	Philosophy and Psychology (human behavior, excludes psychiatry)
200-299	Religion (history, law, mythology)
300-399	Social Sciences (economics, education, occupations)
400-499	Languages and Communication (linguistics, grammar, dictionaries)
500-599	Pure Sciences (botany, chemistry, physics)
600-699	Technology, Applied Sciences (business, farming, medicine, psychiatry)
700-799	Fine Arts and Recreation (music, sports)
800-899	Literature (plays, poetry, speeches)
900-999	History (biography, geography, and travel books)

In the area of educational research are some specific sources that will assist researchers in locating the information that they need. These sources are:

- *Child Development Abstracts.* Is useful for studies on younger children, and summarizes published articles related to education and child development.

- *Psychological Abstracts.* Can also be searched by computer (PASAR) and contains educational concerns with psychological implications. Hard copy references are quickly becoming outdated, and it has been noted that many reflect an author's particular point of view that is selected to support specific research evidence while excluding contradictory evidence. In many instances, a review of the article's summary is of value, and it might contain all the information you need.

- *Encyclopedias.* These references contain alphabetically listed collections of information that

- ranges from the general to the specific and in most instances the information is cross-referenced. The researcher might also want to review the *Encyclopedia of Educational Research.* This reference contains articles written by experts who review and analyze pertinent educational findings. It is however, a somewhat limited resource, but it does give several valuable citations related to the subjects that would allow for additional follow-up. Other encyclopedias include: (1) Comparative Education, (2) National Systems of Education, (3) Early Childhood Education, (4) Educational Evaluation, (5) Psychology, (6) Special Education, (7) School Administration and Supervision, (8) International Encyclopedia of Education, (9) International Encyclopedia of Teaching and Teacher Education, and (1) Specialized Subject Fields.

- *ERIC.* Educational Resources Information Center is a network of sixteen clearinghouses located across the country, whose purpose is to screen, index, and provide information on educational reports and documents. Most journal articles in education are included in ERIC files. Also included in ERIC is *Current Index to Journals in Education.*

- CIJE. Current Index to Journals in Education, is an index that provides extensive listings of articles in education. In many instances, this printed information can be accessed by computer.

- Card Catalog. The card catalog is a master key to quick and efficient use of a library. The arrangement of the card catalog is very similar to that of a dictionary or telephone directory. This alphabetical listing covers a vast array of material including periodicals, encyclopedias, and microfilms which can assist the researcher in locating information relevant to his/her study.

Use of these cited library resources can aid the researcher in conducting a variety of research methods recorded below. There are eight key forms of research and they are:

1. Action Research - Documentation to change or improve inappropriate behavior(s) in the class or school.
2. Applied Research - To seek solutions to practical educational problems.
3. Basic Research - To increase knowledge and understanding of phenomena.
4. Evaluation Research - Documentation to make specific and generic decisions about programs or activities.
5. Experimental Research - Documentation to determine and support the causal relationship between two or more phenomena by direct manipulation of these factors.
6. Non-experimental Research - To describe and predict phenomena, without manipulating factors that influence the phenomena.
7. Qualitative Research - To provide rich narrative descriptions of phenomena that enhance understanding with words.
8. Quantitative Research - To describe phenomena numerically to answer specific questions or hypotheses. Computer base research can facilitate literature searches.

Computer-Based Technology

Currently, libraries use a combination of the Library of Congress (LC) and the DD systems. Many libraries are in the process of converting to computer-based inquiry systems. Over the last twenty (20) years, computer-based technology has proven a major advancement in library research and reference work. Computers have opened doors to fundamental changes in the way we communicate, access, and analyze information. Computers placed massive amounts of information at everyone's fingertips, through the availability of data banks on thousands of topics (refer to Chapter 3 for a detailed discussion relevant to computer technology).

The delivery capability for high-speed searches makes computers more efficient and time saving than traditional methods of library research. Computers reduce the amount of time spent on generic details, allowing more time for creativity and concentration on research. Traditional indexing and information retrieval systems are marked by time lags between dates of publication and indexing for public use. Time saved, combined with accuracy and the ability to navigate through the vast quantity of library materials has made computerized systems popular.

Use of Computers

Computers are available for storing, retrieving, and manipulating information. Some computers can search or execute more than fifty million instructions per second. This speed and precision has made them ideal instruments for quickly locating and retrieving needed research materials. Additionally, if an electronic source has a print equivalent, it is also listed in the annotation. Chapter 3 lists major databases the researcher may use in conducting research. These databases are available in many private and public libraries and in some instances, a small fee may be imposed for accessing and using them.

Both the traditional type of library resources and the computerized database type are at the disposal of the researcher. An understanding of their locations and uses are necessary in conducting any type of research. An understanding of their locations and uses are necessary in conducting any type of research. We have devoted Chapter 3 to discuss computer usage in greater detail.

A computer search can be conducted at a minimum cost at public, universities, and personal computers on a variety of CD-ROM terminals which operates compact disks. Many of the data bases cited in Chapter 3 can be downloaded and printed. The information may also be downloaded on a diskette to be used later. The speed of the computer saves time by searching out a printing data in a matter of minutes. The computer is designed to do several tasks as the same time while simultaneously searching for information several subject headings and different years of publications can be searched simultaneously, thus, saving valuable time (Gall, Borg, & Gall, 1996).

Some Recommended Steps in Conducting a Computer Search

We have listed a variety of data bases in Chapter 3 which one might research. It is recommended that the researcher should have a plan in mind when conducting a computer search. The plan should include the following:

1. The research problem should be clearly defined. A short concise problem will aid in reducing the number of data bases researched. The question should describe the problem clearly and the terms and variables used will assist in focusing the research.
2. Succinctly state the purpose of why the research is being conducted. Some possible reasons may be to summarize the state of the art, to update a previous review, to learn more about a problem, to provide research evidence to support a view, to provide information to revise or adapt a new program, to test a new approach to solving a problem, and to verify or refute other research findings.
3. As we have articulated earlier, select the data bases you which to employ. Select from the list of data bases provided to support your research. By selecting major or minor descriptors your data bases can be reduced by using major descriptors. Some descriptors, such as the author's name, name of the journal, words that appear in the abstract may be used, as well as a combination of descriptors by using "and" and "or." These connectors increase the number of references that the computer will select to research for any data bases. Searches can also be limited by dates. Researchers frequently want the most recent research findings, unless historical research is being attempted.

Both qualitative and quantitative data sources can be easily located within public and private agencies, including college and university libraries, public libraries, and specific agencies in the community serving under-represented groups. Researchers should be aware of problems in documenting information on the Internet and if used, proceed with caution (Hahn & Stout, 1994).

Recently, researchers have used meta analysis strategies to review studies similar to those under investigation.

Meta-Analysis

Meta-analysis research may be defined as a review of literature that synthesizes previous quantitative research by employing statistical procedures to analyze the results of numerous studies concerned with the same problem (Gall, Borg, & Gall, 1996). In using this method, the following steps are recommended for the researcher:

1. Select the topic and studies you wish to investigate;
2. Review and analyze each study, record results and attributes;
3. Choose a statistical technique to determine the "effect size."

The "effect size" indicates how well the group that receives the experimental program does relative to the control group. The "effect size" is computed by taking the difference between the mean score of the experimental treatment and the mean score of the control
group on a criterion measure and dividing the difference by the standard deviation of the scores for the control group.

An illustration for computing meta-analysis follows:

Experimental	x = 46.2	46.2
Control	x = 41.2	-41.4

5.0 4 = 1.25

Standard Deviation = 4.0

An "effect size" of 3.3 or larger is generally considered to indicate a difference that has practical significance.

In choosing studies to use in meta-analysis the researcher should, as much as possible, select studies which are well constructed, and employ the scientific methods in conducting the study, analyze whether appropriate methods and procedures were employed, and determine whether or not appropriate hypothesis, treatment, and statistical tools were applied (Slavin, 1986).

According to Gall, Borg & Gall (1996) when examining large numbers of related studies, the average "size effect" may be computed. An average "size effect" score of at least .33 would imply that there was difference between the experimental and control group. An "effect size" less than .33 would imply that there is no difference of scores earned by the experimental and control groups. Researchers using meta-analysis must be aware that the larger the standard error, the more the "effect size" varies across studies. It is a time consuming process in that an exhaustive review of the literature must be conducted.

For several decades, meta-analysis has been widely used by researchers. It is a technique widely used for synthesizing the statistical research of a group of studies on the same research being investigated. Gall, Borg & Gall (1996) wrote that meta-analysis has the following advantages over using other statistical methods:

1. It focuses on the magnitude of the effect observed in each study to be synthesized;
2. It provides a metric, called an "effect size," that can be applied to any statistic technique;
3. It allows the researcher to determine whether certain features of the study included in the review affect the results that were obtained.

Summary

Methods and procedures for conducting the various research methods have been addressed in Chapters 3, 5, and 6. There are commonalities used in conducting any type of research such as design, methods and procedures, analyzing data, interpreting data, and using meta-analysis in both quantitative and qualitative inquiries and research methods. The use of effective library tools are essential in conducting any type of research. A comprehensive review of the literature is the foundation and cornerstone of any research study. Without this comprehensive review, the research process can not proceed in an orderly and systematic way (Buttlar, 1989; Cooper, 1989; Cooper & Hedges, 1994).

References

Buttlar, L.J. (1989). Education: *A guide to reference and information sources*. Englewood, CO: Libraries Unlimited.

Cooper, H. M. (1989). *Integrating research: A guide for literature review* (2nd ed.). Newburg Park, CA: Sage Publications.

Cooper, H. , & Hedges, L. V. (Eds.). (1994). *The handbook of Research synthesis*. New York: Russell Sage Foundation.

Gall, M. D., Borg, R. W., & Gall, M. P. (1996). *Educational research* (6th ed.). White Plains, NY: Longman Publishers.

Glaser, B. G. (1978). *Theoretical sensitivity: Advances in the methodology of ground theory*. Mill Valley, CA: Sociology Press.

Hahn, H., & Stout, R. (1994). *The internet complete reference*. Berkeley, CA: Osborne McGraw Hill.

Slavin, R. E. (1986). Best-evidence synthesis: An alternative to meta-analytic and traditional reviews. *Educational Researcher, 15* (9), 5-11.

Taylor, G. R. (2000). *Integrating quantitative and qualitative methods in research*.   Lanham, MD: University Press of America.

Chapter Three
Using Electronic Databases in Quantitative and Qualitative Research
Anthony R. Curtis, Ph.D.

INTRODUCTION

Collecting and storing information is an old idea. Aristotle's knowledge classifications in *Physica* are data management. Babbage's 19th century analytical engine stored and sorted data. The Jacquard loom used holes punched in paper cards to control a loom. Herman Hollerith sorted punched cards for the 1890 U.S. census. Large businesses stored records on magnetic tape in the 1960's. American Airlines opened its Sabre reservation's system in 1964 to coordinate information about hundreds of daily flights across the continent. NASA, the Atomic Energy Commission, the National Institutes of Health, and the National Science Foundation built databases. A database for personal computers, *dBASE*, designed in 1976 by an NASA software engineer, became a bestseller.

Database. Does the word database, sounding technical and forbidding, make you uncomfortable? It shouldn't because we use databases comfortably every day. In fact, we use them so much, we don't even think about the fact that we are using databases. Typical databases that you might use on any given day include a telephone directory, a dictionary, an encyclopedia, an airline flight guide, or a bibliography. In fact, now that you think about it, you can see that databases have been used to store all kinds of knowledge that we retrieve on a regular basis.

So what is it? A database is a large organized list of facts and information. A database usually contains text and numbers, but it also can contain still images, sounds, and even video film clips. What's the difference between a list and a database? A database permits its user to extract a specific group of disparate facts from a collection of facts. That elaborate paper filing system in your office is a kind of database. However, the databases under discussion here are constructed on computers where pieces of software such as a *database management program* help people design and construct collections of data.

Wedding invitation lists, tax expense records, and club members names and addresses, are databases kept by individuals on their home computers. Office workers tap databases of budget information and business contacts. Businesses maintain data banks of credit information, while government agencies offer data banks of legal citations and technical data. Academic researchers reach into scholarly journal databases to build *bibs* for their papers and dissertations. (Examples are provided in Appendix C.)

One kind of database known as an *expert system*, presents information on a specialized field. For example, medical information databases gather expertise from physician specialists, as well as specific facts about drugs, and package the information in a database as a substitute for direct contact with the physicians themselves. Users can be connected to all of this vase centralized databases by computer modem and telephone lines.

Searching a database. A typical database is designed around a central set of facts. All databases permit users to add new information or to update old facts. In an electronic database stored in a computer, the order of information can be rearranged, sorted, quickly. To help people retrieve and print facts, computer databases use commands for sorting lists into reports. An electronic database can be searched rapidly for specific items of information. Often, the search commands incorporate *Boolean* logic based on Boolean algebra allowing users to screen out unwanted entries. A full-text database incorporates large files of text such as paragraphs or chapters in a book. By searching for combinations of words that might appear in a text, a user can call forth an entire chapter.

CD-ROM or Internet. The CD-ROM. A CD-ROM (Compact Disc Read-Only Memory) is very much like a popular-music compact disc (CD). It is a laser-read B sometimes said to be optically read data warehousing device on which text, audio and video can be stored. A CD-ROM is a medium for the storage of massive amounts of information accessed through the CD-ROM drive in a computer. Today, one CD-ROM can store 600 megabytes (a million bytes) of data, although the advance of technology will multiply that capacity several fold in the near future.

A *computer network* is formed when many computers are interconnected for the sharing of resources. In a computer network, the individual stations are called *nodes*. A network can provide access to one or more databases. You might like to think of a network as an information highway over which data is transported. Recently, networks have changed our ideas of what computing is, from number-crunching to communicating. Networks have spawned a new *on-line* industry, which is a collection of organizations providing information services to remote customers via dial-up modems and a variety of telephone lines and other transmission media spanning states, countries and the entire globe.

For the most part today, electronic databases are stored either on a CD-ROM disk or on computers serving the Internet. As personal computers have become more powerful in their document storage and retrieval capabilities, sounds, graphics, animations, still photos, and video film clips have been added to CD-ROM and Internet databases. Internet and CD-ROM databases usually contain *hypertext links*. These are cues inserted into text by a database designer which allows a user to jump from one point in a database to another. For example, in a database of magazine articles, articles on sailing might include links to an article about the Chesapeake Bay.

The Internet is an international conglomeration of hundreds of thousands of government, education, and business computer networks. From only a thousand interconnected computer networks in the mid-1980's, the Internet has grown to hundreds of thousands of interconnected networks available to millions of people worldwide. It has become a repository of data for educational institutions, government agencies, and businesses as well as an information-sharing viaduct for thousands of discussion groups with specialized interests. For example:

- The U.S. government posts more and more information on the Internet, such as a new patent filing and NASA, Commerce Department and Social Security data.
- Many universities are converting libraries to electronic documents. For instance, the Union Institute (in Ohio) is storing its Cincinnati library of 4,000 Ph.D. dissertations as electronic documents. Cornell University is converting 100,000 books printed more than a century ago, on the development of the U.S. infrastructure of bridges, roads, and other public works, to electronic format.
- Businesses market their goods and services on the Internet with advertisements and catalogs interspersed with database information. On-line ordering of products has become overwhelmed with popularity.

World Wide Web. The World Wide Web B often referred to as the Web or WWW B is a service that allows computer users to *browse* or *surf the net* (the Internet) to view and download information. Using a software *browser* such as the commercial program *Netscape*, a computer owner can navigate the Internet quickly and easily via hypertext links. Web users jump from one document to another, simply by pointing to a highlighted phrase, or link, and clicking a computer mouse-button.

For instance, a person reading through a document in California about tuberculosis might come across a link to a document in New York about AIDS. When a person clicks on the AIDS link in the tuberculosis document, the AIDS document appears on the computer screen. The Web has fueled rapid growth of the Internet in the latter part of the 1990's by attracting millions of individual users with modem-equipped personal computers. Those users subscribe to local networks that provide a connection to the global Internet.

Many individual persons, as well as educational institutions, government agencies and businesses, create their own *home pages* as points of access through which anyone on the Internet can view and download information from their *servers*. A server is a computer that stores and delivers documents to users. The Web is by far the fastest growing service on the Internet. By the end of 1997, there were an estimated 50 million documents, or pages being served to the Web community by 500,000 servers.

On-line Service. Many databases today, including computerized (digitized) versions of reference books, are part of electronic information services people can reach by dialing a telephone number through a computer modem. The information supplier is referred to as an online database, online service or interactive service. Information providers and service providers also have been called content suppliers. Online services sell data to individual users and deliver the information through a computer and a two-way communication system such as a telephone. Host computer servers store the sellers' information. If direct access to a database by telephone is offered, a system operator enables the user to connect with,
or *log on to*, the information service and navigate through the system by means of keyboard and mouse.

Web Access. Most online service operators now offer their customers connections via the World Wide Web segment of the Internet. The Internet is the international web of interconnected computer networks sometimes referred to as the Information Superhighway. To obtain Web access, the user connects with an Internet Service Provider (ISP) and then navigates the Web to the home page of the online database service. A previously purchased password is required for deep access into such a commercial Web site.

Well Known Online Services. The largest U.S. online systems for consumers include America Online, CompuServe, and Prodigy. DIALOG and OCLC are examples of mammoth online information retrieval services for libraries, each providing online access to hundreds of electronic databases referencing millions of documents in a wide variety of subject areas.

Online Database Searching. An online database search is simply bibliographic research which is performed by an individual scholar or librarian using a computer and the Internet. By connecting with a database research service, millions of records in hundreds of databases can be searched for material on a topic. Citations found for relevant items, usually journal articles, can be printed. Those journals or books not available in the library, can be requested through Interlibrary Loan (ILL). Sometimes, article reprints can be ordered through the online research service.

As an online database search saves time and effort, searching a database is an effective, efficient means of searching for information in ways that may be difficult or impossible to duplicate with printed resources. An online database search is a convenient way to produce a bibliography customized to individual research needs for complex topics or topics covering long time periods.

Intranet. Businesses are creating *Intranet* on their private networks. Using Internet technology, they link databases with networking applications. For example, an Intranet can connect a warehouse, a manufacturing site, a retail store, and a customer via ordinary Internet browsers.

Commercial Databases. Anyone can *download*, or electronically copy data from the Internet. Businesses with data for sale see protection of copyrighted material as a necessity. Some companies *encrypt* the data they sell on the Internet. To do so, they provide decoding keys to buyers of the data. Of course, that scheme doesn't prevent buyers from repackaging and reselling the data.

Privacy. There also are questions about personal privacy. Safeguards against tampering with information exist, but there are few safeguards against human errors. Experts have said that credit information, airline flight records, and crime data, should not be merged into other databases. In corporations, control over databases has legal implications. Users have to discern where database information has come from and how reliable it is.

Natural Language. Database design is moving into natural-language programming through which software sees meaning in ordinary sentences and can search for information without requiring technical languages.

Internet II. Researchers conducting complex projects require greater capacity than the current Internet provides. In 1995, the National Science Foundation began to meet that need by converting the Internet *backbone* B the electronic pipeline among the five supercomputer communications hubs B into a system many times more powerfully than the current Internet, but available only to medical researchers, astrophysicists, and other specialists. The managers and users of this new network, called the Very-High-Performance Backbone Network Service, are increasing its fiberoptic linkages and adding technically-advanced switches and routers to the system.

Bulletin Board System. A computer bulletin board system (BBS) is a computer and software forming an online database which allows people at distant computers to telephone in to retrieve information files. The person maintaining a BBS is the system operator or *sysop*. A BBS usually is a free standing entity and not part of the global Internet. However, some BBS's provide an auxiliary connection to the Internet for a fee. Many BBS's are devoted to specific topics. Some BBS's are offered by commercial information utilities that charge access fees. A few businesses and government agencies operate BBS's, while some are open to the public. There still may be as many as 50,000 BBS's operating in the United States, but the huge growth in the World Wide Web has brought a rapid decline in public interest in BBS's.

Academic Research Libraries. Academic research libraries subscribe to various electronic databases of use to scholars. Most can be accessed either by visiting a library's CD-ROM database room B sometimes called an Electronic Resources Section B or by accessing the databases via the World Wide Web. Many such electronic resources contain full-text versions of articles originally published in scholarly journals and other media. Typically, subscription resources are available only to a subscriber's students, faculty, and staff who access the CD-ROM databases from campus computers or via the Internet using special-access password accounts.

Most commercially-available electronic databases are described in the alphabetical listing of 112 information resources described below:

Alphabetical Listing of Electronic Databases

- *ABI/Inform. A full-text database most useful for research in business, economics and statistics.* More than 800,000 business and management citations from 1,000 U.S. and international publications. Covers nearly every aspect of business, including company histories and new product development. Citations include abstracts and indexes of significant articles from nearly 1,000 current business and management periodicals. Provides access to the ASCII full-text of articles from 570 journals. From August 1971. Updated weekly and published by UMI. Part of the FirstSearch collection of databases

- *Abstracts of Music Literature. A database most useful for research in arts and humanities.* See: RILM Abstracts of Music Literature.

- *AGRICOLA. A database most useful for research in physical sciences, technology, health sciences, life sciences, social sciences, and sociology.* The database includes more than three million citations, not only on agricultural topics such as agricultural engineering and marketing, animal breeding, entomology, environmental pollution, farm management, foods and feeds, pesticides, veterinary medicine and water resources, but also chemistry, energy geography, human nutrition, life sciences, natural resources and rural sociology. It indexes journal articles, audiovisual materials, book chapters, computer databases, conference proceedings, maps, manuscripts, monographs, serials, software, sound recordings, and technical reports. From 1970. New records added monthly. Published by the National Agriculture Library. Part of the FirstSearch collection of databases.

- *AIDS and Cancer Research. database most useful for research in health sciences, physical sciences, technology and social sciences.* Index of cancer and AIDS research gathered from worldwide scientific literature summarized in Virology & AIDS Abstracts, Oncogenes & Growth Factors Abstracts, and Immunology Abstracts. The database covers the current year plus the five preceding years. Updated monthly. Published by Cambridge Scientific Abstracts. Part of the FirstSearch collection of databases.

- *America: History and Life. A database most useful for research in humanities and social sciences.* Bibliographic citations and abstracts on research articles from more than 2,100 international journals studying United States and Canadian history from prehistoric times to the present. Includes citations for dissertations, book, film, and video reviews. From 1982. See: *Historical Abstracts,* for research literature on the history of other countries.

- *American-Indian Multimedia Encyclopedia.A full-text database most useful for research in humanities and social sciences.* Hypertext-linked information on American Indian tribe histories, folklore and religions. Includes biographies. More than 300 full-text documents such as treaties and relevant legislation, glossaries, timetables, and a directory of relevant United States and Canadian museums and societies. Includes color videos, sound files, illustrations, maps, and historical photographs. Keyword and Boolean searching of text and multimedia files.

- *Applied Science and Technology Abstracts.A database most useful for research in mathematics, computer science, physical sciences and technology.* Abstracts from more than 350 international English-language periodicals, covering engineering, mathematics, physics, and computer technology. Latest findings in every area of science, engineering, and technology. Covers trade and industrial publications, journals issued by professional and technical societies, and specialized subject periodicals. Includes articles, interviews, meetings, conferences, etc. From October 1983 with abstracts beginning March 1993. Updated monthly. Published by H.W. Wilson Company. Part of the FirstSearch collection of databases.

- *Art Abstracts. A database most useful for research in arts and humanities.* Comprehensive, authoritative information about arts from architecture to video. More than 250 key international English-language arts periodicals, yearbooks, museum bulletins, competition and awards notices, exhibition listings, interviews, film reviews, and more. A comprehensive record of art reproductions that appear in the indexed publications. Indexing from September 1984. Abstracts from Spring 1994. Updated monthly. Published by H.W. Wilson Company. Part of the FirstSearch collection of databases.

- *ArticleFirst. A general reference most useful for research in arts, humanities, business, economics, statistics, education, psychology, current events, physical sciences, technology, health sciences and social sciences.* Bibliographic citations describe items listed on the table of contents pages of more than 13,000 journals in science, technology, medicine, social science, business, the humanities and popular culture. From 1990. Updated daily. Published by OCLC. Part of the FirstSearch collection of databases.

- *Arts and Humanities Search. A database most useful for research in Arts and Humanities.*More than 1.4 million records referencing more than 1,300 of the world's leading arts and humanities journals. From 1980. Updated weekly.

- *Bartlett's Familiar Quotations, 9th Ed., 1901. A full-text database most useful for research in humanities and social sciences.*Electronic versions of Bartlett's Familiar Quotations, 9th Edition. Part of Columbia University's Project Bartleby which is a large collection of public hypertext literature on the World Wide Web.
- *Basic BIOSIS. A database most useful for research in life sciences, physical sciences, technology and social sciences* More than 300,000 records from 350 of the basic core of life science journals found in college and university libraries. From 1994. Provides information on developments in 96 subject areas of the biological and biomedical sciences covering the most prestigious journals. Updated monthly. Formerly known as BIOSIS/FS. A subset, by journal title and year, of BIOSIS Previews. Published by BIOSIS. Part of the FirstSearch collection of databases.
- *Biography Index. A general reference most useful for research in the arts, humanities, business, economics, statistics, education, psychology, current events, and social sciences.* Biographical index to more than 2,700 English-language periodicals plus biographical materials in 1,800 books. Includes autobiographies, bibliographies, individual and collective biographies, critical studies, fiction, drama, pictorial works, poetry, juvenile literature, obituaries, journals, collections of letters, book reviews and interviews. More than 1,800 books added each year. From July 1984. Updated monthly. Published by H.W. Wilson Company. Part of the FirstSearch collection of databases.
- ***Biological and Agricultural Index Abstracts.*** *A database most useful for research in life sciences, physical sciences, and technology.* Some 250 English-language periodicals in life sciences and agricultural subjects, published in the U.S. and elsewhere. Includes book reviews. Provides information from groundwater pollution to genetic engineering and covers the entire range of sciences related to biology and agriculture. From July 1983. Updated monthly. Published by H.W. Wilson Company. Part of the FirstSearch collection of databases.
- ***Biology Digest (BioDigest).*** *A database most useful for research in life sciences, health sciences, physical sciences, and technology.* More than 8,500 journal article abstracts written in nontechnical style covering botany, health, life sciences, medicine, zoology and environmental science. Access to new scientific developments, with comprehensive abstracts of articles in more than 300 journals. From September 1989. Updated monthly, September through May. Published by Plexus Publishing. Part of the FirstSearch collection of databases.
- *Book Review Digest. A general reference most useful for research in arts, humanities, education, psychology, social sciences and current events.* Index with abstracts to book reviews appearing in some 100 periodicals in the U.S., Canada, and Great Britain, covering more than 7,000 adult and children's books each year. Includes English-language fiction and nonfiction. Concise critical evaluations from 95 selected journals in the humanities, sciences, and social sciences, as well as library review media. From January 1983. Updated monthly. Published by H.W. Wilson Company. Part of the FirstSearch collection of databases.
- *Books In Print. A general reference most useful for research in humanities, life sciences, technology, social sciences, and current events.* Information on 2,000,000 in-print, out-of-print and forthcoming books from more than 44,000 North American publishers. Publisher-verified information on all U.S. books in print. Includes more than 900,000 new or revised records each year. Covers scholarly, technical, popular, adult, juvenile, and reprint titles. Publisher information. Updated weekly. Published by Reed Reference Publishing. Part of the FirstSearch collection of databases.

- *BPI. A full-text database most useful for research in business, economics and statistics.* See: Business Periodicals Index.
- *Britannica.A general reference full-text database most useful for research in the humanities, social sciences, life sciences, physical sciences, technology, health sciences, and current events* This multimedia hypertext version of Encyclopedia Britannica has the full-text contents of thelatest Encyclopedia Britannica including maps, charts, and graphs. Includes Merriam-Webster Collegiate Dictionary 10th Edition. Keyword and natural-language searching of text files.
- *Business Dateline.A full-text database most useful for research in business, economics and statistics.* More than 500,000 citations on regional business activities and trends as well as major stories on local firms, their products and executives. Citations from more than 450 business sources. Access to and full-text articles from some 450 newspapers, city business magazines, wire services in the United States and Canada. A business information tool for monitoring the latest trends in industry, health, environmental issues and education. From 1985. Updated weekly. Published by UMI. Part of the FirstSearch collection of databases.
- *Business and Industry. A full-text database most useful for research in business, economics and statistics.* A multi-industry, international database that provides access to company, industry, market, and product information. Covers more than 600 leading trade and business sources. Facts, figures and events dealing with all manufacturing and service industries, public and private companies, products and markets at an international level. B & I focuses on a body of literature that includes leading trade magazines, newsletters, general business press and international business dailies. From 1994. Updated daily. ASCII full-text articles are available online from more than half of the sources. Published by Responsive Database Services, Inc. Part of the FirstSearch collection of databases.
- *Business Index. A database most useful for research in business, economics and statistics.* Bibliographic citations with abstracts of 950 international business, management and trade journals. Subjects include business, economics, finance, management and current events. From 1982. Updated daily. Published by Information Access Company.
- *Business Organizations, Agencies, and Publications Directory. A database most useful for research in business and economics.* A guide to international business information sources. Lists contact name, address, telephone, fax numbers, and a description of the organization's founding, membership, activities, and sources. Published by Gale Research, Inc. Part of the FirstSearch collection of databases.
- *Business Periodicals Index (BPI). A full-text database most useful for research in business, economics and statistics.* BPI offers full-text of some 400 journals and business magazines with full images. BPI offers extensive cross-referencing, articles indexed under specific business headings, title enhancement providing supplementary information for article titles, complete bibliographic data, name authority control, and citations to book reviews.
- *Business Yellow Pages of America. A database most useful for research in business, economics and statistics.* Database of more than 200,000 American businesses.
- *CARL UnCover. A general-reference full-text database most useful for research in the arts, humanities, business, economics, statistics, education, psychology, social sciences, and current events.* Provides access to contents of 17,000 current English-language journals. More than 7,000,000 articles are available with 5,000 being added daily. UnCover addresses virtually all fields of study. This commercial document delivery service provides free table of contents information for each journal. If an article was published with an abstract, UnCover

provides the abstract. Search the database by subject or name, or view the contents of particular issues after choosing a journal title. While there is no fee for using the UnCover search capabilities, there are fees for articles ordered through the service.

- *Census/Population-Housing 1990. A database most useful for research in business, economics, statistics and social sciences.* See: U.S. Census of Population and Housing, 1990.
- *Chicano Database. A general reference most useful for research in education, psychology, social sciences, and current events.*
  Chicano Database (CDB) contains more than 42,000 bibliographic citations describing the Mexican-American (Chicano) experience. Also, describes the broader Latino experience including Puerto Ricans, Cuban Americans, and Central American immigrants. Reference books, Chicano journals, mainstream journals, anthologies and other forms. A comprehensive bibliographic resource for information about Mexican-American topics. From 1992. Published in English and Spanish by Chicano Studies Library University of California, Berkeley.
- *CIA World FactBook. A general reference full-text database most useful for research in economics, social sciences, statistics, technology and current events.* Electronic version of the FactBook printed annually by the Central Intelligence Agency for U.S. Government officials. Information provided by the American Geophysical Union, Bureau of the Census, Central Intelligence Agency, Defense Intelligence Agency, Defense Mapping Agency, Defense Nuclear Agency, Department of State, Foreign Broadcast Information Service, Maritime Administration, National Science Foundation Polar Information Program, naval Maritime Intelligence Center, Office of Territorial and International Affairs, U.S. Board on Geographic Names, U.S. Coast Guard, and others.
- *CINAHL. A database most useful for research in health sciences, life sciences, physical sciences, and technology.* Cumulative Index to Nursing and Allied Health Literature covers 950 English-language nursing, allied health, biomedical and consumer health journals, publications of the American Nursing Association, and the National League for Nursing. Database contains more than 250,000 records. Adds 30,000 a year. Subjects include aging, AIDS, cancer, diseases, health care, information sciences, medicine, nursing, public health, rehabilitation, biomedicine, management, behavioral sciences, health sciences librarianship, education, and consumer health. Bibliographic database provides references to new books, book chapters, pamphlets, audiovisuals, dissertations, educational software, selected conference proceedings, standards of professional practice, nurse practice acts, critical paths, and research instruments. Indexing from 1982. Abstracts from 1986. Updated twelve times a year. Published by CINAHL Information Systems.
- *Code of Federal Regulations (CFR). A full-text database most useful for research in arts, business, economics, education, government regulation, health sciences, humanities, life sciences, physical sciences, psychology, social sciences, statistics, technology and current event.* CFR database contains rules and regulations established by the executive departments and agencies of the federal government divided into 50 Titles representing broad areas subject to federal regulation. Once a regulation appearing in the Federal Register becomes effective, it is published in the Code of Federal Regulations. CD-ROM updated monthly.
- *Commerce Business Daily. A full-text database most useful for research in business, economics and statistics.* CBD offers the complete text of the print publication Commerce Business Daily which announces products and services wanted or offered by the U.S. government. Information on all proposed procurements of $25,000 or more by civil and

military agencies, including potential research interests; procurement surplus U.S. government; special notices, occasional announcements of business related events; and more.

- *Compact Disclosure/Securities and Exchange Commission. A full-text database most useful for research in business, economics and statistics.* Compact D/SEC database contains financial and management information on more than 12,000 public companies extracted from annual and periodic reports filed with the U.S. Securities and Exchange Commission (SEC). To be included in the database, a company must have at least 500 shareholders of one class of stock, at least $5,000,000 in assets, and file either a 10K, 20F, or appropriate Registration Statement with the SEC in the last 18 months. Directory information on a company and the rank of certain companies within a particular industry as specified by certain criteria (e.g., sales, net assets, gross profit, etc.). Searchable by company name; type of business (using SIC code); geographic area; financial information; full text fields; number of shares/employees; owners, officers, directors; stock exchange; fortune number. There are no records in the database for management investment companies. Real estate limited partnerships, oil and gas drilling funds, or mutual funds.

- *Computer Select. A full-text database most useful for research in computer science, mathematics, physical sciences, technology, business an d statistics.* Full text of 100 computing journals including articles, product specifications, industry information and definitions relating to all areas of computers. The database delivers 12 months of full text articles from more than 70 computer publications; twelve months of abstracts from more than 40 computer publications; more than 1,000 articles with informational graphics; specifications for more than 70,000 hardware, software, and communications products; and contacts and profiles of more than 12,000 vendors and manufacturers.

- *Consumers Index. A full-text database most useful for research in social sciences, current events, business, economics and statistics.* A subject index to the contents of more than 100 periodicals. The database provides information categorized from general (the home) to the specific (automobiles), by periodical (Consumer Reports) or by brand name (Coca-Cola). The information includes consumers, librarians and library users, business professionals, and educational instructors. Some records are linked to full-text articles. Published by The Pierian Press, Inc. Part of the FirstSearch collection of databases.

- *Contents First (Contents 1ˢᵗ). A general reference most useful for research in education, humanities, social sciences, life sciences, psychology and current events.* Table of contents page and holdings information for 13,000 journals in science, technology, medicine, social science, business, the humanities, and popular culture. Some journals in other languages are included. From January 1990. Updated daily. Published by OCLC. Part of the FirstSearch collection of database.

- ***DataTimes EyeQ****. A general reference most useful for research in social sciences, business, technology, and current events.* Indexes articles in 100 newspapers from major U.S. cities and regions including Commerce Business Daily, Investor's Business Daily, and the Christian Science Monitor. International titles include 34 publications from Canada, Europe, Middle East, Asia and Pacific Rim. Articles, reviews, editorials, and commentaries. From February 1, 1996. Updated daily. Published by the Data Times Corporation. Part of the FirstSearch collection of databases.

- *Disclosure Corporate Snapshots. A full-text database most useful for research in business, economics and statistics.* A database of corporate and financial information on more than 11,000 corporations filing with the SEC whose shares are traded in the United States.

Database contains summary data, at least two years of selected balance sheets and income statement items, segment data, five-year summaries, price/earnings/dividend data, comments, subsidiaries, filings, lists, and offer tables. Indexed fields include auditor, comments, company name, city, state, zip code, description of business, stock exchange, fortune number, officers, SIC codes, and subsidiaries. Updated weekly. Published by Disclosure, Inc. Part of the FirstSearch collection of databases.

- *Dissertation Abstracts. A general reference useful for research in any field including the arts, business, current events, economics, education, health sciences, humanities, life sciences, psychology, social sciences, statistics, and technology.* Abstracts of dissertations accepted at accredited institutions since 1861. Includes the complete range of academic subjects. Covers every doctoral dissertation completed in the U.S. at accredited institutions. Includes some master's theses and foreign language dissertations. Updated monthly. Published by UMI. Part of the FirstSearch collection of databases.

- *Dow Jones News Retrieval Service. A general reference full-text database most useful for research in the arts, humanities, business, economics, statistics, education, psychology, social sciences, and current events.* Dow Jones Publications Library is a resource of more than 60,000,000 documents and more than 3,400 trade and business publications including 48 of the top 50 newspapers. Uses the Publications Information on just about any subject, region, industry, company or person. Trade publications cover everything from farming to pharmaceuticals, bits to banking, mining to marketing.

- *EBSCO MasterFILE. A general reference full-text database most useful for research in the arts, humanities, business, economics, statistics, education, psychology, social sciences, and current events.* Index to 2,300-plus business, humanities, general science, social science, health, and trade periodicals. The complete text of the articles from many of these periodicals may be available through this database with the earliest coverage, beginning in 1990. Abstracting began in 1984. Updated weekly.

- *Economic Literature (EconLit). A database most useful for research in business, economics, statistics, and social sciences.* Subject indexing and citations with abstracts to articles from more than 400 economics journals, more than 500 collective volumes per year, plus books, dissertations, and working papers. Subject indexing and abstracts of books and subject indexing of dissertation titles are included. From January 1969. Updated monthly. Published by American Economic Association. Part of the FirstSearch collection of databases.
1983. *Education Abstracts. A database most useful for research in education and psychology.*
1984. Indexing more than 400 English-language periodicals and yearbooks published in the
1985. U.S. and elsewhere. Subjects include administration, teaching methods and
1986. curriculum, literacy, government funding, and more. From June Abstracts from
1987. August 1994. Updated monthly. Published by H.W. Wilson Company.Part of the
1988. FirstSearch collection of databases.

- *eHRAF. A full-text database most useful for research in social sciences.* See: Human Relations Area Files.

- *Encyclopedia Britannica. A general reference full-text database most useful for research in the humanities, social sciences, life sciences, physical sciences, technology, health sciences, and current events.* See: Britannica

- *Engineering Information Village (EiVillage). A full-text database most useful for research in physical sciences and technology.* The EiVillage website offers a wide range of information related to the field of engineering including Compendex Plus, a comprehensive interdisciplinary engineering database.

- *Environment. A database most useful for research in physical sciences, technology, and social sciences.* Environment (Environmental Sciences and Pollution Management) is an index of comprehensive, multidisciplinary coverage of relevant fields across the environmental sciences from all the primary sources for 11 abstracts journals for the current year plus five previous years. Updated monthly.

- *Environmental Periodicals Bibliography. A database most useful for research in physical sciences, technology and social sciences.* More than 450,000 bibliographic citations. References include papers and reports on air, water, and land pollution, energy issues, human ecology, and nutrition and health. From 1972. Updated twice a year. Published by the Environmental Studies Institute, Santa Barbara, CA.

- *Environmental RouteNet. A full-text database most useful for research in physical sciences, technology, and social sciences.* Bibliographic and full-text sources of interest to environmental science and accessible through 23 environmental subject categories. RouteNet includes daily news highlights, research, statistics, standards, patents, legislation, regulations, site-specific information, publications, information on education, grants and funding, etc.

- *Environmental Sciences and Pollution Management. A database most useful for research in physical sciences, technology, and social sciences.* A database of environmental science, including toxic hazards of chemicals, pharmaceuticals, and other substances; air, marine, and freshwater pollution, as well as biochemical applications in water treatment and pollution. Published by Cambridge Scientific Abstracts. Part of the FristSearch collection of databases.

- *Educational Resources Information Center (ERIC). A database most useful for research in education, psychology, and social sciences.* More than 800,000 bibliographic references to published and unpublished sources on thousands of educational topics. Includes journal articles, books, theses, curricula, conference papers, and standards and guidelines. Information from *Resources in Education* (RIE) and *Current Index to Journals in Education* (CIJE). From 1966. Updated monthly. Published by U.S. Department of Education. Part of the FirstSearch collection of databases.

- *EventLine. A database most useful for research in current events, the humanities, business, economics, physical sciences, social sciences, and statistics.* A multidisciplinary, multinational database of past and coming events. Covers all the sciences, industry and business, and major sporting events. Data on conventions, symposia, exhibitions, trade fairs, and major sporting events. Dates and locations of meetings, marketing strategy planning, travel planning assistance, statistics on meetings trends. Published by Elsevier Science Publishing Company. Part of the FirstSearch collection of databases.

- *Expanded Academic Index and Full-Text ASAP. A general reference full-text database most useful for research in the arts, humanities, social sciences, business, economics, statistics, and current events.* See: InfoTrac SearchBank.

- *FactSearch. A general reference full-text database most useful for research in business, economics, the humanities, statistics, social sciences, government information and current events.* A guide to statistical statements on current social, economic, political, environmental, and health issues from 1,000 newspapers, periodicals, newsletters and documents such as *The Christian Science Monitor,* the *Congressional Record*, congressional hearings, daily press briefings of the White House, State Department, and Department of Defense. Some links to free full-text documents. Covering 1984 to present. Updated every six weeks. Based on the publication *A Matter of Fact.* Published by The Pierian Press, Inc. Part of the FirstSearch collection of databases.

- *FastDoc. A full-text database most useful for research in the arts, humanities, social sciences, business, economics, and statistics.* The database covers more than 900,000 articles in all disciplines from more than 1,000 journals. Companion to ArticleFirst database. Published by OCLC. Part of the FirstSearch collection of databases.

- *General Science Abstracts. A database most useful for research in physical sciences and technology.* Index to more than 150 journals and magazines from the U.S. and Great Britain covering such subjects as anthropology, astronomy, biology, botany, chemistry, computers, earth sciences, environmental issues, health, mathematics, medicine, physics, and zoology. Includes articles, reviews, biographical sketches, and letters to the editor. From May 1984. Abstracts from March 1993. Updated monthly. Published by H.W. Wilson Company. Part of the FirstSearch collection of databases.

- *GEOBASE. A database most useful for research in physical sciences, technology, and social sciences.* More than 600,000 abstracts covering worldwide literature of geography, geology, ecology, international development and related disciplines. Subjects include cartography, climatology, energy, environment, geomorphology, hydrology, photogrammetry, sedimentology, geochemistry, geophysics, paleontology, petrology, volcanology. More than 2,000 journals fully covered and an additional 3,000 selectively covered. From 1980. Updated monthly. Published by Elsevier Science Publishers. Part of the FirstSearch collection of databases.

- *GeoRef. A database most useful for research in the physical sciences and technology.* Index to more than 2,000,000 geology and earth science references and the index terms that describe them. More than 4,000 journals in 40 languages are searched regularly along with new books, maps and reports. North America from 1785. Entire world from 1933. Updated bimonthly. Published by American Geological Institute. Part of the FirstSearch collection of databases.

- *GPO Access. A full-text database most useful for research in government information.* Index to more than 450,000 records for documents including all types of U.S. government documents such as the Federal Register, the web version of *The Monthly Catalog*, congressional reports, hearings, debates, and records; judiciary materials; documents issued by executive departments such as Defense, State, Labor, Office of the President, etc. From July 1976. Updated monthly.

- *GPO Monthly Catalog. A full-text database most useful for research in government information and social sciences.* Index to more than 450,000 U.S. government documents such as congressional reports, hearings, debates, and records; judiciary materials; executive department documents such as Defense, State, Labor, Office of the President, etc. From July 1976. Updated monthly. Published by U.S. Government Printing Office. Part of the FirstSearch collection of databases.

- *Historical Abstracts. A database most useful for research in the humanities and social sciences.* Bibliographic citations and abstracts of thousands of world history (from c.1450) research journal articles from more than 2,100 international journals in 50 languages (excluding the U.S. and Canada) covering prehistoric times to the present. Also cites dissertations and book reviews of recently published books. Abstracts are in English. Searchable by subject, author, title and time period. From 1982. Updated three times a year.

Published by the American Historical Association. See : *America: History and Life,* for research literature on the history of the United States or Canada.

- *HRAF. A full-text database most useful for research in the social sciences.* See: Human Relations Area Files.

- *HealthSTAR. A database most useful for research in health sciences, medicine, physical sciences, psychology, and technology.* More than 2.4 million bibliographic citations of journal articles, monographs, monographic series, technical and government reports, meeting abstracts, conference papers, book chapters and newspaper articles. More than 70,000 new health sciences and health care records added annually. HealthSTAR merges contents of HEALTH database with HSTAR database with a focus on clinical and non-clinical aspects of health care delivery. Database cites literature on health care administration, economics, planning and policy as well as health services research, clinical practice guidelines and health care technology assessment. Updated monthly. Produced by the U.S. National Library of Medicine.

- *Humanities Abstracts. A database most useful for research in the arts and humanities.* Index to more than 400 periodicals in archaeology, art, classics, film, folklore, journalism, linguistics, music, the performing arts, philosophy, religion, world history, and world literature. Compliments the monographs accessible via WorldCat. Indexing from February 1984. Abstracts from March 1994. Updated monthly. Published by H.W. Wilson Company. Part of the FirstSearch collection of databases.

- *Human Relations Area Files (HRAF CD-ROM and eHRAF Internet). A full-text database most useful for research in the social sciences.* Information on a broad range of cultures worldwide, from scholarly books, dissertations, journal articles and conference papers. Disciplines covered include anthropology, geology, history, psychology, medicine, ethnic studies, fine arts, literature, social work, law, and archaeology.

- *H.W. Wilson Select. A full-text database most useful for research in the humanities and social sciences.* Database includes more than 430 periodical titles. All records have companion ASCII full-text. Published by H.W. Wilson Company. Part of the FirstSearch collection of databases.

- *Ideal. A general reference full-text database most useful for research in business, economics, statistics, education, psychology, social sciences, and current events.* International Digital Electronic Access Library. (IDEAL) contains the full-text of all 175 primary research journals from *The Academic Press* beginning with 1996 issues. Articles are in Adobe Acrobat PDF format.

- *Index to Legal Periodicals and Books. A database most useful for research in business, economics, statistics, social sciences and the law.* Article indexing from some 620 legal journals, yearbooks, institutes, bar association organs, law reviews, and government publications originating in the United States, Canada, Great Britain, Ireland, Australia, and New Zealand. Covers all areas of jurisprudence including court decisions, legislation, and original scholarship. Includes book reviews. From August 1981. Updated monthly. Published by H.W. Wilson Company. Part of the FirstSearch collection of databases.

- *InfoTrac SearchBank. A general reference full-text database most useful for research in the arts, humanities, social sciences, business, economics, statistics, physical sciences, technology, and current events.* InfoTrac SearchBank's Expanded Academic Index and Full-Text ASAPincludes full-text articles from more than 500 academic periodicals and indexing and abstracting for nearly 1,600 scholarly and general interest periodicals. Database includes the New York Times, Wall Street Journal, Congressional Quarterly weekly report, Newsweek and the Harvard Business Review. SearchBank's Business & Company ProFile ASAP provides full text business journals and current company data. Indexing and abstracting for approximately 900 business and trade periodicals, and full text for 460 titles. From 1980. Updated daily. Published by Information Access Company.

- *INSPEC. A database most useful for research in electrical engineering and electronics, computing and information technology, and physics and physical sciences.* The largest English-language file of bibliographic information and abstracts on the world's output of published works in electrical engineering and electronics, computing and information technology, and physics. Covers scientific and technical journals and conference proceedings. Includes some books, reports, and dissertations. Published by the Institution of Electrical Engineers (IEE). Part of the FirstSearch collection of databases.

- *International Index to Music Periodicals. A database most useful for research in the arts and humanities.* IIMP draws content from 400 international music periodicals from more than 30 countries. Covers music from scholarly studies to fads.

- *Kirk-Othmer Encyclopedia of Chemical Technology. A full-text database most useful for research in chemistry.* Compilation of applied chemical science and industrial technology on CD-ROM database offering comprehensive information on coating processes, combustion, synthetic elastomers, electroplating, liquid separation absorption, biopolymers, and other topics.

- *LEXIS-NEXIS. A general reference full-text database most useful for research in the arts, business, economics, education, government information, health sciences, humanities, life sciences, physical sciences, psychology, social sciences, statistics, technology, and current events.* LEXIS offers full-text of legal materials, court cases, state statutes, federal agency materials, and the United States Code. NEXIS news and business information service provides full-text of international, national and regional newspapers, news wires, magazines, trade journals and business publications, including the New York Times and the Des Moines Register. NEXIS has more than 7,100 sources, of which, 3,700 provide their entire publications online.

- *Library Literature. A database most useful for research in computers, education, information science, library science, psychology and social sciences.* More than 220 library and information-science periodicals published internationally in the library and information science fields, along with more than 600 books and 600 monographs per year. From December 1984. Updated monthly. Published by H.W. Wilson Company. Part of the FirstSearch collection of databases.

- *Linguistics and Language Behavior Abstracts (LLBA). A database most useful for research in communication, linguistics, psychology, and the social sciences.* Includes all aspects of linguistics and language including interpersonal behavior and communication and nonverbal communication. From 1967.

- *Maps & Facts. A database most useful for research in business, economics, education, geography, humanities, social sciences, statistics, and current events.* A world atlas with hundreds of detailed maps and a database of statistical information for 227 countries.

- *MathSciNet. A database most useful for research in mathematics, physical' sciences and technology.* MathSciNet is the searchable Web database providing access to more than 55 years of mathematical reviews and current mathematical publications from 1940. Both bibliographic data and review texts are available from 1980 to present. Bibliographic data is available from 1940-1979. Items listed in the annual indexes of mathematical reviews but not given an individual review are also included.

- *Matter-of-Fact Database. A general reference full-text database most useful for research in the arts, business, economics, education, environment, health sciences, humanities, life sciences, physical sciences, political science, psychology, social sciences, statistics, technology, and current events.* Contains original quotes from speeches and written works containing statistics on current social, economic, political, health, environmental, and public policy issues. Twenty-five percent of the abstracts are derived from congressional hearings, 15% from the *Congressional Record*, and the remainder from general interest and specialized periodicals, newsletters, and newspapers. Many records contain World Wide Web addresses for access to the full text of the *Congressional Record*, debates of the Canadian House of Commons, and Handsards of the Australian House of Representatives and Senate. Also included are speeches of the President, White House press briefings, State Department daily press briefings and background notes, electronic newsletters of the World Health Organization, and many other national, regional, and international resources. More than 80,000 bibliographic records with more than 12,000 new records added annually. From 1984. Updated quarterly. Published by the Pierian Press, Inc.

- *MDX Health Digest. A database most useful for research in the health sciences, physical sciences, and technology.* A consumer health database with bibliographic citations with abstracts of health articles written for the general public. Records are drawn from 200 regularly reviewed publications including newsletters, general interest magazines, medical journals, medical school and hospital publications and bulletins, and newspapers. From January 1988. New records added monthly. Published by Medical Data Exchange. Part of the FirstSearch collection of databases.

- *MEDLINE. A database most useful for research in health sciences, life sciences, medicine, physical sciences, psychology, public health and technology.* Bibliographic data with abstracts from more than 3,700 journals published in 70 countries, covering all areas of medicine. Most of the nearly 9.000,000 records include abstracts. Subjects include anesthesia, dentistry, health sciences, health care, life sciences, medicine, nursing, psychiatry, public health, research and development and veterinary medicine. Citations and abstracts to worldwide biomedical literature including research, clinical practice, administration, policy issues, and health care services. Chapters and articles from selected monographs. Searchable by index terms, synonyms, and subject headings found in the U.S. National Library of Medicine's Medical Subject Headings (MeSH) thesaurus. From 1965. Author abstracts are available for about 60% of the citations since 1975. Updated monthly. Published by the U.S. National Library of Medicine.

- *Mental Measurements Yearbook. A database most useful for research in education and psychology.* MMY describes more than 1,850 standardized educational, personality, vocational aptitude and psychological tests published commercially. Lists authors, publishers, time requirements, score descriptions, intended populations, validity/reliability data and critical reviews. Published by the Buros Bureau of Mental Measurements.

- *Microcomputer Abstracts (MicrocompAbs). A database most useful for research in computer science, mathematics, physical sciences, and technology.* Index to more than 75 popular magazines and professional journals on micro computing in business, education, industry, and the home. Includes abstracts for feature articles, news, columns, programs, buyer and vendor guides, product announcements, and reviews of software, hardware, and books. From

January 1989. Updated monthly. Published by Learned Information, Inc. Part of the FirstSearch collection of databases.

- *MLA International Bibliography. A database most useful for research in the arts, humanities, language studies and social sciences.* The MLA International Bibliography provides easy access to a vast spectrum of subjects, from the prose of Machiavelli, to the poetry of Adrienne Rich; from genres to literary forms, from national literatures to regional dialects. Includes the MLA Bibliography Thesaurus. Indexes critical literary and language scholarship on modern language, literature, linguistics, drama and folklore in more than 4,000 journals and serials published worldwide, as well as books, monographs, essay collections, working papers, proceedings, dissertations and bibliographies. Some 500,000 records with 45,000 added annually. Updated quarterly. From 1963. Published by Modern Language Association of America. Part of the FirstSearch collection of databases.

- *Moody's Company Data with EDGAR. A database most useful for research in business, economics, and statistics.* Information on more than 10,000 domestically-based companies on all of the NYSE, AMEX, NMS, NASDAQ-NMS, OTC   and regional exchanges. Business and financial database allows searching on any word or phrase through more than 140 financial variables, rank or sort by any variable, customize viewing and output, export to spreadsheet, software, and more.

- *Music Literature Abstracts. A database most useful for research in the arts and humanities.* See: RILM Abstracts of Music Literature.

- *National Newspaper Index. A general reference full-text database most useful for research in the social sciences, technology, business, economics, humanities, statistics, and current events.* Bibliographic index of five national newspapers: *The New York Times, Wall Street Journal, Christian Science Monitor, Washington Post* and *Los Angeles Times.* Covers most recent four years. Updated daily. Published by Information Access Company.

- *National Trade Data Bank. A database most useful for research in government information.* NTDB contains U.S. import and export information including balance of payments; international investment in the U.S. and U.S. investment abroad; operations of U.S. affiliates of foreign companies; national and international labor; economic, demographic, and energy statistics; international price indexes; world agricultural production and commodity status reports; trade projections and barriers; stock price indexes for G-10 countries; currency exchange rates; and U.S. export manuals. Published by the U.S. federal government.

- *NetFirst. A general reference full-text database most useful for research in the arts, humanities, business, economics, statistics, education, psychology, social sciences, government information, and current events.* Database contains bibliographic citations, abstracts, summary descriptions, subject headings, and classification codes for Internet resources including World Wide Web pages, interest group listservs, library catalogs, FTP sites, Internet services, Gopher servers, electronic journals, and newsletters. Includes location information to connect with resources of interest. Updated weekly. Published by OCLC. Part of the FirstSearch collection of databases.

- *New York Times. A general reference full-text database most useful for research in social sciences, technology, business, economics, humanities, statistics, and current events.* Full-text of *The New York Times* newspaper articles within 90 days. Abstract and index database covers international, national, business and New York regional news as well as sciences, medicine, arts, sports, and lifestyle news. Articles are from the *Late City Edition,* the same edition as produced on microfilm.   Abstracts accompany all other articles. From 1994. Updated daily. Published by the New York Times. Part of the FirstSearch collection of databases.

- *Newspaper Abstracts (NewsAbs). A general reference most useful for research in the social sciences, humanities, business, economics, statistics, and current events.* Indexes significant stories in 50 national and regional newspapers, including *the New York Times, the Los Angeles Times, Washington Post, Boston Globe, San Francisco Chronicle, USA Today, and the Wall Street Journal.* From 1989. Updated weekly. Published by UMI. Part of the FirstSearch collection of databases.

- *Nineteen-Ninety (1990) Census/Population-Housing. A database most useful for research in the social sciences, statistics and government information.* See: U.S. Census of Population and Housing, 1990.

- *OCLC Union Lists of Periodicals. A general reference union catalog most useful for research in current events, the arts, humanities, education, psychology, social sciences, government information, and information technology.* Database includes more than 7,000,000 listings linked to more than 750,000 bibliographic records in WorldCat, and the OCLC Online Union Catalog. Listings of journals owned by OCLC member libraries provide local holdings information so users can search for locations of periodicals in libraries. Published by OCLC. Part of the FirstSearch collection of databases.

- *PAIS Decade. A database most useful for research in business, economics, statistics, government information, and social sciences.* Public Affairs and Information Service database includes more than 200,000 records representing articles, books, conference proceedings, government documents, book chapters, and statistical directories about public affairs. Covers the most recent 10 years. Updated monthly.

- *PapersFirst. A general reference most useful for research in the social sciences and current events.* Database indexes more than 580,000 papers included in every congress, conference, exposition, workshop, symposium, and meeting worldwide and received by the British Library Document Supply Centre's proceedings collection. From October 1993. Updated monthly. Full text of papers cited may be ordered. Companion to ProceedingsFirst database. Published by OCLC. Part of the FirstSearch collection of databases.

- *Periodical Abstracts (PerAbs). A general reference most useful for research in the social sciences, humanities, psychology, business, economics, statistics, women's studies, and current events.* Abstracts of more than 1,500 general periodicals and academic journals, covering business, current affairs, economics, literature, religion, psychology, women's studies, and others. Included are transcripts of more than 80 news-oriented television and radio shows. Full text of articles from 530 journals. From January 1986. Updated weekly. Published by UMI. Part of the FirstSearch collection of databases.

- *Philosopher's Index. A database most useful for research in humanities.* Citations and abstracts from books and more than 270 journals of philosophy and related interdisciplinary fields. From 1940.

- *Predicasts F & S Indexes Plus Text. A full-text database most useful for research in business, economics and statistics.* Facts and figures about companies, products, markets, and applied technology in all manufacturing and service industries worldwide. Database shows one and two line summaries, abstracts from the PROMT (Predicasts Overview of Markets and Technology) database, and some full-text articles.

- *PRO CD Biz. A database most useful for research in business and statistics.* Contains 18 million records of white page listings for businesses compiled from current white page listings in the U.S. telephone directories updated annually. Published by PRO CD, Inc. Part of the FirstSearch collection of databases.
- *PRO CD Home. A database most useful for research in business and statistics.* Contains 80 million records of white page listings for residences compiled from current white page listings in U.S. telephone directories. Updated annually. Published by PRO CD, Inc. Part of the FirstSearch collection of databases.
- *ProceedingsFirst. A general reference most useful for research in the social sciences, humanities, psychology, statistics and current events.* More than 19,000 citations and tables of contents of papers presented at every congress, symposium, conference, exposition, workshop and meeting worldwide and received at The British Library Document Supply Centre's collection of conference proceedings. Lists papers presented at each conference. From October 1993. Updated monthly. Companion to PapersFirst database. Published by OCLC. Part of the FirstSearch collection of databases.
- *Project Muse. A general reference full-text database most useful for research in the arts, humanities, education, psychology, mathematics, social sciences, computer science and current events.* Full-text access to 42 scholarly journals in the humanities, social sciences and mathematics including two electronic-only journals: *Postmodern Culture* and *Theory & Event.* From Johns Hopkins Press.
- *PsycFIRST. A database most useful for research in education, psychology and the social sciences.* More than 1,300 journals on psychology and related fields. Coverage is current year plus the most recent three years. Updated monthly.
- *PsycINFO. A database most useful for research in business, education, medicine, psychiatry, psychology and sociology.* This bibliographic database with abstracts is the master source from which the subset PsycLIT is derived. Contains nearly a million records covering the same types of literature, and materials from the same relevant disciplines as PsycLIT. More than 60,000 new records added annually. PsycINFO provides indexes to journals, book chapters and books plus dissertations and technical reports not found in PsycLIT. Journals indexed from 1974. Books and chapters from 1987. Updated quarterly. Published by the American Psychological Association.
- *PsycLIT. A database most useful for research in business, education, medicine, psychiatry, psychology and sociology.* This bibliographic database with abstracts is a major subset of the PsycINFO database. PsycLIT contains more than 760,000 records covering the same types of literature and materials from the same relevant disciplines as PsycINFO. More than 52,000 new records added annually. PsycLIT provides indexes to journals, book chapters and books. However, PsycINFO's dissertations and technical reports are not included. Journals indexed from 1974. Books and chapters from 1987. Updated quarterly. Published by The American Psychological Association.
- *Reader's Guide Abstracts. A general reference most useful for research in the arts, humanities, education, psychology, social sciences, technology, and current events.* Abstracts of articles published in popular U.S. and Canadian periodicals. Includes current events and news, fine arts, fashion, education, business, sports, health and nutrition, consumer affairs, and others. From January 1983. Updated monthly. Published by H.W. Wilson Company. Part of the FirstSearch collection of databases.

- *RILM Abstracts of Music Literature. A database most useful for research in the arts and the humanities.* International bibliography of scholarly writings on music and related disciplines in 202 languages, including original language titles; title translations in English; full bibliographic information; abstracts in English.   Includes all forms of scholarly works. Published by Musicale Literature International de Repertoire.   Part of the FirstSearch collection of databases.
- *Social Sciences Abstracts. A database most useful for research in the social sciences and social work.* Index to more than 400 international, English-language periodicals in anthropology, criminology, economics, geography, international relations, political science, social work, sociology, and the law.   Describes feature articles, biographical sketches, interviews, obituaries, scholarly replies, and book reviews longer than one-half page.   Book reviews of government documents and letters to the editor are not included.   Each record contains a bibliographic citation and library holdings for the journal.   Indexing from February
- 1983.   Abstracts from January 1994.   Updated monthly.   Published by H.W. Wilson Company.   Part of the FirstSearch collection of databases.
- *Social Work Abstracts Plus. A database most useful for research in the social sciences and social work.* Subjects include alcohol abuse, crime, gerontology, psychology, public health, social issues, social sciences, sociology and welfare in tow distinct bibliographic databases: Social Work Abstracts and The Register of Clinical Social Workers.   Social Work Abstracts contains information on the fields of social work and human services from 1977 to present. The database provides exceptional coverage of more than 450 journals in all areas of the profession, including theory and practice, areas of service, social issues, and social problems. The Register of Clinical Social Workers is a directory of clinical social workers in the United States.   It contains the name, address, telephone number, employer, education, and employment history as well as type of practice and licensing information.   Social Work Abstracts Plus offers more than 58,000 records with more than 2,500 added annually. Updated semiannually.   From 1977.   Published by the National Association of Social Workers.
- *Sociofile. A database most useful for research in social sciences and social work.* Bibliographic data on the latest international findings in theoretical and applied sociology, social science, and policy science.   Subjects include aging, AIDS, alcohol abuse, anthropology, cities, communications, counseling, crime, culture, death, demography, drugs, education, emergency response, ethics, gerontology, health, healthcare, industry, law, medicine, philosophy, planning, political science, psychiatry, psychology, public administration, public affairs, public health, rehabilitation, religion, social issues, social sciences, sociology and welfare.   Database combines Sociological Abstracts with Social Planning Policy and Development Abstracts (SOPODA).   SOPODA enhances the theoretical focus of sociological abstracts by adding the applied aspects of sociology. References journal articles, dissertations, book abstracts, chapter abstracts and association paper abstracts as well as citations from books, films, and software.   Some 400,000 records with more than 15,000 new records added annually.   Updated quarterly.   Abstracts from 2,300 journals published since 1974.   Enhanced bibliographic citations for dissertations added since 1986.   Published by Sociological Abstracts, Inc.
- *Sociological Abstracts (SocioAbs). A database most useful for research in the social sciences.* Database indexes and abstracts more than 1,900 English-language journals in sociology, social work, and related disciplines including anthropology, criminology, demography,

education, law and penology, race relations, social psychology, and urban studies.   From 1963.   Updated six times per year.   Published by Sociological Abstracts, Inc.   Part of the FirstSearch collection of databases.

- *Statistical Masterfile. A full-text database most useful for research in business, economics, statistics, social sciences and government information.* Statistical data published in the U.S. by international intergovernmental organizations in the areas of population, business and financial activities, domestic and international trade, government programs, health, and other economic, demographic, social, and political issues.   Comprises *American Statistics Index, Index to International Statistics,* and the *Statistical Reference Index.*   Subjects include international station government and other publications containing these types of data: population, business and financial activities, domestic and international trade, government programs, health, and other economic, demographic, social, and political trends.

- *STAT-USA/Internet. A full-text database most useful for research in business, economics, statistics and government information.* More than 300,000 reports and statistical series, including press releases, trade leads, and reports that are released on a daily or weekly basis. STAT-USA/Internet databases include: The National Trade Data Bank (NTDB), the National Economic Social and Environmental Data Bank (NESE-DB), the Economic Bulletin Board, and the Global Business Opportunities Service.

- *Thomas Register. A database most useful for research in business, economics and statistics.* Product information for North American manufacturing companies.   Information on all product and supplier alternatives for U.S. and Canadian markets.   Public and private company information for 148,000 manufacturers, classified under more than 50,000 product classes and more than 110,000 brand names.   Some or all of this information: company name, address, SIC codes, number of employees, exporter status, and executive name.

- *Ulrich's Plus. A general reference most useful for research in communications, mass media, physical sciences, technology, social sciences, and current events.* Listing of currently published periodicals.   International in scope.   Access to 200,000 entries of 67,000 publishers and corporate authors from more than 200 countries around the world.   More than 127,000 periodicals in more than 700 subject areas and 60,000 serials, annuals, continuations, conference proceedings, and other publications issued irregularly or less frequently than twice a year.   Updated information on 66,000 periodicals per year, and about 11,000 irregular serials or annuals and new titles per year.   More than 1,600 cross-referenced subject headings including annotations for about 50,000 titles.   Complete names and addresses of serial publishers and distributors. Updated quarterly. Published by Bowker Electronic Publishing.

- *Union Lists of Periodicals. A general reference union catalog most useful for research in current events, the arts, humanities, education, psychology, social sciences, government information and information technology.* See: OCLC Union Lists of Periodicals.

- *U.S. Census of Population and Housing, 1990. A database most useful for research in the social sciences, statistics, and government information.* Social, economic, population and housing statistics from the 1990 U.S. Census. Geographic areas covered for various statistics include the entire U.S. as well as states, counties, county subdivisions, census tracts/block numbering areas, metropolitan areas and urbanized areas.   Population and housing characteristics measured by the Census are as diverse as occupation, ancestry, age, and telephones per housing unit.

- *U.S. Patent Search. A full-text database most useful for research in business, economic and government information.* Citations with abstracts and exemplary claim to U.S. patents published since 1975. Search by title, patent number, date of issue, inventor, state or country of residence of first inventor, assignee, application serial number and filing date, classification, keyword, abstract, exemplary claim, and status. Source is the complete text of patents issued electronically by the U.S. Patent and Trademark Office.

- *Wilson Business Abstracts.A database most useful for research in business, economics and statistics.* Citations and abstracts for more than 345 international English-language business magazines, covering accounting, finance, management, personnel, and small business. Library holdings information on each journal. Book review cites from January 1986. Article abstracts from June 1990. Updated monthly. Published by H.W. Wilson Company. Part of the FirstSearch collection of databases.

- *WorldCat. A general reference union catalog most useful for research in the arts, humanities, education, psychology, social sciences, government information and current events.* WorldCat, the OCLC Online Union Catalog, contains more than 35 million bibliographic records in 370 languages and covering information from 4,000 years of knowledge. The database describes books, periodicals and other materials owned by libraries around the world. WorldCat tells which library owns a particular title. The title then can be requested via Interlibrary Loan (ILL). Does not include individual articles, stories in journals, magazines, newspapers, or book chapters. Updated daily. Published by OCLC. Part of the FirstSearch collection of databases.

- *Worldscope GLOBAL. A full-text database most useful for research in business, economics and statistics.* Financial information on 9,000 of the world's largest companies in 32 countries derived from corporate annual and 10K reports, disclosure statements, newspapers, and wire services. Coverage includes industrials, utilities, transportation, banks, insurance and others. Describes the business and shows selected financials, key ratios, and officers. Updated weekly. Published by Disclosure, Inc. Part of the FirstSearch collection of databases.

- *World Almanac and Book of Facts. A general reference full-text database most useful for research in the arts, business, economics, education, health sciences, humanities, life sciences, physical sciences, psychology, social sciences, statistics, technology, and current events.* Database first published in 1868. Covers arts, entertainment, U.S. cities and states, people in the news, nations of the world, sports, the environment, vital statistics, science, technology, computers, taxes, etc. Published by K-III Reference Corporation. Part of the FirstSearch collection of databases.

- *Zoological Record. A database most useful for research in physical sciences and technology.* Global coverage of zoological literature with emphasis on systematic taxonomic information. Thesaurus provides easy viewing of subject, geographical, palaeontological and taxonomical hierarchical vocabularies. Users control terms best suited for their subjects. From 1978. Updated quarterly.

How To Access Electronic Databases

Electronic databases are published by commercial firms that distribute them on CD-ROM and via the Internet. Public libraries and college libraries purchase rights to receive and use the information stored in an electronic database. Database information is made available selectively by college and university libraries to students and faculty and by public libraries to the patrons they serve. A user can obtain access to a database by visiting a library and using a computer to read a CD-ROM, or by traversing the World Wide Web to a server computer which stores a database for retrieval on the World Wide Web.

Activity: Using a database to solve a problem.

Database used in this example: Internet Grateful Med.

Published by the U.S. National Library of Medicine, Internet Grateful Med (IGM) is a World Wide Web application running on a gateway system at the U.S. National Library of Medicine. We'll use IGM because it's free and available to any personal computer with Internet connection. Internet Grateful Med's World Wide Web address is:

http://igm.nlm.nih.gov

Internet Grateful Med helps a user create and refine a search, then submits the search to retrieval engines. It searches MEDLINE, which contains 9,000,000 citations to biomedical literature of the world dating back to 1966, and 10 other databases B AIDSLINE, AIDSDRUGS, AIDSTRIALS, DIRLINE, HealthSTAR, HSRPROJ, HISTLINE, OLDMEDLINE, PREMEDLINE, and SDILINE.

Searching is free, but there are charges for ordering actual printed documents for delivery through a medical library. Internet Gratefu l Med is available 24 hours a day, seven days a week. The IGM server computers regularly handle more than 400 simultaneous users during much of a working day and an average total of 375,000 users connected each weekday.

Recommended Web Browser Software

Current versions of Netscape Navigator, Netscape Communicator, Microsoft Internet Explorer, or the America Online web browser work well. Citations retrieved in a search can be e-mailed free to you or someone else. In Netscape navigator 3.x, use Mail Document under the File command. In Netscape Navigator 4.x, use Send Page under the File command. The document will be in HTML tagged format, not in ASCII text format. Microsoft Internet Explorer 3.x does not offer this feature. In Internet Explorer 4.x, use Send...Page By Email under the File command.

Logging on the Internet Grateful Med

The Uniform Resource Locator (URL) or World Wide Web (WWW) address for Internet Grateful Med is: *http//igm.nlm.nih.gov*. When you open your web browser and go to that URL, the Internet Grateful Med introductory screen will be displayed. You need only click Proceed to go on to the Search Screen. Several hyperlinks on the introductory screen can lead you to other information.   In particular, the name AInternet Grateful Med in the sentence AInternet Grateful Med is a product of the U.S. National Library of Medicine at the lower part of the screen is a hyperlink to a 19-slide show giving an interesting overview of the system.

(Source for this searching example: *Internet Grateful Med: New User's Survival Guide,* U.S. National Library of Medicine. Internet document posted November 26, 1997, and retrieved January 29, 1998, at the uniform resource locator): http//igm.nlm.nih.gov/splash/igm_20/IGM.survival.guide.html

How To Search

Looking at the Internet Grateful Med search screen, you will see a row of action buttons across the top. Below that, in an area marked Enter Query Terms, is a set of three empty text boxes where you can enter words or phrases to search for. Whatever you enter in those boxes can be searched as subject, author name, or word in title. The box with the default Subject on it is a pull-down menu. Click your mouse button on it to open it.

At the lower part of the screen is an area of pull-down menus marked Apply Limits. Open them to see options. Limits are useful when a search is conceptually on target, but is retrieving too much information because there is so much in MEDLINE on the subject. MEDLINE is constantly growing as new citations are added, so don't be surprised when the numbers of citations retrieved by the search examples below increase as time goes by.

Using the same searching example found on IGM, let's select the phrase magnetic resonance imaging for a search. Enter magnetic resonance imaging in the first query term box. Click Perform Search. In a few seconds, Internet Grateful Med will have sent the search to NLM's mainframe computer and will return the first eight of more than 27,000 hits. This is probably more than you wanted, so click Return to Search Screen.

Applying Limits

Go to the Apply Limits area of the screen. Limit languages to English. Limit publication types to Randomized Controlled Trial. Limit study groups to Human. Limit age groups to All Child. Then, again click Perform Search. You will see duplicate action buttons at the bottom of the screen for convenience. Now there's a much more manageable total of 48 hits.

Search Results

The Internet Grateful Med Results screen has a number of actions at the top. The information icon takes you to help text which explains the possible actions. Each title retrieved is itself a web hyperlink. Click on one of the titles. Internet Grateful Med displays the long record for that citation with its abstract, if there is one. You can tell which of the long records will have abstracts by looking for the indicator, abstract present to the right of the NLM citation ID at the bottom of a short record.

You can mark several of the short records to be expanded into long records as a group by clicking on the select box to the left of the short record. Mark the first and second short records. Then issue a Fetch for Display command with the action button at the top of the screen. Long records for the two citations you selected will be displayed together.

Click Return to Results. Click Next Records. The next group of eight short records will be displayed. Click Details of Search.Internet Grateful Med displays the number of citations each of your terms found, the number of citations retrieved by the combination of terms, and the way each limit applied reduced that number. There are times when this is very helpful.

Click Return to Results. Click Other Years. Internet Grateful Med shows you that this search retrieved 48 citations in the 1994-97 years and offers to run the same search in earlier years. Click on A1990-93. The search is run against those years, resulting in 11 more hits.

Click Return to Search Screen. Click Clear Search. You will have an empty search screen with everything set back to the defaults, ready for the next search.

Try the Help Text

Click on the little blue is information icon next to Enter Query Terms. Internet Grateful Med will display its help text for that action area. All the help text (more than 30 context-sensitive help files) is in this format. It starts by saying where you were when you clicked the i. It says very briefly what you can do there. Then it offers hyperlinks to additional information, beginning with more detail.

We have worked hard on the help text. Those who use it will benefit significantly by getting better searches. Those who don't will never know the power of the assisted searching Internet

Grateful Med can provide. Click you web browser's Back button at the top of your web browser window to return from the help text to wherever you came from. In this case, you will return to an empty Search Screen.

Author and Title Word Search

Enter Donald Lindberg in the first query term box. Pull down the menu (marked Subject by default) and select Author Name. Next, enter Betsy Humphreys in the second query term box. Pull down the menu to the right of that query term box and select Author Name. Enter medical informatics in the third query term box. Pull down its associated menu and select Title Word. You have set up a search for citations by Donald Lindberg and Betsy Humphreys which contain the word medical and the word informatics in the title.

Click Perform Search. You should get two hits, both from JAMA, the Journal of the American Medical Association. Click Return to Search Screen. Click Clear Search to set up for another search.

Explore the Metathesaurus

Internet Grateful Med offers an amazing array of search formulation assistance in a layered approach. But if you never use the Metathesaurus-with the "Find MdSH/Met"a Terms command you may never know it. MeSH stands for Medical Subject Headings. Metathesaurus is a significant resource. The 1997 version contained 739,000 names for 332,000 concepts from more than 30 biomedical vocabularies, thesauri and classifications.

Fact sheets available from the IGM introductory screen discuss NLM's Unified Medical Language System (UMLS) and the Metathesaurus in some detail. Start exploring Metathesaurus by entering a word or phrase in a text box on the Query Screen, then click on Find MeSH/Meta Terms. For practice in retrieving some interesting hits, try entering one of the terms in the next paragraph as a Query Term on the IGM Search Screen. Then click Find MeSh/Meta Terms:

> *Interesting terms: Lyme, tick, hearing, emotion, monkey, fish, frog, horseshoe crab, heart, coagulation, hemorrhage, vehicle, politics, street, crack cocaine, retardation, laser, nutrition, food, diabetes, neuropathy, serodiagnosis, contraception, death, mortality, computer, artificial intelligence, neural networks, imaging, aspirin, toxin, neurotoxin, epilepsy, sleep, ergonomics, ear wax, ventilation, or sclera.*

When you are presented with a list of concepts, try clicking on one of the underlined concepts to see where it takes you. Anything underlined is a hyperlink and will take you to additional information-including the MeSH trees.

MeSH is NLM's hierarchical-controlled vocabulary used for indexing articles in MEDLINE and other MEDLARS databases. Every term in the tree displays itself as a hyperlink. It's simple to back up the tree to a more general term and grab it for your search by clicking the green light go icon. For instance, try entering aspirin in the first query term box on the Search Screen. Click on Find MeSH/Meta Terms. You will see the Metathesaurus Browser Screen showing the concept hit list for aspirin.

Aspirin itself is a hyperlink near the top of the list. Click on it. You'll be taken to the Metathesaurus Information Screen for aspirin. Look at the definition. Look at the MeSH tree displays. The term aspirin appears in three different places in MeSH, so there are three tree contexts you can open with a click.

Every term in the trees is a hyperlink that will refocus the whole display around that term if you click on it. Don't click on a term in the trees yet. Scroll down to Other Metathesaurus Information. Click on Qualifiers applied with this concept. You'll get a list of all the subheading qualifiers NLM's indexers attached to the term Aaspirin when they used it to index an article in MEDLINE. Each is itself a hyperlink. Click on therapeutic use. You will see the co-terms. The MeSH headings our indexers used as central concepts of an article when aspirin qualified by therapeutic use was also a central concept of the article.

At the top of the list is Myocardial Infarction. If you are interested in that triad (*Aspirin/therapeutic use AND *Myocardial Infarction), just click on the green light go icon to the left of Myocardial Infarction. The whole triad will be pulled to the Search Screen. The default action is to search MEDLINE, so all you have to do now is click Perform Search. If it gets too many hits, add a limit. The whole idea of Internet Grateful Med is to bring an enormous knowledge source to your fingertips and make its power accessible.

MeSH Vocabulary

Every term entered in a query term box on the Search Screen is automatically compared with all of MeSH. If it is a MeSH heading, it is searched both as a MeSH heading and as a text word or text words. If it is a MeSH heading which is explodable, it is automatically exploded so any more specific terms indented under it in the hierarchy will be included in the search. Use the Details of Search button to see exactly what IGM sent to the retrieval engine for your search.

If you go to the Metathesaurus, all kinds of additional information about your term and related terms will be available. Even the MeSH annotations are there...see the Additional MeSH Information hyperlink under Other Metathesaurus Information on the Metathesaurus Information Screen.

Using Metathesaurus

Here's another practice search. There were news articles about mad cow disease in Great Britain and the fatal human condition Creuzfeld-Jakob Syndrome. Enter mad cow in the first query term box. It is not helpful to enter the word disease when searching the Metathesaurus because that word appears more than 40,000 times. It isn't specific enough to be useful in retrieving concepts. Just enter mad cow and click Find MeSH/Meta Terms. Internet Grateful Med checks all 739,000 names for 332,000 concepts in the Metathesaurus and returns a ranked concept hit list. Look at the top of the list.

The Metathesaurus goes from the lay term mad cow disease to the medical term Encephalopathy, Bovine Spongiform. This is exactly the right term for searching MEDLINE for citations dealing with this neuropathy. You can either select the term immediately by checking the select box to its left and clicking on Continue formulating search or you can hyperlink on the term itself for more information. For the purposes of this example, click on "Encephalopathy, Bovine Spongiform." Internet Grateful Med displays its Metathesaurus Information Screen for the term. The definition notes that this is a scrapie-like disorder of cattle.

The term appears in two places in the hierarchical trees of the MeSH controlled vocabulary. The first of the two MeSH tree contexts is open. Everything in that display is a dynamically created hyperlink. You can refocus the whole display around any of those terms by clicking on it, but don't do that now. Use the scroll bar on the right side of your web browser window to scroll further down in this record, past the tree display. You will come to a section marked, Other Metathesaurus Information. Click on Co-terms applied with this concept (descending frequency.)

Internet Grateful Med tells you that the list you will receive is 38 Kbytes long, so those on modems can gauge how long it might take to download. Creuzfeld-Jakob Syndrome is the first term on the co-term list. The help text invoked by the blue information icon at the tope of this screen explains in detail what is meant by co-terms. Click on the green light icon left of Creuzfeld-Jakob Syndrome. Note that Internet Grateful Med goes straight to the search screen and fills both those terms for you. Both terms have been given asterisks, which tells the system AI want only articles for which both these terms were considered major topics of the article by NLM's indexers.

Click Perform Search, and note that Metathesaurus has helped by finding what was needed when we knew only a lay term rather than the right biomedical concept name to use in searching for articles about the disease. More than 100 good citations were retrieved. Click Return to Search Screen. Click Clear Search.

Subheadings and Major Topic Restriction

For another experience, type telemedicine in the first query term box. Click Find MeSH/Meta Terms. The Metathesaurus hit-list is presented. Telemedicine is at the top. Select it by clicking on the radio button to its left. This is not the same as hyperlinking on the term itself. Click Continue formulating search. A new screen is displayed, where you can add the major topic restriction or add subheadings as qualifiers. Click the radio button to the left of Must be major topic of citations. Click on Select qualifiers to focus search.

A list is presented of the subheadings allowed as qualifiers with the concept Telemedicine. Click the radio button to the left of trends. Trends is a hyperlink. Clicking on it will get you an explanation of how NLM uses that qualifier when indexing articles. Use your web browser's Back button to return from that explanation if you go there.

You have selected the subheading trends. Click Return to Major Concept Screen. From that screen, click Return to Search Screen. Internet Grateful Med fills the screen with your term, the subheading qualifier you added, and the asterisk that indicates that you want to retrieve only articles for which that term was a major topic of the articles. Click Perform Search. The first 8 of 45 retrieved citations on trends in telemedicine are displayed. Click Return to Search Screen. Click Clear Search.

Qualifier Cross-Reference Automatic Mapping Search

For another practical example, enter nutritional management in the first query term box. Enter hypertension in the second query term box. Click Perform Search. The first 8 of 226 retrieved citations are displayed. Click Details of Search. Note that Internet Grateful Med has converted the term nutritional management to a better term, the subheading diet therapy. It then OR'ed the text words nutritional and management into the search as well. This automatic mapping will bring better retrieval results. Click Return to Results. Click Return to Search Screen. Click Clear Search.

Full-Text Clinical Practice Guidelines

Here is yet another search to try. Enter bedsores in the first query term box. Click Find MeSH/Meta Terms. Internet Grateful Med goes to the medical term, Decubitus Ulcer. Hyperlink on Decubitus Ulcer. Internet Grateful Med displays the Metathesaurus Information Screen for this concept with a definition. Use your web browser's scroll bar to scroll down past the MeSH tree display, past the Other Metathesaurus Information section, to the bottom of the page.

Notice the Links to Other Database(s). Clicking on Clinical Practice Guidelines Supported by Agency for Health Care Policy and Research will lead you to the clinical guideline titled, Treatment of Pressure Ulcers. This is the full-text document coming delivered by a different web server at NLM. You can search within it, or view its Table of Contents and look at sections that way. Use your web browser's Back button to return to Internet Grateful Med. You may have to use the button several times.

Images from the History of Medicine (IHM)

More than 60,000 online images from the History of Medicine Division of NLM are available. Type in a term on the Internet Grateful Med search screen. Go to the Metathesaurus by clicking Find Related. Scroll down to the Links to Other Databases section at the bottom of the Metathesaurus Information Screen and click Images from the History of Medicine.

The term will be sent to another retrieval engine at NLM, which will attempt to find matches among the words in brief records cataloging thousands of images. If there are matches, that system offers to display them (the default is batches of seven thumbnail-sized images). Click on a thumbnail image to see it full size. Hyperlink on the title of the image to invoke a Scan Results screen from which you can see its catalog record. The IHM retrieval engine uses a Boolean AND operation so single-word terms may get more successful retrieval than multi-word terms. Use the web browser Back button to return to Internet Grateful Med. You may have to use the button several times.

Analyze Search Function

A useful feature of Internet Grateful Med is its ability to analyze a search and suggest things that might improve it. Much of the analysis depends on relationships in the Metathesaurus, so it works best on terms you pick from a Metathesaurus concept hit list after using the Find MeSH/Meta Terms button.

If you're interested in exercise as a therapy for hypertension in geriatrics, enter exercise in the first query term box. Enter hypertension in the second box. Enter geriatrics in the third box. Click Perform Search. Internet Grateful Med notes that the search resulted in no retrieval. It shows the term-by-term details of the search. All three terms individually had hits, but the combination got nothing. You can try searching in other years, or try modifying the search. Click Return to Search Screen. Click Analyze Search. Internet Grateful Med looks at all the terms of the failed search and tries to offer related terms which might augment retrieval, or substitute terms which might result in retrieval when one of the terms was getting nothing.

IGM offers related terms for exercise. One of them is Physical Fitness. Select it. The related terms for hypertension aren't helpful, so leave them. The last is the key one. Internet Grateful Med has recognized that the term geriatrics is what NLM calls an occupational specialty heading. It will retrieve articles about the profession of geriatrics, not articles about older patients. Follow the suggestion, and replace the term geriatrics with Aged. Two things have been selected on this screen: Physical Fitness, and Aged. Click Return to Search Screen. The search has been modified with Internet Grateful Med's help and now will find articles on exercise OR physical fitness, AND hypertension, AND aged. Click Perform Search.

A search which initially got no retrieval at all now gets 271 hits. Internet Grateful Med can recognize 78 occupational specialty headings. This is an example of how an intelligent retrieval system with vast knowledge sources at its disposal can help users find what they need in large databases. Click Return to Search Screen. Click Clear Search.

Associated Expression

Here's another example. Enter abuse control in the first query term box. Click Perform Search. The first eight of 576 retrieved citations are displayed. Click Details of Search. Internet Grateful Med has identified the term abuse control B which is not a MeSH heading and therefore not going to get optimal retrieval in MEDLINE B and mapped it to the MeSH heading Child Abuse qualified by the subheading prevention & control OR elder abuse qualified by prevention & control OR Spouse Abuse qualified by prevention & control. There are some 5,000 such Associated Expression mappings in Internet Grateful Med.

Printing and Downloading What You've Found

You can print retrieved sets of citations using the Print command in your web browser. Internet Grateful Med has an option for downloading part or all of the retrieval set at once, rather than looking at them eight at a time. On the Results Screen, one of the actions is Download for Disk. When you take that action, Internet Grateful Med displays a Download Action Screen. You can set up Internet Grateful Med to download consecutive records B the default is 25 records starting with the first one your search retrieves B or only selected records you have chosen from the IGM Results Screen(s). You can then choose from three levels of detail: short records, long records with abstracts but without MeSH headings, and long records
with abstracts and MeSH headings. Click the Select Format button to go on to the next screen.

On the IGM Download Format Screen, you choose whether you want the records in easy-to-read IGM format or in tagged MEDLARS format for loading into a reference manager program such as Endnote. Click Download Now. Internet Grateful Med will go to one of NLM's main retrieval systems for the records you requested, set up a file containing them on the Request Manager gateway, and initiate an automatic file transfer protocol (FTP) transfer over the World Wide Web to your computer.

Chapter Four
Establishing A Conceptual Framework For Conducting Research
George R. Taylor, Ph.D.
Kriesta L. Watson, Ph.D.

INTRODUCTION

Empirical research requires that a systematic plan of operation be in place. In order to achieve this goal, some type of master or blue print should be developed to organize, control and conduct the process. Frequently already constructed quantitative and qualitative research designs do not meet the many unique research studies designed by students. This necessitates that the student develop his/her own framework or paradigm for conducting research in one of the paradigms.

A conceptual framework may take several forms. It may be a model, flow chart, graph or a paradigm. It may be elementary or sophisticated, descriptive or causal, graphic or narrative. The conceptual framework developed in Figure 4.1 is more descriptive and causal and is represented by a wheel. The components should not be considered static, rather, they should be considered as fluid. The model rests upon ideas, concepts, and observations. They provide the necessary thought and intuition to propel and drive the wheel. Those components provide the initial approach to begin scientific inquiry. Once the initial problem has been perceived, complete infusion can only take place through systematically perusing the professional literature which is the anchor for the framework.

The conceptual model may provide some orderly and cohesive manner for conducting scientific and empirical research. Whether the research is qualitative or quantitative is not an issue. Most models can be adapted for use with either type of research because all research follows a basic strategy designed to seek solutions to problems. The constructed conceptual framework is based upon this supposition.

Initially, the student should have some concept, idea, or problem he or she wishes to investigate (see Fig.4.1). Once the problem area has been identified, the student must explore ways of answering the many questions posed. Several techniques may be employed such as seeking reactions from colleagues, academic advisors, and faculty committee members seeking expert advice, scanning his/her own needs, interests, and experiences, and observing phenomena.

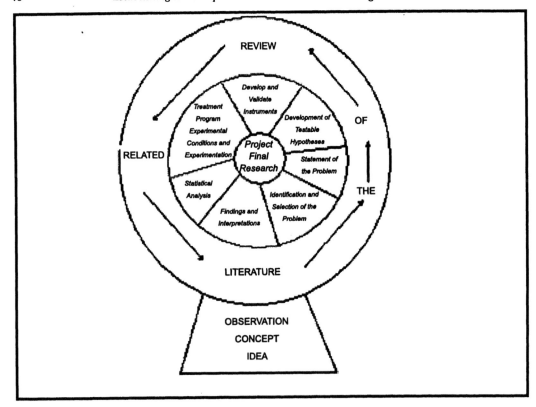

Figure 4.1: Conceptual Framework for Conducting Research

Review of the Literature

The review of the literature is the power source of the conceptual framework in conducting both quantitative and qualitative research. Refer to Appendix D for details. A comprehensive review of the literature is of prime importance before conducting quantitative or qualitative research. Once ways have been explored to ascertain the feasibility of the identified problem and the need for the investigation, attempts must be made to verify the need for the study in the available literature.

Reviewing the literature is important for several reasons. First, it provides an overview of contributions made by others; it can show how to use innovative and connotative intervention strategies. It also can reveal procedures for selecting the random sample. It can indicate how instruments were constructed, modified, or adapted. It may also provide a source for constructing hypotheses. It may indicate appropriate types of statistics to employ. It can indicate the feasibility of conducting the research. It may indicate successful, as well as non-successful methods and procedures. It may indicate a yardstick by which one may judge his/her research as well as what controversies currently exist in the field.

If the review of the literature is inadequate, the total framework is weakened. All of the component parts are related and integrated with the review of the literature. The review is conducted prior to methods and procedures, or in the beginning for quantitative research, and the reverse is true when conducting qualitative research. The relationship between the review of the literature and other research components follow.

Identification, Selection, and Statement of the Problem

These critical areas are frequently minimized in the research process. Generally, students tend to overstate the problem areas or do not offer a valid rationale for selecting or accepting it. A review of the literature will assist students in making direct and clear statements by providing a model for them to emulate in the formation of their problems and subproblems.

Students, through the use of reviewing previous research, will be equipped to:

1.   Analyze the problem and relate the findings to their initial questions
2.   Find a variety of sources for research topics
3.   See how topics are delimited and clarified
4.   State the problem in a complete grammatical sentence with such clarity that an independent researcher will be able to understand it.

Of particular importance in research studies is the construction of realistic questions. If research questions are posed that the researcher is unqualified to answer, his answers may be guesses and are almost certainly invalid. Even though questions may be valid in some situations, in others, they may not be. Some respondents may intentionally or accidentally give untruthful answers to personally threatening questions. The authors of many studies concluded that truthfulness of respondents or subjects is vulnerable particularly when they are employed for the purpose of the collection of personal information, or when subjects who see, or imagine they see an opportunity to advance their personal interests by means of the returns made by them. The review of the literature will provide guidance in the area by assisting the researcher in locating problems and subproblems which are properly stated.

Subproblems

Subproblems are the total sum of the parts, that is, each subproblem assists in solving the major problem part by part. The researcher can get a general view of the major problem through its component parts. In constructing subproblems, the researcher should be aware of the following characteristics (Leedy, 1996):

1.   They would be a completely researchable unit. Each subproblem should stand on its own and communicate effectively to others. Subproblems are usually written as questions because questions tend to focus the attention of the researcher more directly upon the research.
2.   All subproblems are not necessarily researchable. Researchers must safeguard against pseudo subproblems which have no direct bearing on the research process. There are logistical problems which must be addressed because the research cannot begin without this information such as the best way to choose the sample, what instruments to use, how should certain attributes be measured, the size of the sample, etc., just to name a few.
3.   Within subproblems, interpretation of the data must be apparent.
4.   Researchers must control the number of subproblems stated. Some factors to be considered in delimiting the number of subproblems reported are: (a) the researcher should not confuse his personal problems with problems for research; (b) the researcher should not attempt to fragment the true subproblem(s); and (c) there may be a mixture of the preceding errors.
5.   Due to unrealistic goals, many researchers tend to overstate the subproblems and state goals which are impossible to attain.
6.   Subproblems may be effectively used in both quantitative and qualitative research methods.

Development of Research Questions and Testable Hypotheses

Research studies reported in professional literature provide a wealth of information relevant to constructing, defining, development, and testing various research questions and hypotheses. A good research document will reveal: (a) how research questions and hypotheses are stated, (b) the relationship of data sources to research questions and to hypotheses, (c) the different kinds of research questions and hypotheses, (d) how research questions and hypotheses are tested, (e) how hypotheses provide a mechanism for solving the problem, (f) the relationship of research questions and hypotheses to the statement of the problem, and (g) ways of constructing and testing valid research questions and hypotheses.

Research questions and hypotheses are essential in guiding the research process and providing solutions to solving problems in both quantitative and qualitative research. There are usually assumptions and propositions advanced by researchers in order to accept or reject them. Consequently, research questions and hypotheses should not be designed to be proved or disapproved. Attempting to prove or disapprove research questions and hypotheses may lead to the researcher biasing the facts by looking for data that will support the research questions and hypotheses.

Validating Pre/Post Instruments

This aspect of the research process frequently constitutes the greatest problem for many researchers, unless an existing instrument is used. In this case, validity and reliability have already been established. Validity and reliability are not necessary prerequisites in conducting qualitative research methods. We have addressed this issue in greater detail in Chapter 12. A review of the literature will indicate to what degree validity and reliability have been established. A comprehensive review of the literature will also reveal the following:

1. The type of instrument used, questionnaires, sources,   interviews,
   checklists, tape recorders, rating scales, or standardized instruments.
2. Samples of the instruments used.
3. Samples of how to construct instruments.
4. The type of measuring scale used.
5. The purposes and objectives for constructing the instrument.
6. Procedures for validating the instrument.
7. Type of statistical analysis employed.

In the event that the researcher wishes to modify or adapt the instrument, information is given relative to whom to contact. Researchers wishing to construct their own instruments will be exposed to the various procedures employed to validate them. The review will also provide information on pre/post testing of instruments. This aspect is necessary in establishing validity, rewriting items, reclassifying categories, improving format, reformatting scales, selecting samples to participate and directions for administration and scoring.

Treatment Program/Experimental Conditions

In many studies, treatment programs in quantitative research may be referred to as intervention, experimental program, experimental design, research design, etc. Guidelines and time lines are usually reported in the review of the literature with resources needed to effectively conduct the program. Field testing may be employed in some instances, with methods and procedures well articulated. The researcher will be provided with standard operating procedures for implementing and conducting the research. The various types of research designs are usually summarized with a rationale for their selection and use, subject selection, specific intervention strategies, resources (human and physical) and data analyses needed to implement, conduct, and evaluate the effectiveness of the intervention, are provided. Experimental conditions are not a prerequisite for conducting qualitative research. However, in spite of beliefs held by some individuals, qualitative research methods also employ the scientific methods in the solution of problems. The chief differences lie in controlling the variables in the study. Chapters 6, 14, and 15 expand this concept further.

Statistical Analysis

The review of the literature will indicate the type of statistical analysis employed. It will also show the relationship of one type of data source to another. It may provide certain techniques and statistical tools to test data (quantitative, qualitative, parametric, and non-parametric). It may reveal various methods and procedures for testing different types of experimental designs. Studies may provide a mechanism for arranging and formatting data. Analysis from review of the literature will assist the classifying data (nominal, ordinal, ratio, and interval) and indicate the appropriate type of statistics to use with each type. Unique ways of presenting data are reflected in some reviews.

The two major types of statistics are descriptive and inferential. Descriptive statistics describe data through the use of graphs, charts, percentage, central tendency, and correlations. Inferential statistics are used to determine whether or not to accept or reject hypotheses. Probability is also used to assist the researcher in reaching a decision relative to what the data are trying is depict, or tell the researcher the difference between two or more groups. In Chapters 8, 9, and 10, we have given specific examples of using descriptive and inferential statistics.

Findings/Results

Research findings reported in the literature will demonstrate how practical applications can be made of the findings. Limitations of the research may also be revealed and succinctly synthesized. Possible recommendations and suggestions for further research are frequently advanced. Good research will indicate to what degree the research questions and hypotheses have been accepted or rejected, how data should be organized and presented, and the selection and rationale for selecting the type of hypothesis.

The Conceptual Framework summary was designed to show the importance of the review of the literature and the research process. A systematic review of the literature will provide the researcher with in-depth information that bears on the topic under investigation. Some of that information is suggested methods of research, formulation and testing of hypotheses, interpretation of results, intervention strategies, sampling techniques and statistical analyses. Information found in the review of the literature is extensive and indispensable to the researcher.

Components outlined in the Conceptual Framework are designed to provide a model or blue print to guide the researcher successfully through the research process. It is our hope that researchers will apprise themselves of the vast amount of information found in the review of the literature and to objectively select those studies which have references for their work. In our view, a conceptual framework or a modular research paradigm is a prerequisite to selecting appropriate statistical tools. Statistics does not operate in a vacuum. A framework or model must be evident, a design must be developed, instruments must be identified, treatment or intervention should be evident, and some type of analysis and interpretation could be attempted. All of the aforementioned components may be reflected in a conceptual framework or model. Both quantitative and qualitative research may be conducted using the framework. Some of the experimental conditions outlined may be deleted when conducting qualitative research. Refer to Chapter 15 for additional details.

Statistical concepts are the last techniques to employ in conducting qualitative or quantitative research. They are considered to be the mathematical tool of research through which statistical data are gathered, manipulated, and analyzed. Statistics provide a mechanism for extracting out of a mass of data, the truths. It sets up a process for (a) assembling data, (b) recording it, (c) classifying it, and (4) order data. In essence, the major purposes of statistics are:

1.   To describe, generalize, and measure the relationships between variables.
2.   To generalize from small populations limited observations and characteristics about large populations.
3.   To determine whether there is any relationship between two or more factors which are presented in an experiment.

The conceptual framework appears to be an initial step in employing the scientific method in conducting both quantitative and qualitative research.

The Scientific Method

The conceptual framework outlined can be used in conjunction with the scientific method in the solution of problems in the social sciences. The steps involved according to Leedy (1996), Dowdy and Wearden (1991), and Gall, Borg, and Gall (1996) are:

1. Definition of the problem.
2. Statement of the hypothesis.
3. The deduction of observable consequences of the hypothesis.
4. Design of the experiment, survey.
5. Deductive reasoning.
6. Collection and analysis of data.
7. Confirmation or rejection of the hypothesis.

Steps in the scientific method are similar to those outlined in the conceptual framework. Both models are designed to provide insight to complex problems through using deductive and inductive thinking processes. Research conducted under each paradigm follow the same basic format. Both paradigms begin with observations and proceed through empirical testing, answering research questions, accepting or rejecting hypotheses, and interpreting data.

Gravetter and Wallanau (1996) provided us with additional clarity regarding the scientific method, they wrote that an important aspect of the science method is that the researcher must be objective, by not letting biases affect his decisions concerning the outcome of a study. In essence, the researcher should confirm or reject the hypothesis based upon the following steps in the scientific method.

A working knowledge of research methods, both quantitative and qualitative, including the scientific method, as well as statistics are needed. This book attempts to integrate all of the aforementioned research strategies as evidence in the conceptual framework. A detailed explanation of the scientific method is not within the scope of this text. The reader is referred to the listed sources at the end of this chapter.

Chapter Four Research Exercise

1. State your research problem in the form of a question. Include at least two variables.
2. How many subproblems can you derive from the major problem? List them and give justification for data needed for their solutions.
3. List and describe the major components of research design.
4. Which sources will you seek in defining your problem? Check all that apply and give a rationale for each case:
    _____ Reactions from colleagues
    _____ Academic Advisor
    _____ Expert Opinions
    _____ Review of the Literature
    _____ Observations
    _____ Interests and experiences
    _____ A solution to a problem
5. Topic: What is the relationship between teaching competencies and standardized test results?
6. Answer the following questions:
    a. Is this a research topic:
    b. Can the topic be transformed into an effective research problem?

c.　　What are some possible subproblems which could be developed?

d.　　What type of hypothesis will best accept of reject the research?

References

Dowdy, S., & Wearden, S. (1991). *Statistics for research.* New York: John Wiley and Sons.

Gall, M. D,, Borg, W. R., & Gall, J. P. (1996). *Educational research: An introduction* (6th ed.). White Plains, NY: Longman Publishers.

Gravetter, F. J., & Wallinau, L. B. (1996). *Statistics for the behavioral Sciences* (4th ed.). New York: West Publishing Company.

Leedy, P. (1996). *Practical research: Planning and design.* New York: MacMillan Publishing Company.

Chapter Five
Quantitative Research Methods
George R. Taylor, Ph.D.
Jacqueline H. Williams, Ed.D.
Thomas James, J.D.

INTRODUCTION

The major purpose of quantitative research is to make valid and objective descriptions on phenomena. The researcher is attempting to show how phenomena can be controlled by manipulating the variables. Attempts are made to discover principles and laws which can be generated to the larger population. The researcher attempts to achieve objectivity by not letting his personal biases influence the analysis and interpretation of the data. Personal contacts with subjects are kept at a minimum. Researchers seek to understand phenomena by isolating and examining the interrelationship among and between variables in a controlled setting.

Quantitative research methods cannot address the full range of problems in the behavioral sciences as well as in the physical sciences. Several problems are associated with this premise: (1) complete control and objectivity cannot be successfully achieved in the behavioral sciences, (2) data gathering instruments do not frequently answer all of the questions posed by the researcher in the behavioral sciences. Premised upon the above, it is our view that quantitative research cannot successfully evaluate the full range of human behavior. We have reserved Chapter 6 to discuss the value and importance of using qualitative research methods in the evaluation of human behavior. We attempted to show how both methods can be integrated in Chapter 15.

Quantitative research methods include historical, descriptive, correlational, causal-comparative, experimental, action research, and development (Charles, 1988). These methods yield numerical data and are evaluated by utilizing descriptive or inferential statistics. Statistical treatment of data through the use of descriptive or inferential means, are used to test hypotheses and determine if significant relationships or differences exist. The findings are generated to the population. Quantitative research methods have a lot in common due chiefly to the fact that all research follows a common process:

(1) Research questions or hypotheses are developed to guide the research.
(2) Data sources are identified depending upon the type of research being conducted.
(3) Research tools are identified, such as surveys, questionnaires, standard tests, interviews, rating scales, inventories, and check lists, are to name but a few.

(4)   Establishing methods and procedures, specific steps are outlined for conducting the research.

(5)   Analysis of data; what statistical procedures will be employed.

Interpretations of data are employed to report the findings as well as to determine what research questions or hypotheses are significant. Appropriate statistical procedures to employ with each of the research methods are outlined in Chapters 5 and 6.

Use quantitative research methods in market research when:

- You want to know "how many" and/or "how often"
- You want to profile a target audience by determining what proportion of the audience has certain behaviors, behavioral intentions, attitudes, and knowledge related to the health concern, and whether specific determinants predict behaviors at a statistically significant level.

Quantitative market research generally involves:

- Surveying a large group of people (usually several hundred) and
- Using a structured questionnaire that contains predominantly closed-ended, or forced-choice questions.

To design and conduct a quantitative survey, you should consider getting input from a survey expert. Together you will need to consider issues related to designing an appropriate sample, using valid and reliable measures, and conducting a pretest before the survey study is launched. Most surveys are custom studies designed to answer a specific set of research questions. Some surveys are omnibus studies, in which you add questions about your topic to an existing survey.

Surveys can be conducted face-to-face, by mail or telephone, or by computer. They can be self-administered or administered by an interviewer. Tools such as computer-assisted telephone interviewing or touch-screen surveys via a Web site can be useful.

- When the survey involves a convenience sample (e.g., a mall intercept study), data can be collected and analyzed fairly quickly.
- When the survey involves a statistically valid random sample, the results from the sample can be generalized to the entire population if the response rate is high enough.
- Surveys can provide reliable (i.e., repeatable) direction for planning programs and messages.
- Surveys can be anonymous, which is useful for sensitive topics.
- Like qualitative research methods, surveys can include visual material and can be used to pretest prototypes.
- You can generalize your findings beyond your participant group.

Cons

- They have a limited ability to probe answers.
- People who are willing to respond may share characteristics that don't apply to the audience as a whole, creating a potential bias in the study.
- They carne be very costly.

Common Uses

- Assess the proportion of your target audience within a community.
- Assess the proportion of a target audience that practices a behavior-Donald Campbell.
- Qualitative research involves analysis of data such as words (e.g., from interviews), pictures (e.g., video), or objects (e.g., an artifact.
- Quantitative research involves analysis of numerical data.
- The strength and weaknesses of qualitative and quantitative research are a perennial, hot debate, especially in the social sciences. The issues invoke classic 'paradigm war.'

- The personality/thinking style of the researcher and/or the culture of the organization is under-recognized as a key factor in preferred choice of methods.

Overly focusing on the debate of "qualitative versus quantitative" frames the methods in opposition. It is important to focus also on how the techniques can be integrated, such as in mixed methods research. More good can come of social science researchers developing skills in both realms that debating which method is superior.

Quantitative Experimental Design

The paradigm for scientific method in research is the true experiment or randomized control trial (RCT). Typical examples of RCT's include drug trails. Experimental designs are set up to allow the greatest amount of control possible so that causality may be examined closely. The three essential elements of experimental design are:

Manipulation: The research does something to at least some of the participants in the research.

Control: The experimenter introduces one or more controls over the experimental situation.

Randomization: The experimenter assigns participants to different groups on a random basis.

Features of Quantitative Research:

- The aim is to classify features, count them, and construct statistical models in an attempt to explain what is observed.
- Researcher knows clearly in advance what he/she is looking for.
- Recommended during latter phases of research projects.
- All aspects of the study are carefully designed before data is collected.
- Researcher uses tools, such as questionnaires or equipment to collect numerical data.
- Data in the form of numbers and statistics.
- Objective – seeks precise measurement and analysis of target concepts, e.g., uses surveys, questionnaires, etc.
- Quantitative data is more efficient, able to test hypotheses, but may miss contextual detail.
- Researcher tends to remain objectively separated from the subject matter.

Research must be conducted in the setting where all the contextual variables are operating. Past researchers have not been able to derive meaning from experimental research. The research techniques themselves, in experimental research, can affect the findings. The lab, the questionnaire, and so on, can become artifacts. Subjects can become either suspicious and wary, or they can become aware of what the researchers want and try to please them. Additionally, subjects sometimes do not know their feelings, interactions, and behaviors, so they cannot articulate them to respond to a questionnaire. One cannot understand human behavior without understanding the framework within which subjects interpret their thoughts, feelings, and actions. Researchers need to understand the framework (Siegle, D, n.d.)

Qualitative vs. Quantitative

Qualitative	Quantitative
The aim is a complete, detailed description.	The aim is to classify features, count them, and construct statistical models in an attempt to explain what is observed.
Researcher may only know roughly in advance what he/she is looking for.	Researchers knows clearly in advance what he/she is looking for.
Recommended during earlier phases of research projects.	Recommended during latter phases of research projects.
The design emerges as the study unfolds.	All aspects of the study are carefully designed before data is collected.
Researcher is the data gathering instrument.	Researcher uses tools, such as questionnaires or equipment to collect numerical data.
Data in the form of words, pictures or objects.	Data is in the form of numbers and statistics.
Subjective – individual's interpretation of events is important, e.g., uses participant observation, in-depth interviews, etc.	Objective – seeks precise measurement and analysis of target concepts, e.g., uses surveys, questionnaires, etc.
Qualitative data is more 'rich' time consuming and less able to be generalized.	Quantitative data is more efficient, able to test hypotheses, but may miss contextual detail.
Researcher tends to become subjectively immersed in the subject matter.	Researcher tends to remain objectively separated from the subject matter.

HISTORICAL RESEARCH

Historical research is designed to portray a complete and accurate description of historical events. It attempts to summarize significant past events or principles are valuable in assisting humankind to profit from past mistakes and planning appropriately for the future. Historical research may be focused toward conception ideas, institutions, or individuals. These factors seldom operate independently of each other. Rather, they are usually infused. An example of interrelation between concepts, institutions, and individuals, would be the civil rights movement. The basic concept was to improve the civil rights of African-Americans. The movement was directed at improving conditions for African-Americans in institutions in both the private and public sectors. The individual who led the movement was the late Dr. Martin Luther King, Jr.

Historical research, like all other research, follows the scientific method. It requires that a problem be identified, that a research problem or hypotheses be developed, that data be collected, organized, verified, validated, and analyzed. The final part of the scientific method is to verify the research question or hypothesis and write the final report. Historical research may be quantitative or qualitative or a combination of both methods.

Historical data sources of data are basically of two types, primary and secondary. Secondary sources are frequently used when primary sources cannot be secured. Primary data sources include any firsthand data such as oral or written documents including court records, diaries, office records, letters, autobiographies; local, state and national documents, individuals and relics, such as photographs, tools, war machinery, fossils, books, clothing, art and paintings, are to name but a few. Attempts are made by researchers to seek primary, original firsthand sources of information.

Secondary data sources include second hand information such as individuals who relate the experiences of others, authors who quote what others have written. Most newspapers and reference books which report events and contributions of others. Caution should be exercised in using secondary data sources because of frequent errors and mistakes made when information is exchanged or is passed from one person to another. Consequently, historical documents must be examined to validate their authenticity and accuracy before they can become reliable data sources. The process is referred to as *historical criticism*. Historical criticism is divided between *external* and *internal* criticisms (Borg, Gall & Gall, 1993). In external criticism, the researcher poses questions relevant to the nature of the document such as: Is it genuine? Is it the original copy? Who wrote it? Where? When? Under what conditions? It is important to ask these questions and to seek valid answers in order to validate the documents.

Internal criticism involves evaluating the accuracy and worth of the statements in a document. The researcher usually poses the following questions: What is the probability that the events occurred in the way described? Do the numerical data in the census report seem accurate? Does the author appear biased or prejudiced? Individuals may distort data to support their views or philosophy.

Descriptive Research

Descriptive research describes and interprets the present. Its primary purpose is to analyze trends that are developing, as well as current situations. Thus, data derived can be used in diagnosing a problem or in advocating a new or approved program. In essence, descriptive research is designed to solve present day problems. Solutions of present day problems will assist in projecting goals and directions for the future, as well as information relevant to how to reach designated goals. Information relevant to the present condition is a prerequisite in solving problems. Descriptive research may also aid in identifying goals and objectives while indicating realistic means for reaching them (Borg, Gall & Gall, 1993).

Prerequisite to conduct descriptive research is to operationally define terms and measures so than an adequate description can be given for the phenomena under study. Hypothetically, suppose a researcher wanted to study the relationship between democratic and autocratic leadership styles. An adequate description of leadership styles must be evident. Attitudes of employees must be assessed to assist in determining how leadership styles are viewed by the employees. As in historical research, descriptive research follows the scientific method. It involves more than collecting and tabulating data. Statistics such as frequencies, percentages, averages, graphs, sometimes variability and correlations, are used to analyze and interpret data. These statistical procedures are conducted to provide meaning, understanding, and solutions to present day problems.

Sources of data are numerous in descriptive methods. They include surveys, case studies, comparative studies, time-and-motion studies, document analyses, follow-up studies, trend studies, and predictive studies. All of the aforementioned methods can be valid techniques providing that they are properly constructed and used. Validity and reliability of instruments are beyond the scope of this text, refer to the following sources. *

CORRELATION RESEARCH

Correlations attempt to show relationships between two or more variables. They are classified as negative or positive and tend to show strong or weak relationships. These relationships assist the researcher in explaining, controlling, and predicting phenomena. Correlations do not show cause and effect. They simply indicate that relationships occur between two or more variables. The method permits the researcher to analyze several variables at once or a combination of variables to determine how they may affect certain behavior. Correlations assist us by explaining, predicting, and controlling conditions that affect us in our society.

The scientific method is employed in correlational research. Subproblems are not usually reported since the major problem can be investigated directly. Major questions are usually converted to null hypotheses. Null hypotheses usually indicate what the researcher hopes to discover. They are either accepted or rejected and determine the degree of relationship between two or more variables. The statistical process employed in the correlational method is referred to as a correlational coefficient. The procedure is expanded in greater detail in Chapter 8.

Source of Data

Unlike historical and descriptive research methods, correlational research requires few data sources. Only two data sources are needed depending upon the variables under investigation. Commonly used data sources include test scores, dichotomies, and ranking of attributes. Samples in correlational research, based upon the central limit theorem, should at least consist of thirty individuals.

EXPERIMENTAL RESEARCH

Experimental research follows the scientific method more closely than any other method. Conditions are rigorously controlled. The researcher is able to manipulate the experimental variables. Cause-effect relationships can be demonstrated using the experimental methods. It describes what will be when conditions are scientifically controlled (Borg, Gall, & Gall, 1993).
Direct manipulation of the independent variable and control of extraneous variables are necessary when conducting experimental research. Attempts are made by the researcher to keep constant all variables with the exception of the independent variable. Extraneous variables must be controlled so that the researcher will be able to determine to what degree the independent variable is related to the dependent variable.

Differences in the variation of the independent variable must be noted and the researcher must have the flexibility to manipulate and control the time that the subjects are exposed to the independent variable. A researcher may design a study to determine the effects of massive dosages of Vitamin C on reducing colds. The experimental group would be given massive doses of Vitamin C over a designated time. The control group would be given no Vitamin C. The results would be compared and the differences in the amount of colds experimental subjects contracted in comparison to the control group. Any differences noted in the experimental group may be attributed to the dependent variable (massive doses of Vitamin C). It should be noted that the researcher must consider such factors as age, gender, and other characteristics in drawing conclusions relevant to the impact of massive doses of Vitamin C on reducing colds

---

* Litwin, Marks (1995). How to Measure Survey Reliability and Validity. Thousand Oaks, CA: Sage Publications.

*McNamara, James F. (1994). Surveys and Experiments in Educational Research. Lancaster PA: Technomic Publishing Company.

Sources of Data

Data used in experimental methods includes standardized test results, assessment data, rating scales, interviews, surveys, questionnaires, personality tests, and informal tests, are to name but a few instruments. These instruments are frequently administered on a pre-post basis. Differences are determined by analyzing the differences between the pre-post test. If significant differences are noted, they are usually attributed to the experimental condition manipulated by the researcher.

Casual-Comparative

Casual-comparative research methods attempt to show cause-and-effect relationships. Researchers are attempting to discover how one variable influence another one. They are chiefly concerned with the factors which produced the cause-effect condition. Causal-comparative research should be used when the cause cannot be manipulated. The researcher is simply trying to establish cause-effect relationship (Best, 1959). An example of cause-effect relationship would be, for instance, a researcher finds during the early years of development, girls usually have a greater facility for language development than boys. There is nothing that the researcher can do to change the effect. This causal-comparative research is frequently referred to as *ex post facto* research. Boys' language development sequence cannot be changed to match girls. However, results may be used to change and provide additional instructional procedures for boys, making educators more aware of developmental differences between boys and girls during this stage and explaining the differences in language development between boys and girls. In essence, causal-comparative research yields data which may be used to predict, modify, and plan, to change directions and approaches.

Sources of Data

Assessment data, scores, ratings, and all types of instruments and measures are used to obtain data for causal-comparative research. Differences between the two groups are analyzed and there is no attempt to manipulate the variables.

ACTION RESEARCH

Action research basically follows the same format as experimental research. It is the application of the scientific method to practical problems requiring action solutions (McKay, 1992.) Stringer (1996), asserted that an action research project consists of gathering initial information, describing the situation, exploring and analyzing what is happening, and interpreting and explaining how and why things occur through the acts of planning, implementation, and evaluation.

Action research is not a method of research but an approach to research designed to solve practical problems. It is directed toward developing a greater understanding and improvement of practice over a given period of time. This type of research is a collaborative approach that permits individuals with the means to take action to resolve specific problems. This approach favors consensual and participatory procedures that enable people to (a) investigate systematically their problems and issues, (b) to formulate powerful and sophisticated accounts of their situations, and (c) to devise plans to deal with the problems at hand. Action research focuses on methods and techniques of inquiry that examines interactional practices, and perceptions about practice. Stringer (1966), asserted that action research is presented in such a way that its findings can be easily understood by both professional practitioners and lay individuals. Ary, Jacobs, and Asghar (1990), reported that action research has five advantages for researchers. They are:

1.   Action research contributes to the theory and knowledge base for enhancing professional practice. Researchers learn to reconstruct educational theory in

terms that are understandable, which may lead to more effective practice in their work setting.

2. Action research supports the researchers by assisting them in understanding and utilizing research findings.
3. Action research builds a collegial networking system which proves communication and reduces the isolation often experienced by researchers.
4. Action research helps practitioners identify problems and seek solutions in a systematic fashion.
5. Action research can be used at all levels in all areas of society.
6.

Sources of Data

Data sources are similar to those employed in experimental research. Sources depend upon the nature and type of study being investigated. Field tests are the procedure usually employed. In field testing, the project or program with primary data are used. Secondary data may be used in the absence of primary data.

Summary

All research methods follow a similar format regardless of the type whether it be historical, descriptive, correlational, experimental, action, causal-comparative, or research and development. All methods aid the researcher in understanding past and present events, analyze the relationships between factors, describe what will be, and tests the effectiveness of various approaches and needs in our society. All research demands standards and the employment of scientific and systematic procedures such as the identification of the problem, formulating and testing the hypotheses, collecting, organizing, validating and interpreting data, and generating the final reports.

Some common pitfalls to avoid when conducting any type of research:
1. Not choosing instruments, which are designed based upon the goals and objectives of the study.
2. Not demonstrating a comprehensive knowledge of the literature.
3. Not comparing scores to established by a different norm group. The problem is that the group being compared may not have the same traits and characteristic as the norm group.
4. Not choosing research topic where there is no personal interest.
5. Not using appropriate statistical tools.
6. Not assessing the importance of the topic
7. Not field and pilot testing instruments may result in constructing instruments which are not valid for the sample or population under study.
8. Not developing a sound theoretical framework for conducting the study.
9. Not considering the expense and costs before conducting the research.
10. Not considering timing employed in treatment and intervention techniques.
11. Not choosing inappropriate research methods.
12. Not considering ethics issues in conducting research, and
13. Not avoiding the "Hawthorne" effect.

CHAPTER FIVE RESEARCH EXERCISE

1. You are interested in determining the effects of parental involvement on school attendance.
   a. What type of quantitative method would you use to address the problem?
   b. What justification would you give for selecting the method?
   c. How would you state the hypothesis?
   d. What type of statistical tool would you employ? Justify the choice.

2. Assuming that you wanted to design a study to determine if social skills' intervention taught to primary boys would have an effect upon their interpersonal relations.
   a. What type of quantitative research methods would you select?
   b. Develop a research design to investigate the study?
   c. What type of statistical tool would you use? Explain.
3. Discuss how you would develop a sound theoretical framework for a study?
4. Distinguish between primary and secondary sources in historical research.
5. If a school teacher noticed that most of her children were two grade levels below in reading, and he/she wanted to improve their reading levels as quickly as possible, which research method would he/she use? Justify your choice.

Filed tests are the procedure usually employed. In field testing, the product or program with primary data are used. Secondary data

References

Aneshensel, C. S. 2002. Theory Based Data Analysis for the Social Sciences. Pine Forge Press.

Ary, D. , Jacobs, L. C., & Asghar, R. (1990). Introduction to Research In Education. New York: Holt, Rinehart, and Winston, Inc.

Babbie, Earl. (2001). The Practice of Social Research. (9th ed.). Belmont, Ca: Wadsworth/ Thompson Learning.

Bell, J. (1987). Doing Your Research Project: A Guide for First-Time Researchers in Education and Social Sciences. (3r ed.). Buckingham: Open University Press.

Benyon, D., Turner, P., & Turner. Systems People, Activities, Context, Technologies. London: Pearson Education Limited.

Best, J. W. (1959). Research in Education. Englewood Cliffs, NJ: Prentice-Hall, Inc.

Borg, W., Gall, J. P., Gall, G., & Gail, M. D. (1993). Applying Education Research. New York: Longman Publishing Company.

Charles, C. M (1988). Introduction to Educational Research. New York: Longman Publishing Company.

Creswell, J. W. (20020. Research Design: Qualitative, Quantitative, and Mixed Methods Approaches. Thousand Oaks, CA: Sage Publications.

Gefen, D., Straub, D., & Boudreau, M. C. (2000). "Structural Equation Modeling and Regression: Guidelines for Research Practice," Communications of AIS, Vol. 4, No. 7, pp. 1-80.

Litwin, M. (1995). How to Measure Survey Reliability and Validity. Thousand Oaks, CA: Sage Publications.

McKay, J. A. (1992). Professional Development Through Action Research. Journal of Staff Development, 13 (1), 18-21.

McNamara, J. F. (1994). Survey and Experiments in Educational Research. Lancaster, PA: Technomic Publishing.

Miller, Delbert C (2002). Handbook of Research Design and Social Measurement (6th ed.). New York: Longman.

Morgan, Susan E., Reicher, Tom, & Harrison, Tyler R. (2002). From Numbers to Words: Reporting Statistical Results for the Social Sciences. Boston: Allyn and Bacon.

Patten, Mildren L. (2002). Understanding Research Methods: An Overview of the Essentials (3rd ed.). Log Angeles: Pyrczak Publishing.

Robinson, Colin. (1993). Real World Research: A Resource for Social Scientists and Practitioner-Researchers. Cambridge: Blackwell Publishers.

Straub, Detmar W., David, Gefen, & Boundreau, Marie-Claude. (2005). "Quantitative Research," In Research in Information Systems: A Handbook for Research Supervisors and Their Students. Elsevier, Amsterdam, 221-238.

Williams, F., & Monge, P. (2001). Reasoning with Statistics: How to Read Quantitative Research (5th ed.). Fort Worth, TX: Harcourt College Publishers. Electronic Glossary of Social Science Computer and Social Science Data Terms

http://odwin.ucsd.edu/glossary/ Online Dictionary of the Social Sciences

http://socialsciencedictionary.nelson.com Rutgers University Research Methods WWW Tutorial http://sociology.camden.rutgers.edu/main.htm.

Social Science Information Gateway http://www.sosig.ac.uk/

Qualitative versus Quantitative http://www.gifted.uconn.edu/siegle/research/Qualitative/qua1quan.htm

Qualitative versus Quantitative Design http://www.kelcom.igs.net/~nhodgins/quant-qual.html

The Qualitative versus Quantitative Debate http://writing.colostate.edu/references/research/gentrans/pop2f.cfm-

Chapter Six
Qualitative Research Methods
Michael Trumbull, Ph.D
Kriesta Watson, Ph.D

INTRODUCTION

Qualitative research is multimethod in focus, involving an interpretive, naturalistic approach to its subject matter. This means that qualitative researchers study things in their natural settings, attempting to make sense of, or interpret, and phenomena in terms of the meanings people bring to them. Qualitative research involves the studies use and collection of a variety of empirical materials-case study, personal experiences, introspective, life story, interview, observational, historical, interactional, and visual texts – that describes routine and problematic moments and meanings in individual's lives (Denzin & Lincoln, 1994; Patton, 2002).

The qualitative approach is inductive, with the purpose of describing multiple realities, developing deep understanding, and capturing everyday life and human perspectives. The research focus will examine full context and interacts with participants while collecting most data face-to-face from participants. The research plan begins with an initial idea that evolves as research learns more participants and setting flexible levels throughout the tentative proposal and data analysis is mainly interpretive and descriptive. It is a process of discovery of the phenomena being studied, consequently, it tends to be guided by broad research questions based upon some theoretical framework. Additionally, it is naturistic in nature and take place in the real world with manipulation by the researcher.

According to Schwandt (1997a) qualitative inquiry is a set of multiple practices in which words in methodological and philosophical vocabularies acquire different meanings in their use or in particular acts of speaking about the meaning of the practice (P.XIV). Kirk and Miller (1968) viewed qualitative research as an approach to study social research that involves watching people in their own territories and interacting with them in their own languages or terms. Jacobs (1988) noted that qualitative research has many varieties that can be identified and used employing different research methods reflecting variable and fluid research strategies.

According to Glaser and Straus (1967) qualitative research is designed to develop theory. These authors named the process "ground theory" which implied that a theory should be developed and defined by continually "grounding" it in data. Before ground theory or any method in qualitative research can be successfully conducted certain prerequisites should be met, such as validity, reliability of data sources must be established.

Validity of Qualitative Research

Data collecting sources in qualitative research such as interviews and observations can not be validated as easy as traditional data sources which yield traditional measurements. However, there are methods that a researcher may employ to improve the validity of data sources: (1) using multiple sources to validate information, an example might be to validate interview information through observations, (2) have participants to review information for accuracy, (3) attempt to keep bias out of the data by reporting only what was observed and told, rather than inferring what was believed to have been told or drawing one's own conclusions. Additionally, validity of instruments depend greatly upon the competence of the researcher as well as established rigor and experience. Patton (2002) has succinctly summarized the major types of data sources used in qualitative research, refer to Figure 6.1.

Patton (2002) wrote that qualitative findings grew out of three kinds of data collection: (1) in-depth, open-ended interviews; (2) direct observations; and (3) written documents. He further articulated that interviews yield direct quotations from people about their experiences, opinions, feelings, and knowledge. On the other hand, data from observations consist of detailed descriptions of people's activities, behaviors, actions, and interpersonal interactions and organizational processes employed to observe human behavior. In contrast, document analysis includes studying excerpts, quotations, or entire passages from organizational, clinical, or program records; memoranda and correspondence; official publications and reports; personal dairies; and open-ended written responses to questionnaires and surveys (p.4).

Interviews

Open-ended questions and probes yield in-depth responses about people's experiences, perceptions, opinions, feelings, and knowledge. Data consist of verbatim quotations with sufficient context to be interpretable.

Observations

Fieldwork descriptions of activities, behaviors, actions, conversations, interpersonal interactions, organizational or community process, or any other aspect of observable human experience. Data consist of field notes: rich, detailed descriptions, including the context within which the observations were made.

Figure 6.1 Three Kinds of Qualitative Data

Documents

Written materials and other documents from organizational, clinical, or program records; memoranda and correspondence; official publications and reports; personal diaries, letters, artistic works, photographs and memorabilia; and written responses to open-ended surveys. Data consist of excerpts from documents captured in a way that records and preserves context.

A significant amount of qualitative research and inquiry are conducted in the field. The field may be classified as an y place that the researcher designates to conduct his/her study, and frequently participates in the investigation under study. Data may be collected from a variety of sources including observations, interviews, examining official documents and records. The process will generate voluminous raw data, which must be analyzed by the researcher into themes and patterns.

Source: Michael Q. Patton (2002). Qualitative Research and Evaluation Methtods (3rd ed.). Thousand Oaks, CA: Sage Publications.

Reliability of Qualitative Research

Several qualitative researchers believe that reliability in their research can be controlled by keeping careful records of interviews and observations. Data gathering procedures should be reliable to the extent that the results obtained from the data can be replicated by other researchers. Borg, Gall, and Gall (1981) supported the above by stating that "to improve reliability the researcher should standardized the timeline for collecting the data, correctly and systematically data from individuals or event measured, specific to the context in which the measurements were made, delineate the procedures employed gain assess to individuals or events, the nature and types of interview questions asked, identify the methods used to record the data, and whether the data collector received special training."

Sampling In Qualitative Research

The researcher conducting qualitative research is attempting to discover as much information as possible about the individual or phenomena under study, by providing detailed narrative descriptions of the phenomena rather than statistics calculations. As a result, the qualitative researcher usually study small groups. Sample size is not a prerequisite. Purposive sample is frequently used with the technique, where the researcher select a case or cases which he/she believes can yield sufficient data to address the research questions. Random sampling procedures may be used in both quantitative and qualitative research. In qualitative research the researcher may select cases or individuals by using random procedures. Refer to chapter 10 for specifics on how to use the techniques.

Qualitative research methods are designed to give real and stimulating meaning to the phenomenon by involving the researcher directly or indirectly in the process. According to Gilqun (1992), qualitative research is not represented by numbers, rather, it is focused on meaning and the involvement of the researcher in the process. The research is usually conducted in a natural setting and premised upon the uniqueness of the individual and his/her environment. A high level of communication and analytical skills are needed to accurately report the full essence of the experience, reflecting holistic and detailed views of the participants. Observations, case studies, interviews, and collection of specific documents constitute the major data sources (Creswell, 1994; Marshall and Rossman, 1989; Morse, 1995).

As with all empirical research, qualitative research begins with the observation of a phenomenon. Data are then recorded, and classified. Themes are developed to organize the massive amount of data generated. Usually, there is no theoretical framework to base the research. The researcher is attempting to discover principles and strategies that can provide valid evidence to develop theory (Borg, Gall & Gall, 1993). Qualitative research may be classified as deliberative, integrative, and historical.

Some research designs emphasize the gathering and manipulation of numerical data; these designs are frequently referred to as quantitative. Other research designs involve the analysis of complex data collected by observations, interviews, or actual participation by the researcher. These designs are frequently referred to as qualitative.

Research designs are constructed plans and strategies developed to seek, explore, and discover answers to research questions. The plan should include a blue print for conducting the research, outlining all of the major steps in the process including stating the hypotheses and their implications to analyzing the data. A research paradigm is presented in Chapters 13 and 15 summarizing major components which should be included.

The major purpose of research designs are to assist researchers to (1) provide answers to assumptions, research questions, or hypotheses, and (2) to control variance. They are constructed to enable the researcher to answer questions posed by the researcher as well as to make inferences from the data. . Research designs also aid researchers in determining the types of observations to make, how to make them, and the type of research to employ (qualitative or quantitative). Specific procedures are outlined to guide the researcher in manipulating and categorizing the variables. Research designs should also indicate appropriate types of statistical and narrative analyses to use as well as anticipate or project conclusions to be drawn from analysis. In essence, it is a systematic plan for conducting or investigating a problem using qualitative or quantitative research methods since both methods have similar components in a research design. In choosing one approach over another, the issue should be to assess which approach will best serve the research under investigation. Chapter 14 outlines similarities and differences between the two approaches.

Qualitative Methods

There are several major qualitative methods which researchers can include: phenomenology, ground theory, ethnography, case study and biographics. The selection of the method depends upon the nature and scope of the problem being investigated, the training and experiences of the researcher, the receptivity of individuals in the field in which the study is conducted, types of participants chosen, and techniques for dealing with one's biases. The methods are inductive and designed to describe multiple realities, deep understandings, and clearly understanding the human experience. Interacting with participants and collect data face-to-face are essential to the process.*

The following qualitative research methods are multimethod in focus, involving an interpretive and naturalistic approach (Lincoln & Guba, 1985). Researchers attempt to make sense of phenomena in terms of the meaning people bring to them. Qualitative research involves the study, use, and collection of case study materials, personal experiences, introspective, life stories, interviews, observations, historical documents, interactional data, and visual texts that describe routine and problematic moments and meanings in individuals' lives (Denzin & Lincoln, 1994, p. 2; Patton, 2002).

We have summarized some of the pros and cons associated with qualitative research methods in Figure 6.2.

[See Next Page for Figure 6.2]

---

*For specific ways to use qualitative methods refer to: Michael Q. Patton, (2002). Qualitative Research & Evaluation Methods. Thousand Oaks, CA: Sage Publishers.

Qualitative Data – PROS and CONS

PRO – Rich data. Qualitative data are complex and rich.

   PRO – Interesting data. People do not get very excited about word   counts! The critics who talked about the authors above relied on their impressions rather than actual work counts, and they would probably have defended this approach to the death.

   PRO – Data focus. If you are interested in a quality of the data,   numbers may not be able to reflect is for you.

   CON – Subjectivity. Qualitative data are usually generated by some method of coding or rating. Unless great care is taken, such methods may reflect only the opinions of one individual. This con can be avoided if raters or coders are tested for agreement with each other, as described in the next chapter.

   CON – Unknown reliability and validity. If we invent a new qualitative data analysis for each new experiment we perform, we will always be working with dubious measurements. This con can be avoided by the use of careful measurement techniques, as discussed in the next chapter.

Quantitative Data – PROS and CONS

PRO – Crispness and clarity. This is the opposite of richness. One or two clean numbers are frequently easier to understand and interpret than 23 coding catgories.

   PRO – Lack of subjectivity (Objectivity), especially if the measure is taken through instrumentation rather than through human judgments. Where humans are subjective, instruments (including tests and scales) are objective.

PRO – Known reliability and validity. Quantitative experiments are often designed around the use of know measures whose reliability and validity has been established. Look, for example, at any subgroup of learning studies (memory, operant condition) and you will always find some type of quantitative measures.

   CON – Data focus. There is not always a nice numerical technique for measuring the data characteristic in which we are interested.

   CON – Inability to convey data richness. This is what we meant when we referred to Louise's data and claimed that only reading teenagers' descriptions could convey the full impact of the data set.

Figure 6.2 Pros and Cons: Quantitative and Qualitative Research Methods

The upshot of this balancing act is the following: if you want richness, complexity, and something that cannot be easily translated into scaled numbers, use qualitative data analysis. If you want clarity, and are a fanatic about the reliability and validity of measurement, use quantitative data analysis. If you are a really open-minded researcher use both or either – as the situation and data demand. Two things you should not do are (1) assume that qualitative data are easier to work with, or (2) imagine that quantitative data are more scientific. As long as they are rigorously applied, the two types of data are equally easy (or difficult) to work with, and equally scientific. Application of these summaries will aid the researcher in selecting a suitable qualitative research method.

Phenomenology

Phenomenology is the science of describing human events and behaviors. A condition for conducting phenomenological research according to O'Mery (1983) is that no preconceived notions or framework are presented to guide the researcher. It involves the systematic searching of a description for the meaning or essence of a phenomenon and is designed to obtain knowledge through lived human experiences. Qualitative researchers do not believe that one can analyze human experiences quantitatively. Bruyn (1966), added to our understanding of this concept by stating that intuition is important in the development of knowledge and human meaning cannot be inferred from sensation alone. He believed that a researcher must look for the total meaning of events. All the knowledge of a human experience is in one person. Questions are open-ended and may be accompanied by guiding sub-questions.

The history, definitions, and methods of phenomenological research and inquiry are detailed and comprehensive, based upon the discipline defining and using it on the philosophy of the researcher using it. This chapter is not designed to accomplish such an awesome task. In phenomenological research, the researcher is looking for feelings, thoughts, and awareness. For instance, if a researcher would like to know about the experience of hopelessness, he will go to a person experiencing hopelessness and interview him or her. Questions are open-ended and not predetermined, but rather flow with clues being generated by the individual being interviewed (Ray, 1994). Answers must be rich and complete. For those researchers interested in the history, definition, and methods of phenomenological research, there are excellent sources devoted to the subject.*

In phenomenological research, the researcher attempts to block out his own personal experiences and remove them from the research process. The researcher describes the experience of others. Data sources may include the use of observations, interviews, tapes, other recording devices, and informal tests constructed by the researcher, poetry and pictures (Ray, 1994). The researcher can ask "what" but not "why". He gets to know "how." He asks the subject to describe his life and how he/she does things. Self is removed. The researcher keeps himself/herself out of the process and writes textual descriptions for each subject or one description for all the subjects which may frequently be subjective. The researcher deciphers meaning from the data and blends the meanings together. There are different models to be utilized in analyzing the data such as grouping, labeling, eliminating irrelevant data, clustering data and identifying common themes in data sets (VanManen, 1990). Phenomenological study involves the use of the researcher, co-researchers , and phenomena.

According to Moustakas (1994), Steward & Mickunas (1990),   there are three phases of phenomenological study:

1.   *Epoche:* Recognizing and suppressing personal biases to reduce impact upon outcome. There is some debate on the possibility of doing this successfully.

---

*Clark, M. (1994). Phenomenology Research Methods. Thousand Oaks, CA: Sage
   Publishing Company

*Natanson, M. (Ed.). (1973). Phenomenology and the social sciences. Evanston, IL:
   Northwestern University Press.

Patton, M. Q. (2002). Qualitative Research and Evaluation Methods. Thousand Oaks,
   CA: Sage Publishing Company.

*Steward, D., & Mickunas, A. (1990). Exploring Phenomenology: A Guide to the
   Field and its Literature (2nd   ed.). Athens, OH: State University Press.

*VanManen, M. (1990). Researching Lived Experiences: Human Science for an Action
   Sensitive Pedagogy. New York: University of New York.

2.   *Phenomenological Reduction:* Bracketing important information for analysis and horizontalizing or setting all remaining material equal in value. The researcher evaluates then he/she *delimits* or brackets once more. He/she pulls out themes and clusters and then writes textual descriptions, i.e., what the subject actually told the researcher. He/she writes textual descriptions for each subject or one complete description for all the subjects. The researcher takes the data, breaks it down to a manageable theme. From the cluster comes the theme.

3. *Imaginative Variation:* This involves reflection, comprehension, and judgment. The researcher merges description with his interpretation in the final output. Poems and pictures are

used. He writes textual descriptions, i.e., based upon the actual story told by the participant.

Numerous authors have articulated their views concerning how to conduct phenomenological research (Tesch, 1990; Giorgi, 1994; Polkinghorne, 1989; and Moustakas, 1994). We have reviewed these views and projections and have summarized them in the steps outlined below:

Steps in Conducting Phenomenological Research
1.   The researcher separates him/herself from the phenomenon.
2.   Epoche–The researcher looks inside self; reduces prejudices.
3.   Phenomenological reduction–identifies data in pure form.
4.   Horizontalize data–examines groups, clusters.
5.   Eliminate–irrelevant, repetitious or overlapping data.
6.   Identify themes.
7.   Textural portrayal of each theme–describe the experience.
8.   Structural synthesis–look beneath for deeper meaning.

Heuristic Research
Heuristic inquiry is a process that begins with a question which the researcher is attempting to answer. The question is frequently one that has been a personal challenge in the search to understand one's self and the world in which one lives. Heuristics is a way of engaging in scientific search through methods aimed at discovery; a way of self-inquiry and dialogue with others.

In summarizing research findings reported by Giorgi   (1985), Moustakas (1990), VanManen (1990), and Douglass and Moustakas (1985), the following are featured in heuristic study:
1.   Personal involvement
2.   Everyday process of self-discovery
3.   Co-researchers

Heuristic study is conducted between the researcher (oneself) and the co-researchers used in the investigation. The researcher organizes the data, listens to the tapes and writes narrative descriptions relevant to the phenomenon under study. This is a time consuming process. The researcher starts with "what" or "how" questions that provide data to write narrative descriptions. In heuristic study, formulating questions for instance, in the case of depression, the researcher asks such questions as:
1.   What time of year depresses people most?
2.   What do people do when they are depressed?
3.   Where do people go to seek professional assistance when they are depressed?

Heuristic study is a form of phenomenological inquiry and involves self disclosure. The researcher is attempting to experience what the subject is experiencing. He explains and compares his own experience with the co-researcher. The researcher is intuitive; he is more involved in the study. Heuristics is an accurate report on the experience of oneself and others (Moustakas, 1990). An example of the difference between phenomenological and heuristic research is sitting on the bank of a river and describing it versus being *in* the river. The latter is heuristic research.

In heuristic research, the researcher identifies co-researchers. The primary researcher has the same experience and reviews the literature. The primary researcher interviews himself through self-dialogue and transcribes the dialogue. The primary researcher also interviews the co-researchers and accurately reports their experiences.

Every feeling is underlined and questions are developed. The questions are very narrow, but a mile deep. For example, one could study only migraine headaches looking at all aspects of a migraine. Heuristic research begins with the following process:

1. Introduction–interest of the researcher and why the subject was chosen.
2. State the question.
3. Review of the literature.
4. Methodology–Data Collection–Interviews
5. Transcribe the information on the tape.

The researcher immerses himself in their experience and becomes a different personality. The researcher then writes a 2-3 page depiction using observations and dialogues with self and others, and interviews of co-researchers which captures the essence of their story. The depiction is sent to the person for their comments and to validate the depiction. When one interview is finished, the researcher goes on to the next interview. An acceptable number of co-researchers is between 6-8 people. Themes begin to emerge so the researcher keeps a record of these and form creative syntheses of the stories (Douglas & Moustakas, 1995).

Heuristic research involves several processes according to Moustakas (1990), and Douglas and Moustakas (1995). They are:

1. *Identifying with the focus of inquiry* allows the researcher to fully achieve an understanding of the experience being investigated. This self-directed search is also an opportunity for the researcher to identify more closely with the question.

2. *Self-dialoging* allows the researcher to engage in dialogue with one's own experience. This experience enables the researcher to depict or explore multiple meanings developed from self-dialoging. Self-dialogue is a critical concept of heuristic research which opens the lines of communication between both the researcher and co-researchers.

3. *Tacit knowing* are experiences that have a vague presence, but we know that the individual qualities or its parts allows one to sense the wholeness of something.

4. *Intuition* makes it possible for the researcher to perceive something from various clues until we are able to determine the truth. The bridge between the explicit and the tacit is the realm of the between, or the intuitive.

5. *In dwelling* refers to the process which allows the researcher to engage in a deeper search for the meaning of a human experience. Out of this process, the researcher moves a step closer toward the explication process. Indwelling is a critical and deliberate process requiring one to be patient and understanding.

6. *Focusing* is a process in which the researcher is able to identify qualities of an experience that have remained out of conscious reach chiefly because the individual has not paused long enough to examine his or her experience of the phenomenon.

7. *Internal frame of reference* provides the researcher with numerous opportunities to express, explore, and explicate the meanings that are one's own experiences. Additionally, an atmosphere of openness and trust must be present so that communication can be expressed freely among co-researchers.

The seven processes outlined above must work in concert with the six phases of heuristic research as propounded by Moustakas (1990). A summary is provided below:

1. *Initial engagement* occurs when the researcher engages himself or herself in the task of discovering the central topic, theme, problem, or question that ultimately leads to a critical area of interest. During this phase of the heuristic process, the researcher is

passionately involve d in selecting a research topic or question
that allows one to explore one's own history, experiences, and
relationships within a social context.

The researcher demonstrates a strong commitment discover the meaning of his or her experiences as it relates to the social context of the research question. The initial engagement phase allows one to fully explore the vast range of one's experiences, and to search inwardly for tacit awareness, intuition to flourish freely, and elucidate the significance of the research question.

2.   *Immersion* occurs when the question is identified and defined by the researcher. During the immersion phase, the researcher is passionately focused on the research question. His or her life evolves around the question. Reviewing all events, people, meetings, readings, and other related experiences provide a myriad of clues for understanding the phenomenon. The immersion process is facilitated by self-dialogue, intuition, and a sustained focus on the question.

3.   *Incubation* is defined as the process in which the researcher detaches himself or herself from the question. The researcher, who is no longer absorbed in the question, engages in other levels of knowledge that contribute to understanding the phenomenon. The new knowledge or growth process is defined as the inner workings of tacit dimension. Incubation is a process in which tacit dimension allows mental functioning to occur at a subconscious level.

4.   *Illumination* occurs when the researcher emerges from the incubation process with a thorough understanding of tacit knowledge and intuition. During this phase, the researcher is disengaged from his or her resting stage and is now ready to tackle the question with a renewed sense of purpose. The researcher returns to a conscious state that invites one to capture the essence of one's experiences by embracing new discoveries, reviewing old experiences, and clarifying missed or distorted core qualities that are essential elements in unveiling deeper meaning of the phenomenon.

5.   *Explication phase* begins when the researcher seeks to understand and explain in detail the various themes, qualities, and meanings that characterize experiences in one's awakened consciousness. This phase requires the researcher to engage in focusing, indwelling, self-searching, and self-disclosure. Focusing and indwelling are recognized as the two most important concepts in explicating a phenomenon. The researcher, when utilizing these concepts, is able to direct his or her full attention on the phenomenon, and paves the way for greater understanding of the entire heuristic experience.

6.   *Creative synthesis* is the final phase of heuristic research which occurs when the researcher thoroughly understands all the data, and can now summarize his experiences utilizing several forms of expressions. Creative synthesis can be in the form of story, painting, poem, or by some other creative form utilizing verbatim material. Preparatory steps for engaging in creative synthesis are knowledge of the data and a period of solitude and meditation. Tacit dimension, intuition, and self-searching are key elements essential in the creative synthesis process.

Hermeneutics

Hermeneutic researchers use qualitative methods to establish context and meaning for what people do. It originated in the study of written texts. Narrative analysis extends the idea of text to include in-dept interviews, life historics, and memoirs. It also involves the art of reading a text so that the intention and meaning behind appearances are fully understood. There is a relationship between a listener's comprehension and literary-historical analysis. This relationship provides a central meaning and unity that enables one to understand the substance and essence of the experience. Interrelationship of science, art, and history is at the heart of hermeneutic design and methodology. The author claims that hermeneutic analysis is required in order to derive a correct understanding of a text. The hermeneutic process involves a circle through which scientific understanding occurs; through which we correct our prejudices or set them aside and hear what the text says to us (Patton, 2002; Schwandt, 2001; Kneller, 1984).

Ground Theory

Ground theory is designed to develop or construct theory related to the phenomenon under study. Ground theory is inductively generated from field work that emerges from the researcher's observations and interviews in the real world rather than in laboratory (Patton, 2002). The researcher's intent to all relevant data germane to the conditions. Data sources include observations, interviews, and field visits as necessary. In analyzing data, the researcher develops and integrates categories and writes theoretical postulates or hypotheses. Combined, these factors are employed in developing a visual picture of the theory under study (Creswell, 1998).

The history and development of ground theory has generated some controversies among researchers. The theory was first developed by Glaser & Strauss (1967) to respond to questions posed by sociologists relevant to the understanding of human behavior assessed by quantitative methods. It was believed that human behavior was too complex to be relegated to basing analyses on averages and statistical manipulations. Rather, human behavior is developed through interaction with others. Symbols in one's environment are used to construct realities. Therefore, individuals must become active participants in creating incoming situations. Quantitative methods and procedures could not accomplish this goal. Refer to Chapter 5 for contrasting views between the two paradigms. In contrast to the above theoretic notation advanced by Glasser and Strauss (1967), they later developed separate views concerning grounded theory. Glasser (1992) strongly criticized Strauss's approach. He maintained that the nucleus of ground theory research is the development of a theory closely related to the phenomenon under study. Strauss and Corbin (1994) disagreed and maintained that the theory should be based upon data generated from the field of sociology. In spite of the controversy in the field, grounded theory has remained a vital research tool. Stern (1994) wrote that both Glasser and Strauss produced scientific work; the differences in their work being the method used. Researchers should clearly indicate the method being employed at all times.

Cresswell (1998) contended that grounded theory study challenges researchers for the following reasons:

- The investigator needs to set aside, as much as possible, theoretical ideas or notions so that the analytic, substantive theory can emerge.
- Despite the evolving, inductive nature of this form of qualitative inquiry, the researcher must recognize that this is a systematic approach to research with specific steps in data analysis.
- The researcher faces the difficulty of determining when categories are saturated or when the theory is sufficiently detailed.

The researcher needs to recognize that the primary outcome of this study is a theory with specific components: a central phenomenon, causal conditions, strategies,
conditions and context, and consequences.   These are prescribed categories of information in the theory.

Ethnography

According to Harris, (1968), *ethnograpy* is   a description   and interpretation of a cultural or social group or system. The researcher examines the group's observable and learned   patterns of *behavior*, customs, and ways of life. Agar (1980) wrote that ethnography is a product of research, typically found in textbook form.   Ethnography includes lengthy observation of group behavior through *participant observation* in which the researcher is immersed in the day-to-day lives of the people. The researcher studies the meanings of behavioral changes of the group being studied.

Historically,   ethnography   had its roots in anthropology during the early 20th century. research using this model was based upon a modified natural science model which did not employ the scientific method (Agar, 1996). During the early 20th century, researchers at the University of Chicago experimented with the anthropological field method to study diverse cultural groups in the country (Bogdan & Biklen, 1992). The approach has been modified to include other aspects of human behavior, social agencies in the community, and other social science fields. The researcher using and ethnographical paradigm observes individuals in interactive settings and uses the data to develop cultural themes and patterns depicting daily living conditions of individuals participating in the study (Spradley, 1980).

Data sources include gathering artifacts, observations, stories, interviews, rituals, myths and cultural themes. In order to gather the above data sources, the researcher must use data from the field extensively to develop cultural patterns. He/she must seek out individuals in the community who are knowledgeable about the social structure and issues and can direct the researcher to key individuals who have knowledge of the cultural group (Wolcott, 1994).

Researchers using ethnographical research should be well versed in cultural anthropologyand have a comprehensive understanding of the cultural system being researched.   They should be aware of the time factor since the ethnographical model requires extensive time in the field to collect, validate, analyze data, and converting and writing narrative in a literary style, reflecting the deep essence of the research (Lecompte & Schensul, 1999). Feagin, Orum, and Sjoberg (1991) defined case study as an ideal methodology when a holistic, indepth investigation is needed.

Case Study

There are many varieties and types of case studies. Merriam and Makower (1988) defined a case study as an   exploration of a "bounded system." The case study is bounded by   time restrictions and place and is commonly used in sociological studies. The researcher sets the standards and conditions for studying the phenomena. The following may be considered by the researcher: (a) they type of case study attempted or (b) programs, events, or individuals. There are two types of case study programs from which the researcher may select. He may select a multi-site design or a single-site design.   The multi-site design involves more than one case and is frequently referred to as a *collective* case study.   Single-site designs are frequently called *intrinsic* case study where some unique aspect of a case study may be investigated, or an *instrumental* case study which emphasizes a certain issue or issues to be explored (Stake, 1995).

Case studies may be used in both quantitative and qualitative research methods (Yin, 1989). They are widely used in the social sciences to solve or to investigate societal problems in their natural settings (Merriam & Makower, 1988; Stake, 1995). The researcher can converse with participants and can interview them in depth to gain insight into certain phenomena. Case studies may involve the use of multiple data sources, such as, total or partial group discussions, interaction between groups or individuals or discussions between different members of the group (teachers and parents). Validity of case study data may be conducted by comparing one data source to another data source on the same phenomena (Merriam, 1988).

The researcher employs several data sources to collect data such as observations, interviews, participant observations, physical artifacts, the use of audio visual materials, official documents, archival reports, and direct observations. These data sources enable the researcher to collect information in an orderly and systematic way, as well as to cross-validate information. These data sources can be holistically analyzed, or specific aspects of the case can be analyzed (Yin, 1989). According to Stake (1995), researchers may use the above data sources to provide a detailed description of the case, as well as to develop themes or issues.

Equally important with collecting and analyzing data sources will be the selection of a sample to participate in the study, as well as the type of case study to select. The purpose of the field sample technique is recommended for the case study method. In using this method, the researcher selects individuals who are considered to be informed on the issues. Selected criteria are developed depending upon the nature and scope of the study. These criteria are used to select participants who show different views on the problem being researched. Caution should be exercised in selecting the type of case study method. As indicated, the approach can be single or collective, intrinsic or instrumental. The researcher must choose an approach based upon his training and experiences with the use of case study strategies as well as his/her knowledge on qualitative research methods, set boundaries for the study, and choose data sources which will provide sufficient data to give a comprehensive picture of the issues involved.

Biographical Study

A biographical study depicts the life experiences of an individual. The method is defined as the study, use, and collection of life documents that describe significant points in an individual's life as reported by others (Denzin, 1989; Smith, 1994). Biographical writings appear in various fields and disciplines and is designed to reflect the history of one's life. The various types of biographical studies are summarized below:

1. A *biographical study* covers the life of an individual and is written by someone other than the individual being studied, living or deceased (Denzin, 1989).

2. An *autobiography* is a self-analysis about one's self.

3. The *life history approach* reports on contributions made by individuals and how these contributions have affected society. Data sources include interviews, tape recordings, conversations with the individuals, letters and photographs (Cole, 1994; Geiger, 1986; Plummer, 1983).

4. *Oral history* involves the researcher collecting personal data on events; the causes and effects as viewed by individuals. Data sources include the use of tape recordings or narrative descriptions of written work from living or deceased individuals (Smith, 1994). There are several specific biographies, *classical* and *interpretive* that researchers may use. In a classical biography, the researcher uses statements about theory. Validity, criticism of materials, and formulation of hypotheses are constructed by the researcher (Denzin, 1989a). Denzin also provided us with a description of interpretive biography. He wrote that interpretive biography is a preferred approach to biographical writing. This type of writing challenges traditional approaches and requests that biographers be cognizant of how studies are constructed and interpreted.

According to Denzin (1989a), researchers using biographical approaches should:

1.   Choose a stage in the life of the subject to investigate, such as childhood, adolescence, or adulthood since such experiences provide a source to gather extensive information.

2. Select the type of contextual biographical material to report or write about the experiences of the subjects in order to develop stories.

3. Organize stories around themes that depict selected events in the life of an individual which explains various components of life.

4. Explore the essence and meaning of the stories as well as searching for multiple meanings.

5. Looking for longer structures to explain the meaning of social interaction in groups, cultural issues, philosophical beliefs, and historical contexts in order to provide an interpretation of life's experiences of the individual.

Characteristics of Qualitative Research

As indicated in Chapter 5 on Quantitative Research Methods, all research follows a basic pattern. This basic premise is also true for qualitative research regardless of the methods employed. Characteristics of qualitative research according to Reisman (1993) include (a) the natural setting, (b) direct data collection, (c) rich narrative descriptions, (d) process oriented, (e) inductive data analysis and (f) participant perspectives:

1. *Nature setting.* Research is conducted in a natural environment. No attempt is made to control conditions and behavior as in experimental research.

2. *Direct Data Collection.* The research is usually an activity participant in the study by interacting directly with the participants under study.

3. *Rich Narrative Descriptions.* Descriptions are expressed in words rather than in numbers as in quantitative research. Some descriptive statistics may be used to clarify the narrative descriptions. A detailed description is needed in order to reflect a clean and complete analysis of the behavior under study.

4. *Process Oriented.* Unlike quantitative research, in qualitative research the researcher is looking for the process through which behavior occurs, not the "why" and "how" as specified in quantitative research methods.

5. *Inductive Data Analysis.* Hypotheses are infrequently used in qualitative research. Researchers usually use research questions. Data are collected and synthesized inductively to formulate theory whereas in quantitative research, the *deductive* method is used and theories are tested.

6. *Participant Perspectives.* Researchers attempt to relate reality as articulated by participants. No predeterminations are made concerning what participants might say. Researchers depend entirely on information provided by participants in analyzing data.

Coding Qualitative Data

There are several problems associated with coding qualitative data. One important factor to consider is the effects of subjective scoring by the researcher. Qualitative data is subject to much criticism because of subjective scoring. Extreme care must be executed by the researcher in collecting data. We have summarized below, guidelines that researchers may employ to make coding and collecting qualitative data more objective:

Guideline 1: Draw a random sample from the qualitative data, usually 10-20%.

Guideline 2: Review the data carefully and consider several possible coding schemes or categories.

Guideline 3: Form initial categories by separating information into subcategories. Researchers who move too rapidly into coding schemes risk finding that they have missed important data that was conveyed in their participant's responses.

Guideline 4: Formalize the coding scheme. Describe the scheme clearly and accurately in order that another coder can use it and arrive at the same conclusions. Give several accurate descriptions of the coding scheme.

Guideline 5: Trial coding. Using the random sample drawn, code all the data according to the scheme developed. Select another coder to validate your process. The coder should be independent of the experiment, but be knowledgeable about coding procedures. Compare information.

Guideline 6: Coding evaluations. Compare your coding to that of the second coder and strive for a percentage agreement between 80-90%. Continue the process until this level is met. Once this level is met, coder reliability will be established and data will not be considered to be subjective. Give a full description of any disagreements noted while establishing reliability.

Guideline 7: Application. Once reliability has been established, all the data may be coded with the assistance of at least one independent rater. If a researcher is coding his/her own data, another independent rater should be used to decrease subjectivity. This process ensures that the richness of the data are preserved, and that subjectivity is reduced.

The researcher is now ready to employ a coding system which can be effectively used in the research.

Summary

As indicated in Chapter 5, Quantitative Research Methods, all research follows a similar format. This premise is also true for the qualitative research methods as outlined in this chapter. All of the qualitative methods addressed in this chapter are designed to assist the researcher in understanding past and present events, developing theories, appreciating the value-laden aspect of inquiry, the personal approach to writing the narrative, the multiple meaning of reality, and employing inductive methodology in research. In order to facilitate the process Patton (2002) articulated that the credibility of qualitative inquiry depends upon the following:

2.   Rigorous methods for doing field work that yield high-quality data that are systematically analyzed with attention issues of credibility;

3.   The credibility of the researcher, which is dependent on training, experiences, track record, status, and presentation of self;

4.   Philosophical belief in the value of qualitative inquiry, that is, a fundamental appreciation of naturalistic inquiry, qualitative methods, inductive analysis, purposeful sampling, and holistic thinking (pp 552-553).

The commonalities among qualitative methods necessitate that the researcher (1) construct and organize information; (2) initially reviews the information and organizes it into sequential parts; (3) develops descriptive phases around which theory is constructed; (4) begins to analyze and categorize data; and (5) writes the final narrative report (refer to Appendix E for a format to use in writing narrative reports).

In qualitative research, organizing and developing an outline is not too important because the researcher should not have preconceived structure for conducting the study. In Patton's (2002) view all qualitative research are affected by intended purposes and targeted audience, but purpose emphasis The research model or paradigm should be constructed to guide the research as outlined in Chapters 13 and 15.

Exercise 6

1.   Choose a topic of interest to you.   Develop a qualitative research design; refer to Chapter 12 for guidance.

2. Select one of the traditional qualitative methods discussed in the chapter. Find a journal article which supports the method. Indicate in specific terms, the relationship between the journal and the qualitative method selected.

3. Summarize the traditional qualitative method and list the data sources you would use to collect data.

4. Construct an interview or an observational schedule. List factors that you would consider in constructing the instrument. Append the instrument.

5. Discuss how the NUD*IST$_4$ program can be effectively used in analyzing qualitative data.

6. Select a traditional qualitative method, different than the one selected in Chapter 2. Use a different journal article and discuss the relationship between the article and the method selected.

References

Agar, M. (1986). Speaking of ethnography. *Qualitative Research Methods Series*, Vol. 2. Beverly Hills, CA: Sage.

Bogdan, R.C., & Biklen, S. K. (1992). *Qualitative research for education.* Boston: Allyn & Bacon.

Borg, W. R., Gall, J. P., Gall, & Meredith D. (1993). *Applying educational research: A practical guide*. New York: Logman.

Bruyn, S.R. (1966). *The human perspective in sociology*. Englewood Cliffs, N.J.: Prentice-Hall.

Clark, M. (1994). *Phenomenology research methods.* Thousand Oaks, CA: Sage.

Cole, A. (1994). *Doing life history in theory and in practice.* Paper prepared for the Annual Meeting of the American Educational Research Association, New Orleans, L.A.

Creswell, J. W. (1994).   *Research Design: Qualitative ad Quantitative Approaches.* Thousand Oaks, CA: Sage Publications.

Creswell, J. W. (1998). *Qualitative Inquiry and Research Design: Choosing Among Five Traditions.* Thousand Oaks, CA: Sage Publications.

Denzin, N.K. (1989a). Interpretive Biography. Newburg Park, CA: Sage Publications.

Denkin, N. K., & Lincoln, Y. (1994). *Handbook on qualitative research.* Thousand Oaks, CA: Sage Publications.

Douglas, B.G. and Moustakas, C.(1985*). Heuristic Inquiry: The internal search to know. Journal of Humanistic Psychology, 25,* (3).

Feagin, J., Orum, A., & Sjoberg, G. (Eds.). (1994). *A case for case study.* Chapel Hills, NC: University of North Carolina Press.

Geiger, S.N.G. (1986). Women's life histories: Methods and content signs. *Journal of women in culture and society*, 11, 334-351.

Gilgun, J. (1999). Finger nails painted red: A feminist semiotic analysis of a hot text. *Qualitative Inquiry,* 5 (2), 181-206.

Giorgi, A. (Ed.) (1985). *Phenomenology and psychological research.* Pittsburgh, PA: Duquesne University Press.

Glaser, B.G. (1992). *Emergence versus Forcing: Basics of Grounded Theory Analysis.* Mill Valley, CA: The Sociology Press.

Glaser, B. G., & Straus, A. L. (1967). *The discovery of ground theory: Strategies for qualitative research.* Hawthorne, NY: Aldine.

Harris, M. (1968). *The rise of anthropological theory.* New York: Cromwell.

Jacob, E. (1998). Clarifying qualitative research: A focus on traditions. *Education Research*, 17 (1), January-February) 16-24.

Kirk, J., & Miller, M. L. (1968). *Reliability and validity in qualitative research*. Beverly Hills, CA: Sage.

Kneller, G. F. (1984). *Movement of thought in modern education*. New York: John Wiley.

Lecompte, M. D., & Schensal, J. (1999). Designing and conducting ethnographic research. *Ethnographer's Tool Kit*, Vol. 1. Walnut Creek, CA: Altalyira.

Lincoln, Y. S., & Guba, E. G. (2000). Paradigmatic controversies, contradictions, and emerging influences. *In Handbook of Qualitative Research* (2nd ed.) pp. 163-188, edited by Norma K. Denzin and Yvonna S. Lincoln. Thousand Oaks, CA: Sage

Marshall, C., & Rossman, G. B. (1989). *Designing qualitative research*. Newbury Park, CA: Sage.

Merriam, J. E., & Makower, J. (1988). *Trend watching: How the media create trends and how to be the first to uncover them*. New York: Tilden Press, American Management Association (AMACOM).

Moustakas, C.(1994). *Phenomenological Research Methods*. Thousand Oaks, CA: Sage Publications.

Morse, J. M., & Field, P.A. (1995). Qualitative research methods for health professional. Thousands Oaks, CA: Sage.

Moustakas, C. (1996). *Heuristic Research: Design, Methodology, and Applications*. Newbury Park: Sage Publications.

Natanson, M. (1973). *Phenomenology and the social sciences*. Evanston, IL: NorthWestern University Press.

O'Mery, A. (1983). *Phenomenology: A Method for Nursing Research*. Advances in Nursing Science. 5, 49-63.

Patton, M. Q. (2002). *Qualitative research and evaluation methods*. Thousand Oaks, CA: Sage Publications.

Polkinghorne, D.E. (1989). *Phenomenological Research Methods*. In R.S. Valle and S. Halling (Eds.) *Existential Phenomenological Perspectives in Psychology*. New York: Plenum.

Plummer, K. (1983). *Documents of Life: An Introduction to Problems and Literature of a Humanistic Method*. London: George Allen and UNWIN.

Ray, M.A. (1994). *The Richness of Phenomenology: Philosophic, theoretic and methodological concerns*. In J.M. Morse (Ed.) *Critical Issues in Qualitative Research Methods*. Thousand Oaks, CA: Sage Publications.

Reisman, C. K. (1993). *Narrative analysis*. Newbury Park, CA: Sage Publications.

Schwandt, T. A. (1997a). *Qualitative inquiry: A dictionary of terms*. Thousand Oaks, CA: Sage Publications.

Schwandt, T. A. (2001). *Dictionary of qualitative inquiry* (2nd ed.). Thousand Oaks, CA: Sage Publications.

Smith, L.M. (1994). *Biographical Methods in* N.K.Denzin & Y.S. Lincoln (Eds.) *Handbook on Qualitative Research*. Thousand Oaks, CA: Sage Publications.

Spradley, J.P. (1980). Participant observation. New York: Holt, Rinehardt & Wilson.

Stake, R. (1995). The art of case study research. Thousand Oaks CA: Sage Publications.

Stern, P.N. (1994). Enroding grounded theory. In J.M. Morse (Ed.) *Critical Issues in Qualitative Methods*. Thousand Oaks, CA: Sage Publications.

Steward, D. and Mickunas, A. (1990). Exploring Phenomenology: A guide to the field and its literature (2nd ed.). Athens, OH: Ohio University Press.

Strauss, A. and Corbin, J. (1990). *Basics of Qualitative Research*. Newbury Park, CA: Sage Publications.

Tesch, R. (1990). *Qualitative Research: Analysis, types, and software tools*. Bristol, PA: Falmer.

Yin, R.K. (1989).   Case study Research: Design and Method. Newbury Park, CA: Sage
    Publications.
VanManen, M. (1990). *Researching lived experience: Human Science for an Action Pedagogy.*
    London, Ontario: Althouse.
Wolcott, H.F. (1994). *Transforming qualitative data: Descriptions, analysis, and interpretation.*
    Thousand Oaks, CA: Sage Publications.

Chapter Seven
Computerized Statistical Packages
George R.Taylor, Ph.D.
Jacqueline Williams, Ed.D.

OVERVIEW

The use of computers in analyzing data have greatly improved over the last two decades. There are highly reliable software available to accomplish the task of data analysis. These software packages are relatively inexpensive and "people friendly." Considerable time can be saved by the researcher using these computerized statistical packages providing that instructions are systematically followed.

Quantitative and qualitative data generated from computerized statistical packages must be analyzed in light of the hypothesis stated. A knowledge of statistics is needed in order for the researcher to adequately interpret the data generated. The computer can only present the results; not analyze *and* interpret them. Therefore, it is incumbent upon the researcher to be versed in statistical data analyses (Blaisdell, 1993). We have devoted a considerable amount of time to this topic throughout the text. Both parametric and non-parametric statistics may be analyzed through the use of the computer software packages. A word of caution is in order for the researcher. The computer is not a "cure all" for data analysis (Patton, 2002). The computer can complete many of the mechanical details, however, the researcher must select the appropriate computer software, code the data, determine how the data will be recorded on the data sheet, what things go together to form categories and themes, how to develop codebooks, indexing, showing multiple text entries, cross-referencing, and cutting and pasting text (Heise, 1988; Devore & Peck, 1986). Fielding and Lee(1991) has added to the list of cautions by stating the software programs vary in how data are entered, stored, coded, organized, data-linking mechanism, ways of browsing, ease of search and retrieval, data display, and tracking, and completing; and complete basic calculations in preparation for using the computer in completing many of the exercises advanced in this text.

It is evident from the above summary of computer software that the researcher must be well versed in the use of these programs. Patton (2002) indicated that computer analysis might not be for everyone and may interfere with the analysis process. Choosing a computer program should be a matter of individual style. Most statistical packages give detail instructions, therefore, the researcher must meticulously refer to, and follow the instructional manual. It is not within the scope of this chapter to present details on setting up computer file, entering data, displaying data and managing data through the use of computers. The reader is referred to the references at the conclusion of this chapter for more detailed information in those areas.

Selection of a software package will depend upon many factors, such as, the type of analyses needed for the study, availability of the computer center to handle the data generated, faculty recommendations, user-friendliness, computer skills of the researcher, and the ability of the software to analyze massive amounts of data are to name but a few factors which should be considered in selecting software (Minitab, 1991). Some of the commonly used software packages and their addresses are:

1. B.M.D.P. Statistical Software, Inc.
   1440 Sepulveda Boulevard
   Suite #316
   Los Angeles, California 90025
2. Genstat, N.A.G. Inc.
   1400 Opus Place
   Suite #200
   Downers Grove, Illinois 60515
3. Minitab, Inc.
   3081 Enterprise Drive
   State College, Pennsylvania 16801
4. N.L.S.S.
   329 N. 100 East
   Kaysville, Utah 84037
5. N.U.D.I.S.T.
   2455 Teller Road
   Thousand Oaks, CA 91320-2218
6. P.Stat, Inc.
   230 Lavertville Road
   Hopewill, New York 08525
7. Statgraphics, Manugistics, Inc.
   2115 E. Jefferson Street
   Rockville, Maryland 20852
8. Statistical Statsoft, Inc.
   2325 E. 13th Street
   Tulsa, Oklahoma 74104
9. Systat, Inc.
   1800 Sherman Avenue
   Evanston, Illinois 60204

Each of the statistical software packages listed can analyze a variety of programs or studies. The researcher is advised to contact the above computer software companies for information concerning whether or not their software packets will perform the type of statistical procedures desired.

SPSS Computer Software Package

We have selected to review the Statistical Package for the Social Sciences (SPSS) statistical software package chiefly due to the fact that this software package will perform most of the statistical analysis outlined in the text. Additionally, it is well used in the social sciences to calculate the effectiveness of study and programs by performing a variety of statistical analyses and procedures. Using the SPSS computer software mandates that the user understand the complex data file management procedures. If researchers have not acquired an understanding of computer software, a consultant is recommended to assist in the management and interpretation of the data generated from the computer software.

The SPSS may be used to analyze a variety of statistical data. Instructions for using the programs are detailed and specific and may be found in the manual. Only minimum computer skills are needed to perform many of the operations although some of the complex operations will require expert assistance. Data fields are large enough to permit small and massive amounts of data to be analyzed. SPSS is a complex program with many programming options. Our intent is not to discuss all of the complex components, but rather to overview those components needed for the beginning researcher. The command "frequencies" is used to generate frequency distributions and curves, and to compute measures of central tendency and variability. "Cross tabs" and "correlations" are used to compute coefficients of relationships for nominal, ordinal, interval, and ratio data. We recommend that beginning researchers experiment with the program for computerized data and examples given in Chapters 8-12.

The program frequently begins with a title command. The purpose is to develop a title which is programmed to appear on each page of the print out. Another line on the program is a Data List command. This command identifies the data sources and informs the researcher within which fields or spaces the information can be located. Names provided for variables will appear on the Data List line. After the researcher has entered descriptive information, the program will allow him/her to examine, select, record, and compute commands which are used to transform the data sets.

- *Data List* defines variables and locates them in columns. In order for the program to work, the variables must be found exactly in the columns specified by this command.
- *Comment* is not an active command. It simply adds comments to the output.
- *Begin Data* indicates the beginning of data.
- *End Data* indicates the end of data.
- *Value Labels* commands can be used to give specific names of labels to categories of nominal variables.
- *Frequencies* produces frequency distributions and curves, and descriptive statistics.
- *Descriptive* produces descriptive statistics for interval/ratio data.
- *Crosstabs* gives a crosstabulation of data and calculates Cramer's V.
- *Nonpar Corr* calculates Spearman Rank Correlations for all named variables.
- *Correlations* calculates Pearson correlations for all named variables.
- *Temporary* follow by
- *Select If* allows the researcher to choose a subsample of data to work with.
- *Recode* allows the researcher to recode or change values of a variable.
- *Compute* computes new variables by manipulating old ones and/or numbers.
- *List* allows the researcher to print a list of data.

SPSS Data Definitions Lines must end with a period. If the data are in an ASCII file, the Data List statement follows the Title line. This statement must contain the number of data records per case. Subsequent parts of the Data List statement contains the format of the data.

The final line in the SPSS program is the Begin Data line. It instructs the SPSS program to identify what data follow and how the data should be read in the format outlined in the Data List statement. A period does not follow the Begin Data line. The researcher should consult the SPSS manual and references listed for procedure used to illustrate and identify Data Lines.

Value Label commands may be employed to classify and name subcategories of variables. Example:

Value Labels: "Job Satisfaction 1," (1)Not Pleased, (2), "Pleased."

The *Frequencies* command will produce frequency distributions for each variable named. A part of the command produces basic descriptive statistics such as the mean, mode, median, and standard deviation. This command may be used to obtain distributions and to obtain measures of central tendency and variability for nominal, ordinal, and interval/ratio scales.

The *Descriptive* command also produces basic information, but without the frequency distribution. It is mainly useful for interval/ratio type data such as correlations. The *Correlations* command produces correlations between all the variables named. The correlations are Pearson product-moment correlations suitable for interval/ratio data. The Spearman-Rho Rank is used for ranked data. The *Correlation* command for the Spearman-Rho Rank produces rank correlations between all the variables named. The computer first ranks the data in each pair of variables and then correlates with a rank correlation. The *Crosstabs* command produces a nominal measure of relationship. This coefficient shows how strongly two nominal variables are related to each other. The command also produces a crosstabulation of nominal variables.

It is possible to conduct analyses with only a subset of the data. If the temporary command is omitted, the computer will permanently discard all cases except those identified to be analyzed. It is possible to recode or rearrange the values of an old variable in itself, or into a new variable. An example would be to name "Job Categories" into "yes" and "no" categories, and the new variable is called "Job Satisfaction 2." For "Job Satisfaction 2" employer (pleased) and employee (not pleased) characters are in one group. Compare the results of the frequency analysis to those obtained in the original analysis above. Note that a new value labels line defines the meaning of values in the new variable *Job Satisfaction.*

It is possible to use the COMPUTE command to create new variables. These could be the sum of old variables, as noted. Compute commands are very versatile and the researcher can use different ones to manipulate data. The command LIST can be used to list all data, or to list only some variables. The command for selected variables is LIST VARIABLES.

Output data generated from the SPSS program or any software program should be reviewed carefully. If the researcher is not competent in analyzing output data from computer software, expert opinions should be sought. We have included some sample data using the SPSS program for the Pearson *r*, the Spearman Rho Rank, Correlation and Analysis of Variance statistics. Pitfalls discussed earlier will also apply to the computerized statistical software summarized.

SPSSX outputs are notated with an * if $p<.05$ and ** if $p<.01$. When computing the Pearson *r* stars imply the rejection of the null or no relationship. This is shown in the correlation matrix below. The command asked for all possible relationships between the variables and in interpreting the output, we have focused on and mentioned relationships that are starred.

Notice that the matrix contains each correlation twice. We could simplify our existence by drawing a diagonal across the box where the 1.000's are (top left to bottom right) and crossing out either the top of the bottom triangle since these contain the same information:

Correlations: Workload, Job Satisfaction, Income, and Years Worked :

Correlation Coefficients

	Workload	Job Satisfaction	Income	Years Worked
Workload	1.0000	.1821	.6548**	.3080*
Job Satisfaction	.1821	1.0000	.3457*	.0419
Income	.6458**	.3457*	1.0000	.2823*
Years Worked	.3080*	.0419	.2823*	1.0000

* - Signif.LE.05** - Signif.LE (2-tailed)

Which correlations are worthy of attention? See below:

- the .31 correlation between workload and years worked ($p<.05$);
- the .28 correlation between income and years worked ($p<.05$);
- the correlation between income and workload ($p<.01$);
- the correlation between income and job satisfaction ($p<.05$).

In each of these cases, the null of no relationship has been rejected. To complete the interpretation, the researcher need only mention the strength and direction of the relationship, as follows:

The Pearson *r* correlation coefficient was used to evaluate inter-relationships among income, workload, years worked, and employee satisfaction. There were weak to moderate correlations between workload and years worked: $r=.31$, p<.05; income and years worked: $r=.28$, p<.05; and income and job satisfaction: $r=.35$, p<.05. There was a positive correlation of moderate strength between income and workload: $r=.65$, p<.01. When describing outputs of a Pearson correlation analysis, the researcher should:

- mention what was inter-correlated,
- point out significant correlations,
- mention the direction and strength of each, adding perhaps an interpretive statement and
- reporting the *r* value itself along with AP.

It is assumed that any correlation the researcher did not discuss was not significant. On the other hand, the researcher is obligated to report all significant correlations, and those correlations should be reported in tables.

For the Spearman Rho correlation, the SPSSX command and its output are as follows:

Job Satisfaction		.1412		
	N(50)			
	SIG .164			
Income	.6667	.2515		
	N(50)	N(50)		
	SIG .000	SIG .039		
Years Worked	.3221	.0309	.3309	
	N(50)	N(50)	N(50)	
	SIG .011	SIG .416	SIG .009	
	Workload	Job Satisfaction	Income	

Rules for interpretation of the Spearman Rho Rank data are exactly the same as those for computing the Pearson *r*, except for the following:

1. The researcher must note that he/she is dealing with a correlation of ranks which require that ordinal data are used, rather than interval/ratio data.
2. Half of the correlation matrix has already been excluded from the output.
3. Instead of marking correlations with stars, the Spearman Rho Rank output gives exact *p* values which are reported as ASIG@ in the second line below each correlation.

For our example, the null of no relationship was rejected for the relationship of Income and Workload (rank correlation = .67, p<.001), Income and Workload (rank correlation = .32, p=.011), Income and Years Worked (rank correlation = .33, p=.009), and Income and Job Satisfaction (rank correlation = .25, p=.039).

SPSSX Commands and Output for a One-Way Analysis of Variance

The SPSSX commands and the output for a simple or one way analysis of variance are as follows:

Source	D.F.	Sum of Squares	Mean Squares	F Ratio	F Prob.
Between Groups	2	30.0962	15.0481	7.1713	.00019
Within Groups	47	98.6238	2.0984		
Total	49	128.720			

Group	Count	Mean	Standard Deviation	Standard Error	95% Conf. Int. for Mean
Grp 1	21	3.9048	1.3749	.3000	3.2789 to 4.5301
Grp 2	15	3.4000	1.4541	.3754	2.5948 to 4.2052

Group					
Grp 3	14	5.3571	1.5495	.4141	4.4625 to 6.2518
Total	50	4.1600	1.6208	.2292	3.6994 to 4.6206

Group	Minimum	Maximum
Grp 1	1.0000	7.0000
Grp 2	2.0000	7.0000
Grp 3	3.0000	7.0000
Total	1.0000	7.0000

The estimates of variance are called MEAN SQUARES. Find the mean square between groups (15.0481). Find the mean square within groups (2.0984). Now notice the *F* ratio, which is actually the first of these numbers divided by the second (7.1793). Finally, look at the probability of *F*. If this number is less than .05, the researcher rejects the null. It is .0019, so the researcher rejects the null, inferring some differences among the three Means. The degrees of freedom (DF) for the *F* ratio are also included in the table. An analysis of
variance was used to compare Job Satisfaction means for employees with one of three kinds of outcomes (income, workload, and years worked. The null of equality of means was rejected ($F[2,47]=7.18$, $p=.002$). The mean for Group 3 was highest (5.4) while the mean for Group 2 was lowest (3.4).

New Computerized Statistical Packages
General Packages: Support a wide variety of statistical analyses.
- Subset Packages: deal with a specific area of analysis, or a limited set of tests.
- Curve Fitting and Modeling: to handle complex, nonlinear models and systems.
- Biostatistics and Epidemiology: especially useful in the life of sciences.
- Surveys , Testing and Measurement: especially useful in the business and social sciences.
- Excel Spreadsheets and Add-ins: you need a recent version of Excel.
- Programming Languages and Subroutine Libraries: customized for statistical calculations; you need to learn the appropriate syntax.
- Scripts and Macros: for scriptable packages, like SAS, SPSS, R, etc.
- Miscellaneous: don't fit into any of the other categories.
- Other Collections of Links to Free Software.

General Packages: No package does everything, but these programs support a wide variety of statistical analyses.

OpenSat - - a general stats package for Win 95/98/NT, developed by Bill Miller of Iowa State University, with a very broad range of data manipulation and analysis capabilities and an SPSS-like user interface. Bill also has provided an excellent downloadable textbook in the form of Adobe Acrobat files.

ViSta - -a Visual Statistics program for Win 3.1, Win 95/NT, Mac and Unix, featuring a Structured Desktop, with features designed to structure and assist the statistical analyst.

OpenEpi Versis 2.2 - - Open Epi is a free, web-based, open source, operating-system-independent series of programs for use in public health and medicine, providing a number of epidemiologic and statistical tools. Version 2 (4/25/2007) has a new interface that presents results without using pop-up windows, and has better installation methods so that it can be run without an internet coneection. Version 2.2 (2007/11/09) lets users run the software in English, French, Spanish, or Italian.

Statext - - Provides a nice assortment of basic statistical tests, with text output (and test-based graphics). Capabilities include: rearrange, transpose, tabulate and count data; random sample; basic descriptive; text-plots for dot, box-and-whiskers, stem-and-leaf, histogram, scatter plot; find z-values, confidence interval for means, t-tests (one and two group, and paired; one-and two-way ANOVA; Pearson, Spearman and Kendall correlation; in ear regression, Chi-square goodness-of-fit test and independence tests; sign test, Mann-Whitney U and Kruskal-Wallis H tests, probability tables (z, t, Chi-square, F, U); random number generator; Central Limit Theorem, Chi-square distribution.

MicrOsiris - - a comprehensive statistical and data management package for Windows, derived from the OSIRIS IV package developed at the University of Michigan. It was developed for serious survey analysis using moderate t large data sets. Main features: handles any size data set; has Excel data entry; imports/exports SPSS, SAS, and Status datasets; reads ICPSR (OSIRIS) and UNESCO (IDAMS) datasets; data mining techniques for market analysis (SEARCH - - very fast for large datasets); interactive decision tree for selecting appropriate tests; database manipulation (dictionaries, sorting, merging, consistency checking, recording, transforming) extensive statistics (univariate, staccerplot, cross-tabs, ANOVA/MONOBA, log-linear, correlation/regression MCA, MNA, binary segmentation, cluster, factor, MINISSA, item analysis, survival analysis, internal consistency); online, web-enabled users manual; requires only 6MB RAM; uses 12MB disk, including manual. Fully-functional version is free; the authors would appreciate a small donation to support ongoing development and distribution.

Gnumeric – a high-powered spreadsheet with better statistical features than Excel. Has 60 extra functions, basic support for financial derivatives (Black Scholes) and telecommunication engineering, advanced statistical analysis, extensive random number generation linear and non-linear solvers, implicit intersection, implicit iteration, goal seek, and Monte Carlo simulation tools.

Statist – a compact, portable program that provides most basic statistical capabilities: data manipulation (recording, transforming, selecting), descriptive stats (including histograms, box & whisker plots), correlation & regression, and the common significance tests (chi-square, t-test, etc.). Written in C (source available); runs on Unix/Linux, Windows, Mac, among others.

OpenEpi Version 2.2 -- OpenEpi is a free, web-based, open source, operating-system-independent series of programs for use in public health and medicine, providing a number of epidemiologic and statistical tools. Version 2 (4/25/2007) has a new interface that presents results without using pop-up windows, and has better installation methods so that it can be run without an Internet connection. Version 2.2 (2007111/09) lets users run the software in English, French, Spanish, or Italian.

Statext -- Provides a nice assortment of basic statistical tests, with text output (and text-based graphics). Capabilities include: rearrange, transpose, tabulate and count data; random sample; basic descriptives; text-plots for dot, box-and-whiskers, stem-and-leaf, histogram, scatter plot; find z-values, confidence interval for means, t-tests (one and two group, and paired; one- and two-way ANOVA; Pearson, Spearman and Kendall correlation; ;lunar regression, Chi-square goodness-of-fit test and independence tests; sign test, Mann-Whitney U and .Kruskal-Wallis H tests, probability tables (z, t, Chi-square, F, U); random number generator; Central Limit Theorem, Chi-square distribution.

MicrOsiris -- a comprehensive statistical and data management package for Windows, derived from the OSIRIS IV package developed at the University of Michigan. It was developed for serious survey analysis using moderate to large data sets. Main features: handles any size data set; has Excel data entry; imports/exports SASS, SAS, and Stats datasets; reads ICPSR (OSIRIS) and UNESCO (IDAMS) datasets; data. mining techniques for market analysis (SEARCH --very fast for large datasets); interactive decision tree for selecting appropriate tests; database manipulation (dictionaries, sorting, merging, consistency checking, recoding, transforming) extensive statistics (univariate, staccerplot, cross-tabs, ANOV.A/MANOVA., iog-linear, correlation/rel ressionMCA, MNA, *bizrafy* segmentation, cluster, factor, MINISSA, item analysis, survival analysis, internal consistency); online, web-enabled users manual; requires only 6M.I3 RAM; uses 12MB disk, including manual. Fully-functional version is free; the authors would appreciate a small donation to support ongoing development and distribution, Gnumeric -- a high-powered spreadsheet with better statistical features than Excel, Has 60 extra functions, basic support for financial derivatives (Black Scholes) and telecommunication engineering, advanced statistical analysis, extensive random number generation, linear and non-linear solvers, implicit intersection, implicit iteration, goal seek, and. Monte Carlo simulation tools.

Statist -- a compact, portable program that provides most basic statistical capabilities: data manipulation (recoding, transforming, selecting), descriptive stats (including histograms, box&whisker plots), correlation & regression, and the common significance tests (chisquare, t-lest, etc.). Written in C (source available); runs on Unix/Linux, Windows, Mac, among others.

Tanagra -- a free (open source) data-mining package, *which* supports the standard "stream diagram" paradigm used by most data-mining systems. Contains components for Data source (tab-delimited text), Visualization (grid, seatterplotss), Descriptive statistics (cross-tab, ANOVA, correlation), Instance selection (sampling, stratified), Feature selection and construction, Regression (multiple linear), factorial analysis (principal components, multiple correspondence), Clustering (kMeans, SOM, LVQ, TIAC), Supervised learning (logistic regr., kNN, multi-layer perceptron, prototype-NN, ID3, discriminant analysis, naive Bayes, radial basis function), Meta-spv learning (instance Spv, arcing, boosting, bagging), Learning assessment (train-test, cross-validation), and Association (Agrawal a-priori). (french-language page here)

Pan -- a statistics and graphics package developed by Susan Bassein for Unix and Limn systems, with conmionly-needed data management, analysis, and graphics (univariate statistics, correlations and regression, ANOV:A, categorical data analysis, logistic regression, and nanparametric analyses). Provides some of the core functionality of SAS, and is able to read and run, many (but not all) S.AS program files. Dap is freely distributed under a GNU-style"copyleft".

A --- a free package for analyzing data from complex samples, especially large-scale assessments, as well as non-assessment survey data. Has sophisticated stats, easy drag & drop interface, and integrated help system that explains the statistics as well as how to use the system. Can estimate models via marginal maximum likelihood (MML), which defines a probability distribution over the proficiency scale. Also analyzes "plausible values" used in programs like NAEP. Automatically provides appropriate standard errors for complex samples via Taylor-series approximation, jackknife & other replication techniques.

I.nstat Plus -- from the University of Reading, in the UK. (Not to be confused with Instat from GraphPad Software.) An interactive statistics package for Windows or DOS.

WlnIDA S -- from UNESCO -- for numerical information processing and statistical analysis. Provides data manipulation and validation facilities classical and advanced statistical techniques, including interactive construction of multidimensional tables, graphical exploration of data (3D scattergram spinning, etc.), time series analysis, and a large number of anultivariate techniques.

SSP Smith's Statistical Paden =e -- a simple, user-friendly package for Mac and Windows that can enter/edit/transform/import/export data, calculate basic summaries, prepare charts, evaluate distribution function probabilities, perform simulations, compare means & proportions, do ANOVA's, Chi Square tests, simple & multiple regressions.

Also, check out *f* and Ox, described in the *Programming Languages* section below.

NCSS 6.4 Junior -- a free, stripped-down version ofNCSS 6.0 for Win 3.1. Has data entry, descriptive statistics, t-tests, multiple regression, tests on proportions, cross tabs, one-way ANOVA, exponential smoothing, *histograms,* scatter plots, and box plots.

Dataplot -- (Unix, Linux, PC-:DOS, Windows) for scientific visualization, statistical analysis, and non-linear modeling. Has extensive mathematical and graphical capabilities. Closely integrated with the NIST/SEMAI'.1_CH Engineering Statistics Handbook

WebStat -- A Java-based statistical computing environment for the World Wide Web. Needs a browser, but can be downloaded and run offline.

EasyStat -- Simple program for Windows and Mac for t-tests, F-tests, simple ANOVA, contingency table, Mantel-Haenszel

Regress+ -- A professional package (Macintosh only) for univariate mathematical modeling (equations and distributions). The most powerful software of its kind available anywhere, with state-of--the-art functionality and user-friendliness. Too many features to even begin to list here.

Scilab -- a scientific software package for numerical computations in, a user-friendly environment.

Available for Windows, Mac and Unix computers, this is a sophisticated programming language with a MatLab-like syntax, hundreds of built-in functions and libraries, 3-d graphics, and symbolic capabilities through a Maple interface.

SIS -- Simple Interactive Statistical Analysis for PC (DOS) from Daan Uitenbroek. An excellent collection of individual DOS modules for several statistical calculations, including some analyses not readily available elsewhere.

Statistical Software by Paul W. Mielke Jr. -- a large collection of executable :DOS programs (and Fortran source). Includes: Matrix occupancy, exact g-sample empirical coverage test, interactions of exact analyses, spectral decomposition analysis, exact mrbp (randomized block) analyses, exact multi-response permutation procedure, Fisher's Exact for cross-classification and goodness-of-tit, Fisher's combined p-values (meta analysis), largest part's proportion, Pearson Zelterrnan. Greenwood-Moran and Kendall-Sherman goodness-of-fit, runs tests, multivariate Retelling's test, least-absolute deviation regression, sequential permutation procedures, LAD regression, principal component analysis, matched pair permutation, r by c contingency tables, r-way contingency tables, and Jonkheere-Terpstra.

IRRISTAT -- for data management and basic statistical analysis of experimental data Windows). Primarily for analysis of agricultural field trials, but many features can be used for analysis of data from other sources. Includes: Data management with a spreadsheet , Text editor, Analysis of variance, Regression, Genotype x environment interaction analysis, Quantitative trait analysis, Single site analysis, Pattern analysis, Graphics, Utilities for randomization and layout, general factorial EMS, and orthogonal polynomial.

Hypercard stack that performs basic statistical analyses. Rums on the Mac (a free HyperCard Player program can be downloaded. from the Apple *web site)*.

SYSTAT 12 -- powerful statistical software ranging from the most elementary descriptive statistics to very advanced statistical. methodology. Novices can work with its friendly and simple menudialog; statistically-savvy users can use its intuitive command language. Carry out very comprehensive analysis of univariate an multivariate data based on linear, general linear, and mixed linear models; carry out different types of robust regression analysis when your data are not suitable for conventional multiple regression analysis;compute partial least-squares regression;design experiments, carry out power analysis, do probability calculations on many distributions and fit them to data; perform m atTix computations. Provides Time Series, Survival Analysis, Response Surface Optimization, Spatial Statistics, Test Item. Analysis, Cluster Analysis, Classification and Regression Trees, Correspondence Analysis, Multidimensional Sealing, Conjoint Analysis, Quality Analysis, Path Analysis, etc. A 30-day evaluation version is available for free download.

Statlets -- a 100% Pure Java statistics program. Should run on any platform (PC, Mac. Unix) that supports Java. The free Academic Version is limited to 100 cases by 10 variables.

STATISTICA from StatSoft -- a fully functional time limited (30 days) desktop version 8 of STA ISTICA Advanced + QC. Contains all modules from Base, Advanced, and QC products: Descriptives, ANOVA, Regression, Nonparametrics, QC Charts, Process Analysis, Design of Experiments, Six Sigma toolbar and calculator, Advanced Linear/Nonlinear Models, Multivariate and Exploratory Techniques, and Power Analysis.

WINKS (Windows KWIKSTAT) -- a full-featured, easy-to-use stats package with statistics (means, standard deviations, medians, eta), histograms, t-tests, cor^{r}elation, chi-square, regression, nonparametrics, analysis of variance (ANOVA), probability, QC plots, epic, graphs, life tables, time series, crosstabs, and more. Works on Windows XP (as well as Windows 2000, NT, 98, ME and 95.) Comes in Basic and Professional editions. Evaluation version available for download.

StudyResult -- General statistics package for: paired & unpaired t-test, one-way ANOVA, Fisher's exact . McNemar's, Chi2, Chi^2 homogeneity , life table & survival analysis, Wilcoxon rank-sum & signed-rank, sign test, bioequivalence testing, correlation &. regression coefficient tests. Special features for interpreting summary data found in publications (pvalues & coat:

intervals from summary statistics, converts p-values to CJ's Se vice versa. what observed results are needed to get a significant result, estimates from. publications needed for sample size calculations). Includes equivalence- and non-inferiority testing for most test *STATGRAPII;.ICS Plus* v5.0 (for Windows) -- over 250 statistical analyses: regression, probit, enhanced logistic, factor effects plots, automatic forecasting, matrix plots, outlier identification, general linear models (random and mixed), multiple regression with automatic Cochrane-Orcutt and Box-Cox procedures, Levene's, Friedman's, Dixon's and Grubb's tests, Durbin-Watson p-values and 1-variable bootstrap estimates, enhanced 3D charts. For *Six Sigma* work: gage linearity and accuracy analysis, multi-vari charts, life data regression for reliability analysis and accelerated life-testing, long-term and short-term capability assessment estimates. Two free downloads are available: full-function but limited-time(30 days), and unlimited-time but limited-function (no Save, no Print, not all analyses).

NCSS-2000 Statistical Analysis System and PASS-2000 Power and Sample Size program for Windows (both programs in one 19-megabyte download) -- Comprehensive, easy to use. Free 30-day evaluation version of NCSS is limited to 1017 rows of data.

StatSimple -- a Mac package that does descriptive statistics, histograms and Box Plots, Student's t-test, Mann-Whitney U-test, paired t-test, Wilcoxon test, linear regression, Pearson's and Spearman's coefficients, ANOVA with post-hoes (multi-comparisons vs control, Bonferroni, Fisher's LSD), Kruslcal-Wallis statistic, and simple ChiSquare. The free version puts limits on dataset *size*.

QuickStat -- a powerful yet very easy to use research tool for MS Windows. Does not assume statistical knowledge. The novice can call up advice on experimental. design, analysis and interpretation from the integrated statistical help system. Results are presented in plain language. For the more experienced user, Arcus is an extremely useful statistical toolbox which covers biomedical statistical methods that are often absent or difficult to access from other statistical packages. The free download is limited to 50 cases, and expires after 3 months.

MiniTab -- a powerful, full-featured MS-Windows package, with good coverage of industrial l quality control analyses. The free Version 12 Demo expires after 30 days.

InStat (Instant Statistics), a full-featured statistics package from GraphPad Software. Demo version disables printing, saving and exporting capabilities. Demo available for Windows only; commercial version available for Windows and Mac.

Prism. -- from GraphPad Software. Performs basic biostatistics, fits curves and creates publication quality scientific graphs in one complete package (Mac and Windows). Windows demo is fully-functional for 30 days, then disables printing, saving and exporting; Mac demo always disables these functions.

CoStat 6.2 -- an easy-to-use program for data manipulation and statistical analysis, from CoHort Software. Use a spreadsheet with any number of columns and rows of data: floating point, integer, date, time, degrees, text, etc. Import ASCII, Excel, MatLab, S+, SAS, Genstat, Fortran, and others. Has ANOVA, multiple comparisons of means, correlation, descriptive statistics, analysis of frequency data, miscellaneous tests of hypotheses, nonparametric tests, regression (curve fitting), statistical tables, and utilities. Has an auto-recorder and macro programming language. Callable from the command line, batch files, shell scripts, pipes, and other programs; can be used as the statistics engine for web applications. Free time-limited demo available.

PS -- a well-implemented Windows program for power and sample size calculations from Vanderbilt Univ Med Ctr. Handles dichotomous, continuous, or survival response measures, which are analyzed by chi-square or Fisher Exact tests, Student t tests, and log-ranks tests, respectively. The alternative hypothesis may be specified either in terms of differing response rates, means, or survival times, or in terms of relative risks or odds ratios. Studies with dichotomous or continuous outcomes may involve either a matched or independent study design. The latest version also handles Mantel-Haenszel tests. Can determine sample size for a specified power, power for a specified sample size, or the specific alternative hypotheses that can be detected with a given power and. sample size. Produces graphs of relationships between power, sample size and detectable alternative hypotheses (with any two of these variables on x & y, and the third variable generating a family of curves on a single graph). Linear or logarithmic *axes* may be specified. Can print professional-quality power charts.

Factor -- a comprehensive factor analysis program. Provides univariate and multivariate descriptive statistics of input variables (mean, variance, skewness, kurtosis), Var charts for ordinal variables, dispersion matrices (user defined , covariance, Pearson correlation, polychoric correlation matrix with optional Ridge estimates). Uses 'MAP, PA (Parallel Analysis), and PA . MISS (with marginally bootstrapped samples) to determine the number of factors/components to be retained. Perfbtms the following factor and component analyses: PCA, ULS (with Heywood correction), EML, MRFA, Sehmid-Leiman second-order solution, and Factor scores. Rotation methods: Quartimax, ,Varimax , Weighted Varimax, Orthomin , Direct Oblimin, Weighted Oblirnin, Pronlax, Promaj , Promin, and Simplimax. Indices used in the analysis: dispersion matrix tests (determinant, Bartlett's, Kaiser-Meyer-Olldn), goodness of fit: Chi-Square ,non-nonmed fit index, comparative ht index, goodness of fit index, adjusted GPI, RMS error of approx, and estimated non-centrality parameter (NCP), reliabilities of rotated components , simplicity indices: Bender's, and loading simplicity index. Provides mean, variance and histogram of fitted and standardized residuals, and automatic detection of large standardized residuals.

KEYFINDER - a menu-driven interactive program for generating, randomizing and tabulating blocked and/or fractional-replicate factorial designs in completely general situations. It can generate blocked and/or fractional-replicate designs with userspecified confounding and aliasing properties. KEYFINDERruns on all versions of Windows. You can download the Version. 3.3 Overview document, in PDF format, here. To obtain a free copy of the progʳam and. manual, send an e-mail to the author: Peter.Zemroch@shefl.con7

Weka -- a collection of machine learning algorithms for data mining tasks, implemented in lava. Can be executed from a command-line environment, or from a graphical interface, or can either be called from your own lava code. Weka contains tools for data pre-processing, classification, regression, clustering, association rules, and visualization, and is well-suited for developing new machine learning schemes.

StaCalc -- a PC calculator that computes table values and other statistics for 34 probability distributions. Also includes some nonparametric table values, tolerance factors, and abivariate normal distribution. A help file is provided for each distribution.

Scientific Calculatar - ScienCalc program contains high-performance arithmetic, trigonometric, hyperbolic and transcendental calculation routines. All the function routines therein map directly to Intel 80387 FPU floating point machine instructions.

Distributions - Windows program allows for the analysis of discrete single dimension distributions. The program is based on various manipulations of the posion, binomial and hypergeometric distribution. Available are the probability of an observed number of cases given a certain null hypothesis, the calculation of exact poisson, binomial or hypergeometric confidence intervals, the exact and approximate size of a population using catch-recatch methodologies, the full analysis of a Poisson distributed rate ratio, Fieller analysis, and two versions of the negative binomial distribution can be used in various ways. Beside the exact procedures there are also various approximate procedures available. From the Downloads section of the QuantitativeSkills web site.

Multinomial - - This Windows program is the exact solution to the Chisquare Goodness of fit test of testing for a difference between an observed and an expected distribution in a one-dimensional array. For example, the test can be used to compare the distribution of diseases in a certain locality with an expected distribution on the ʾbasis of national or international experiences using an ICD classification. In a two-category array the multinomial test provides a two-sided solution for the Binomial test. For example, Multinomial {10 20 0.20 0.80} gives the two-sided probability

(0.105) for the single sided Binomial {0.20 10 30} probability (0.061). The =binomial allows you to work with empty '0' observation cells although you must have an expectation about a cell. From the Downloads section of the QuantitativeSkills web site.

Tables -- a Windows program for the analysis of tables with up to 2*7 and 3 *3 cells. The program allows for exact and approximate statistics to be calculated for traditional, ordinal and agreement tables. Fisher exact, Number Needed to Treat, Proportional Reduction in *Error* Statistics, Normal. Approximations, Four different Chi-squares, Gamma, Odds-ratio, t-tests and Kappa are among the many statistical procedures available. From the Downloads section of the QuantitativeSkills web site.

MorePower -- another well-implemented power/sample-size calculator for any ANOVA design, for I- and 2-sample t-tests, and for 1- and 2sample binomial testing (sign test, chi-square test),

BlockTreat -- a Java program that implements a very general Monte Carlo procedure that performs non-parametric tests (based on random permutations, not ranks) for block and treatment tests, tests with

matching, k-sample tests, and tests for independence between any two random variables. Designs may be incomplete and unbalanced, or even have supernumerary entries. The tests are "exact", in the Monte-Carlo sense -- they can be made as accurate as desired by specifying enough random shuffles.

PEPI -- a collection of 43 small DOS/Windows programs that perform a large assortment of statistical tests. They can be downloaded .individually, or as a single Zipfile,. (A new Windows version is being developed; the test version can be downloaded here,) They were written to accompany the book *Computer Programs for Epidemiologic* Analyses. *PEPI v.* 40, by Abramson and Gahlinger, which is available for purchase. A freely-accessible article describing the new features of WinPEPI can be accessed here. The programs include: p-value adjustments for multiple significance tests; Attributable and Prevented Fractions: Case-Control Studies; Analysis of 2 x 2 Tables; Chi-square Tests of Association; Combining Measures of Association or Probabilities; Confidence Intervals; Aids to Use of Pearson`s Correlation Coefficients; difference Between Rates, Proportions or Means; Direct Standardization; Exact Test for a 2 x K Table; Tests for Goodness of Fit ; Fitting of Poisson and Binomial Distributions; Appraisal of Frequency Distribution ; Indirect Standardization; Agreement Between Categorical Ratings; Life Table Analysis; Logistic Regression Analysis (Unconditional and Conditional); Wilcoxon-Mann-Whitney Test and Related Procedures ; Extended Mantel-Haenszel Procedure: Trend Analysis; Multiple Matched Controls; Cor'ecting for Misclassification in 2 x 2 Tables; Analysis of Paired Samples ; Poisson Probability: Observed vs Expected Events; Poisson Regression Analysis; Power of a Test Comparing Two Proportions or Means; Probability and Inverse Probability Values: Z, t, Chi Square, F; Procedures using Random Numbers; Association Between Ordinal-Scale `Variables; Comparison of Two Rates or Proportions; Comparison of Person-Time Incidence Rates; ower and Sample *Size for* Regression and Correlation Analyses; Comparison of Several Related Samples; Sample Size for Estimation of Proportion, Rate, or. Mean; Sample Sizes for Comparison of Two Samples ; Internal Consistency of a Scale; Screening and Diagnostic Tests ; Seasonal Variation ; Smoothing of Curves and Median Polish Procedure; Kaplan-Meier Life Table Analysis, Log-rank and Logitrank Tests; Calculation of Elapsed Time; Trend Analysis and Multiple Comparisons, arid two special calculators: *WHATIS and WHAT.*

TETRAD (from the TETRAD Project at CMU) -- a free program for creating, simulating data from, estimating, testing, predicting with, and searching for causal/statistical models of categorical (or ordinal) data and to linear models ("structural equation models') with a Normal probability distribution, and to a very limited class of time series models. Provides sophisticated methods in a friendly interface. It performs many of the functions in commercial programs such as Netica, Hugin, LISREL, EQS and other programs, and many discovery functions these commercial programs do no t perform. TETRAD is limited to models The TETRAD programs describe causal models in three distinct parts or stages: a picture, representing a directed graph specifying hypothetical causal relations among the variables; a specification of the family of probability distributions and kinds of parameters associated with the graphical model; and a specification of the numerical values of those parameters, Easy Sample -- a tool for statistical sampling. Supports several types of attribute and variable sampling and includes a random number generator and standard deviation calculator. Has a consistent, easy-to-use interface. Results may be saved or read in CSV (spreadsheet compatible) or XML (Internet compatible) file formats or printed.

EpiData -- a comprehensive yet simple tool for documented data entry. Overall frequency tables (codebook) and listing of data included, but no statistical analysis tools.

Grocer -- a free econometrics toolbox that runs under Scilab. It contains: most standard econometric capabilities: ordinary least squares, autocorelated models, instrumental variables, non linear least squares, limited dependent variables, robust methods, specification tests (multicolinearity, autocorelation, heteroskedasticity, normality, predictive failure,...), simultaneous equations methods (SUR, two and three stage least squares,...), VAR, VECM, VARMA and GA:RCH estimation, the Kalman filter and time varying parameters estimation, unit root tests (ADP, KI⁻SS,...) and cointegration metltod;t (CADE, Johansen,...), HP, Baxter-King and Christiano-Fitzgerald filters. It also contains some rare ·and useful-- features: *ape-gets* device that performs automatic general to specific estimations, and *a contributions* device, that provides contributions of exogenous variables to an endogenous one for any dynamic equation. Has a - rough- interface with Excel and unlike Gauss or Matlab, it deals with true timeseries objects.

BiomapDer -- a kit ()FOB and statistical tools designed to build *habitat suitability (HS)* models *and* maps for any kind of animal *or* plant. Deals with: preparing ecogeographical maps for use as input for ENFA (e.g. computing frequency of occurrence map, standardisation, masking, etc.); Exploring and comparing them by mean of descriptive statistics (distribution analysis, etc.): Computing the Ecological Niche Factor Analysis and exploring its output; and Computing and evaluating a Habitat Suitability map

ROC Curves:- a set of downloadable programs and Excel spreadsheets to calculate and graph various kinds of ROC (Receiver Operator Characteristic) curves.

BKD: Bayesian Knowledge Discoverer -- a computer program able to learn Bayesian Balief Networks from (possibly incomplete) databases. Based on a new estimation method called Bound and Collapse. Developed -within the Bayesian Knowledge Discovery project. *See also the commercial* product, called Bayesware Discoverer, available free for non-commercial use.

RoC: The Robust Bayesian Classifier -- a computer program able to perform supervised Bayesian classification from incomplete databases, with no assumption about the pattern of missing data. Based on a new estimation method called Robust Bayesian Estimator. Developed within the Bayesian Knowledge Discovery project.

DQO-PRO -- a sample-size calculator for MS Windows that performs three types of calculations:

- • determining the *rate* at which an event occurs (confidence levels versus numbers of false positive or negative conclusions),
- o determining an estimate of an averse within a tolerable *error* (given the standard deviation of individual measurements), and
- • determining the sampling grid necessary to detect "hot spots" of various assumed shapes.

Probability Calculator -- Regular (p-value) and inverse calculation for most popular central and non-central probability distributions: Beta, Binomial, Bivariate Normal, Chi Square, Correlation, Fisher F, Gamma, Flypergeometric, Negative Binomial, Normal (Gaussian), Poisson, Student t, Studentized Range, Weibull.

Binomial Probability Program (BPP) is a menu driven program which performs a variety of functions related to the success/ failure situation. Given the probability of occurrence for a specific event, this program calculates the probability that EXACTLY, NO MORE THAN, or AT LEAST a certain number of events occur in a given number of trials for all possible outcomes, and will generate plots for each of these.

The program allows the user to repeatedly combine probabilities in series or in parallel, and at any time will show a trail of the calculations which led to the current probability value. Other program capabilities are the calculation of probabilities from input data, Gaussian approximation, and the generation of a mean time between failure (MTBF) table for various levels of confidence. Up to 2200 trials may be run, limited by ICBM PC BASIC memory utilization. It is assumed that the user is familiar with the theory behind binomial probability distribution.

ADE-4 multivariate analysis and graphical display software package for Mac and Win 95/NT. Includes component analysis and correspondence analysis, spatial data analysis methods (analogous to Moran and Geary indices), discriminant analysis and within/between groups analyses, many linear regression methods including lowest and polynomial regression, multiple and :PINS (partial least squares) regression:and orthogonal (principal component) regression, projection methods like principal component analysis on instrumental variables, canonical correspondence analysis and many other variants, coinertia analysis and the RLQ method, and several three-way table (k table) analysis methods. Graphical displays include an automatic collection of elementary graphics corresponding to groups of rows or to columns in the data table, automatic k-table graphics and geographical mapping options, searching, zooming, selection of points, and display of data values on factor maps. Simple and homogeneous *user* interface.

R (Not to be confused with the "R" statistical programming language!) -- A group of programs (Macintosh and VAX/VMS), originally developed for ecologists, various complex multidimensional and spatial analysis procedures. Contains AutoCorrelation, BioGeo, Chrono, Cluster, Cocopan, COnvert, GeoDistances, Import-Export, K-Means.

Links, Look, Mantel, PCoord, Periodograph, P.nComp, Simil, and VerNornm. Pull documentation is provided.

G*Power -- a general Power Analysis program for DOS and Macintosh. Performs high-precision analysis for t-tests, F-tests, Chi-square tests. Computes power, sample sizes, alpha, beta, and alpha/beta. ratios. Has a comprehensive web-based tutorial and reference manual.

MSBNx -- a component-based Windows application for creating, assessing, and evaluating Bayesian Networks, created at Microsoft Research, Includes complete help files and sample networks. Bayesian Networks are encoded in an XML file format.

QUEST (Quick, Unbiased and Efficient Statistical Tree), and CRUISE (Classification Rule with Unbiased Interaction Selection and Estimation. Two statistical decision tree algorithms for classification and data mining, by Wei-Yin Loh and Yu-Shan Shih.

AMB'IELIA -- A program for substituting reasonable values for missing data (called "imputation")

SPSS Syntax Files. -- a large collection of SPSS routines for randomized study design sampling strategies, meta-analysis, sample size for confidence intervals, correlation tests, psychometry and other areas. The documentation is in Portuguese, but the scripts are usable

assist. You can have AltaVista automatically translate the page into English by going here, but do not use the "translated" scripts!

.A collection of MS-DOS program from the *Downloads* section of the *QuantitativeSkills* web site:

- Hypergeometric -- calculates the hypergeometri.c probability distribution to evaluate hypothesis iii relation to sampling without replacing in small populations

- Binomial -- calculates probabilities for sampling with replacing in small populations or without replacing in very large populations. Can be used to approximate the hypergeometri.c distribution. The binomial is probably the best known discrete distribution.

- Negative binomial -- Also used to study accidents, is a more general case than the Poison, it considers that the probability
  of getting accidents if accidents clusters differently in subgroups of the population. However, the theoretical properties of this distribution and the possible relationship to real events are not well known.
- Negative binomial -- Another version of the negative binomial, this one is used to do the marginal distribution of binomials (try it!). Often used to predict the termination of real time events. An example is the probability of terminating listening to a non-answering phone after n-rings.
- Multinomiai -- Same as the multinomial above, this one for DOS computers.
- Chi-square -- Calculates the Chi-square and some other measures for two dimensional, tables
- CASRO -- Calculates response rates according to different procedures. The CASRO (Council of American Survey Research Organizations) procedure is the 'accepted' procedure for surveys.

Curve-fitting Modeling: EasyReg (Easy Regression Analysis), by Herman J. Bierens, Incredibly powerful and multi-featured program for data manipulation and analysis. Designed for econometrics, but useful in many other disciplines as well. For Win 98/98fNT4.

Compunrine Rule Discovery System -- easy to use data mining software for developing high-quality rule based prediction models, such as classification and regression trees, rule sets and ensemble models. This program is licensed under the P3 license model wick means that it is free to use forever for developing rule-based predictive models, and can be freely downloaded here.

gretl -- a cross-platform (Linux, Windows, Mac, etc.) package for econometric analysis. Has an. intuitive interface (English, French, Italian & Spanish). Supports a wide variety of least-square based estimators, including two-stage & nonlinear least squares, augmented Dickey-Fuller test, Chow test for structural stability, Vector Auto regressions, ARMA estimation. Creates output niodelss as LaTeX files, in tabular or equation format. Has an integrated scripting language: enter commands either via the gui or via script, command commercial package for processing market research data. Available for Windows, Linux, and SunOS. C++ source code also available, under the GNU General Public Licerse.

ProtoGenie -- a free extensible web-based environment for research design and data collection for surveys, experiments, clinical trials, time series, cognitive and vision research, and methods courses. Lets you specify groups and define measurement and treatment events and their sequencing: The goal is to let users move smoothly from research design and data collection to interim and final statistical analysis.

0-Method -- a statistical program for analyzing data from the Q-Sort Technique. Enter data (Q-Sorts) the way they are collected, i.e. as 'piles` of statement numbers. It computes intercorrelations among QSorts, which are than factor-analysed with the Centroid (or, alternatively, PCA) method. Resulting factors can be rotated either analytically (Varimax), or judgmentally with the help of two dimensional plots. Finally, after selecting the relevant factors and 'flagging' the entries that define the factors, the analysis step produces an extensive report with a variety of tables on factor loadings, statement factor scores, discriminating statements for each of the factors as well as consensus statements across factors, etc.

Stats -- Windows program for several commonly-needed statistical functions for marketing researchers; random :numbers; sample sizes needed for surveys; mean, standard deviation, standard error and range for keyboard-entered data; standard error of a proportion; significance testing between two percentages from independent samples; significance between two percentages from dependent samples; significance testing between two averages from independent samples; contingency table analysis (i.e., Chi-Square)

SABRE -- a Fortran program for statistical analysis of binary, ordinal and count recurrent events. Such data are common in many surveys either with recurrent information collected over time or with a clustered sampling scheme. Fit is particularly appropriate for the analysis of work and life histories, and has been used intensively on many longitudinal datasets.

POSDEM -- Uses simulation techniques to analyze and *compare* alternate sampling strategies for surveys. Performs power sample size I precision analyses for different sampling methods: systematic, stratified, random, etc. Windows versions available in Spanish and English.

SSCalculator -- calculates standard scores (z, t, NCE) as well as percentiles and Wechsler test scores. (Mac, 315K)

PopTools -- Windows DILL for Excel 97 and 2000 (PC's only). Facilitates analysis of matrix population models & simulation of stochastic processes. Adds a new menu item and installs many powerful functions: matrix decompositions (Cholesky, QR, singular values, LU), eigenanalysis (eigenvalues and eigenvectors of square matrices) and formulas for generation of random variables (Normal, binomial, gamma, exponential, Poisson, logNormal). Also has routines for iterating spreadsheets to run Monte Carlo simulations, conduct randomisation tests (including the Mantel test) and calculate bootstrap statistics. Some facilities for maximum-likelihood parameter estimation, and some other generally useful functions. Free download from website, which also has documentation, examples, and related links.

SimulAr -- Provides a very elegant point-and-click graphical interface that makes it easy to generate random variables (correlated or uncorrelated) from twenty different distributions, run Monte-Carlo simulations, and generate extensive tabulations and elegant graphical displays of the results.

EZAnalyze -- enhances *Excel (Mac and PC)* by adding "point and click" functionality for analyzing data and creating graphs (no formula entry required). Does all basic "descriptive statistics" (mean, median, standard deviation, and range), and "disaggregates" data (breaks it down by categories), with results shown as tables or disaggregation graphs". Advanced features: correlation; one-sample, independent samples, and *paired* samples t-tests; chi square; and single factor ANOVA.

The *latest version* can create z-scores, percentile ranks, and random. numbers as new variables; has repeated-measures ANOVA.; does simple post hoe tests for single factor and repeated-measures ANCOVA; can graph multiple variables on a single graph, and can add error bars for + 2 SDs; adds *the ,sum* function to the *disaggregate* and *descriptive statistics* functions, and the *mode* function to *descriptive stats;* adds *delete sheets;* adds English & Spanish language options, and works better in international environments; incorporates various bug fixes; and contains an updated user manual.

EZ-R Stats -- supports a variety of analytical techniques, such as: Benford's law, univariate stats, cross-tabs, histograms. Also supports databases such as mySQL, SQLite, MS-Access, MS-SQL. Simplifies the analysis of large volumes of data, enhances audit planning *by* better characterizing data, identifies potential audit exceptions and facilitates reporting and analysis. This language is a Computer Assisted Audit Technique (CAAT) in support of COSO, SAS 78, SAS 99 and analysis required by Sarbanes-Oxley.

SSC-Stat -- an Excel add-in designed to strengthen those areas where *the* spreadsheet package is already strong, principally in the areas of data management, graphics and descriptive statistics. SSC-Stat is especially useful for datasets in which there are columns indicating different groups. Menu features within SSC-Stat can:

- help users manipulate their data (stacking, unstacking columns, 2-way unstacking, lookups, generating factors, etc.);
- generate good graphs (X-Y Scatter Plot, Category-Value Plot, Boxplot, Normal

Probability Plot, Density Estimate), that can be edited and polished like any other Excel graph ;
provide basic statistical analysis (descriptive statistics, summary statistics, I- and 2-sample t tests, 1- and 2-sample tests of proportion).

MIX (Meta-analysis with Interactive explanations) -- a statistical add-in for Excel 2000 or later (Windows only). Ideal for learning meta-analysis (reproduces the data, calculations, and graphs of virtually all data sets from the most authoritative meta-analysis books, and lets you analyze your.own data "by the book"), Handles datasets with dichotomous & continuous outcomes; calculates Risk Diff, RR, OR. Mean Diff, Hedges's g, Cohen's d; performs standard & cumulative meta analysis with CI ,z & p; fixed and random effects modeling; Cochran's Q with p-value; Higgins's 12 and H with CI; and publication bias tests: Rank correlation (tau-b) test with z & p, .Egger's and Macaskill's regression tests with, CI, and Trim-and-Fill. Generates numerous plots: tandard and cumulative forest. p-value function, four funnel types, several funnel regression types, exclusion sensitivity, Galbraith, L'Abbe, 13aujat, modeling sensitivity, and Trim-and-Fill.
OZGRID -- contains over 4000 pages (and growing) of information on Excel and VBA for Excel. Many add-on's are for sale, but there is also an enormous amount of totally free content: downloads, a tree *2417* question and answer support forum MS Office, a free Excel monthly newsletter full of detailed tips, tricks, hacks, and more for Excel and VBA.
Strreadsheet123 -- a collection of over 70 free Excel spreadsheets from financial services provider A&N Poligraph . (These will also run ᵍander an almost-free Excel-like program, Streadsheet Software Developer.) Spreadsheets include: capital budgeting, acquisition/buyout, company valuation, risk analysis, FCFE and FCFF, lease or buy a car, NPV & MR, cash :flow, capital structure, stock & bond valuation financial projections, risk analysis, foreign market exchange, income statement what-if analysis, historical & pro-forma financial statements, template for assessing risk of information technology and data warehousing, IPO timeline, Malcolm I3aldrige quality model, and risk return optimization, among many others.
Very-high-precision Statistical Probability Functions -- Provides double-precision (16 significant figures) mass , density, cumulative, inverse probability distributions, critical values, and confidence bounds for the geometric, negative binomial, binomial, Poisson, hypergeornetric, negative hypergeometric, exponential, normal, children, gamma, Student t, Fisher F and beta; non-central gamma, chi-square, beta, t and F; and the mixed Gamma-Poisson, Beta-Binomial, and Beta-Negative-binomial distributions. The routines are programmed in VBA, embedded within an Excel spreadsheet that illustrates the usage of each of them.
DE Histograms -- an Excel add-in that provides comprehensive descriptives stats, histograms, outlier detection, normality testing, and much more.
Exact confidence intervals for samples from the Binomial and Poisson distributions -- an Excel spreadsheet with several built-in functions for calculating probabilities and confidence intervals. (42k long).
BiPlol -- by Ilya Lipkovich and *Eric P. Smith*., of Virginia Tech. A user-friendly add-in for Excel to draw a biplot display (a graph of row and column markers from data that :forms a two-way table) based on results from principal components analysis, correspondence analysis, canonical discriminant analysis, metric multidimensional scaling, redundancy analysis, canonical correlation analysis or canonical correspondence analysis. Allows for a variety of transformations of the data prior to the singular value decomposition and scaling of the markers following the decomposition.
Essential Regression and Experimental Design – an Excell 95/97 add-in and electronic book package for linear multiple and polynomial regression. Includes significance tests of model and parameters, model adequacy checking, tests for multicollinearity and variance inflation factors, autocorrelation, model optimization, stepwise regression, and experimental design (screening designs, orthogonality and rotatability, and response surface modeling).

Correlation Tests -- EXCEL spreadsheet template which tests the significance of difference between correlations (both independent and dependent). (Mac, 25K)

Receiver Operating Characteristic (IRC) -- EXCEL template, graphs the ROC curve and calculates Area Under the ROC Curve (AUC) using a nonparametric method. Mac, 20K)

Summary

Using computers in research is a recent 20[a] Century development. During this century some segments of humankind has considered the computer a "cure" for all problems. They are widely used in all segments of society from keeping vital statistics to analyzing the most complex types of research in all fields. In spite of the many uses and flexibility of computers, there are many <u>things</u> that they cannot do. In summation, computers can:
1. Handle massive amounts of data with great speed
    and accuracy;
2. Follow verbatim a controlled sequence of instructions for conducting both qualitative and quantitative data;
3. Store and retrieve data for present or historical use;
4. Not think; they have to be programmed to perform accurately.

Computer analysis can save the researcher countless time by reducing the amount of time needed to analyze data by removing most of the tedious work in recording, sorting, tabulating, and analyzing data. For analyzing large amounts of data, software programs are invaluable (Durkin, 1997; Ryand & Bernard, 2000; Fielding & Lee, 1998).

Computers are valuable tools for the researcher. We have articulated throughout this text that computers can only produce what they are programmed to do. They must be told exactly what to do, and appropriate computer software must be used. We chose to summarize the use of the SPSS software package because of the many applications the package can perform. The researcher should review the various types of computer software packages outlined in this chapter and choose appropriate software which has proven its utility in research. If employed correctly, computer software packages can be a vital resource for the researcher.

References

Blaisdell, Ernest A. (1993). *Statistics In Practice.* New York: Sanders College Publishing.

Devore, J. and Peck, R. (1986). *The Exploration and Analysis of Data.* St. Paul, MN:West Publishing Company.

Durkin, T. (1997). *Using compuers in strategic qualitative research.* In Miller and Dingwall (Eds.). Content and method in qualitative research. Thousand Oaks, CA: Sage Publications.

Fielding, N.G. and Lee, R.M. (1991). *Using Computers in Qualitative Research.* Newbury Park, CA: Sage Publishing Company.

Fielding, N.G. and Lee, R.M. (1998). *Computer analysis and qualitative research.* Thousand Oaks, CA: Sage Publications.

Heise, D.R. (1988). *Computer Analysis of Cultural Structures.* Social Science Computer Review. 6, 183-197.

Minitab, Inc. MINITAB Reference Manual (1991). Release 8, P.C. Version. State College, PA: Minitab, Inc.

Patton, M. Q. (2002). *Qualitative research and evaluation methods.* Thousand Oaks, CA: Sage Publications.

Ryan, G. W., & Bernard, H. R. (2000). *Data management and analysis methods.* In Denzin and Lincoln (Eds.). Handbook of qualitative research (2nd ed.). Thousand Oaks, CA: Sage Publications.

Chapter Eight
Descriptive Statistics
Theresa L. Harris, PhD
George R. Taylor, PhD

INTRODUCTION

The field of statistics is generally broken down into two major areas: *Descriptive Statistics* and *Inferential Statistics*. The functions of the two differ. Descriptive Statistics are used to describe quantitatively how a particular characteristic is distributed among a group of people. Inferential statistics are used to determine how likely it is that characteristics exhibited by a sample of people are an accurate description of those characteristics exhibited by the population of people from which the sample was drawn. Since most professional research literature consists of quantitative material, students who have had little experience reading published studies often have difficulty understanding research that is quantitative. Too often, students are used to reading textbooks or journal articles that offer basic descriptions or opinions of subjective matter regarding various aspects of some field of science, technology, education, etc., and not in-depth research materials. These two types of articles basically do not expose students to the objective level of research using a quantitative approach.

Quantitative research articles will contain descriptions of how the researcher (s) collected data and what conclusions were reached after analyzing the data. Usually, the data collected consists of measures of some type of human behavior in which the researcher (s) obtained either by administering a written test to study participants, a survey was conducted, or by directly observing intrusively or non- obtrusively, how the participants behaved under controlled conditions (Snedecor & Cochran, 1956). The student who is unfamiliar with either descriptive or inferential statistics often lacks the skill sets needed to interpret the information recorded in the study and lack the knowledge to analyze and interpret data collected. A discussion of Inferential Statistics is provided in Chapter 13.

As mentioned earlier, researchers use *descriptive statistics* when reporting the findings of certain studies. There are many ways in which the research can be presented and used. The research can be used to organize and present data in a summary format. For example, in a situation where a researcher compares the effectiveness of the language approach versus phonics when used with autistic-like students in two separate high schools in Baltimore City, Group B scored higher than Group A (Francisco, 1992). The average score of students in Group B who used whole language was 45.2 while the average scores of students in Group A using phonics was only 36.9. The average represents a descriptive statistic. On the other hand, inferential statistics is used to determine how probable it is that the characteristics of a sample of people are an accurate description of the characteristics of a population of people from which the sample was drawn.

The average scores of the students in the situation above represent a sample of high school Level V (local education agency classification) autistic-like students' (population) in the Baltimore City Public Schools. The use of inferential statistics provides data results with the average scores of Group B who used whole language as 45.2 and that the average scores of Group A, who used phonics as 36.9. Inferential statistics is used to determine the outcome of the application of statistical tests of significance to the data to determine how likely the results of the study would be applicable to the members of the population who did not participate in the study.

Scales of Measurement

The selection of appropriate statistical tests of significance to analyze data depends upon the scale of measurement associated with the measuring instrument used to collect data. Some measuring instruments use only one particular scale of measurement. However, it is possible to use more than one scale, and not all scales have equally desirable measurement properties.

Someone can apply all kinds of statistics to all kinds of situations and the unskilled or untrained student of statistical analyses probable would have little or no idea whether data have been analyzed by correct statistical procedures or not. There are certain ground rules to follow if statistics are to be applied correctly. Some kinds of statistics can be applied only if it is reasonable to assume that the data are normally distributed. One factor that must always be considered before deciding to use one statistical procedure as opposed to another is how the data have been measured. Different kinds of data are measured by different scales that have different properties. Some are more desirable than others because they permit one to use the most powerful statistical procedures available (Nunnally, 1967). A summary of the various types of measurement scales follows.

Nominal (Consistency) - Data classified into categories which have no mathematical relationship to each other. E.g.: People classified according to color of eyes.

Ordinal (Rank) - Data can be placed into rank order, so that one knows the direction (that one number is greater than another), but not distance (the amount one number is greater than another). E.g.: Finishing positions in a horse race.

Interval (Magnitude) - Distance among data is known in terms of a fixed, well-understood unit or measurement. E.g.: Temperature in terms of degrees Fahrenheit.

Ration - Interval scaled data with a real zero or origin. E.g.: Kelvin scale temperatures.

Multivariable correlation analyses are used when you want to compare more than two variables. Below are two of the most common multivariate analyses. Pearson correlation coefficients are used as input data in these analyses whenever possible. Also, linear correlation coefficients may be used if the assumptions for them are fulfilled and if all of the coefficients in the analysis are of the same magnitude (Harris, 1995; Gravetter & Wallnau, 1996).

Ordinal measures are rare in research applications. Most measurement falls either into the nominal or into the interval ratio categories. The type of statistical tool used will frequently depend upon the scale of measurement selected. Examples include when the median, quartile deviation, or range one used, ordinal data sources are recommended to be used. On the other hand, when non-parametric statistics, such as the chi-square is used, nominal data sources are recommended. Interval/ratio data are primary used with parametric statistics such as the *T*-test. Data sources may be changed from one form to another form.

It is nice to know that with interval/ratio data we could use the techniques developed for ordinal and nominal data if we wished to do so, because we can always change interval/ratio data into ordinal data (by ranking it) or nominal data (by grouping it). Ordinal data can also be turned into nominal data (by grouping). Unfortunately, this process only works in one direction.

Complex data can be reduced to a less complex form, but not vice versa. Nominal data can only remain as nominal data, and ordinal data cannot be changed into interval/ratio data. Table8.1.

shows which methods are appropriate for each scale of measurement when you have questions of centrality, spread, or relationship.

Table 8.1Measures of Central Tendency, Variability, and Relationship for Nominal, Ordinal, and
  Interval/Ratio Scales

	Nominal	Ordinal	Inter V/Ration
Central Tendency	Mode (Most common score or category.)	Median (The score or person with the middle rank.)	Mean (The average.)
Variability	Number of Categories	Range or Quartile Range (Based on ranks that define the 25%, 50%, and 75% cutoffs in the data.)	Standard Deviation (Based on the squared difference of each and every score from the mean.)
Relationship	Coefficient of Relationship (e.g., Cramer's V: Based on how often a subject is found in combinations of categories.)	Spearman Rank Correlation (Based on the agreement between ranks achieved for two different measures.)	Pearson Product Moment Correlation (Based on similarity of z scores for two different measures.)

A researcher should always remain aware of his or her measurement operations, of their strengths, and of their limitations. This awareness should include a clear idea of the operational definition being used and its reliability and validity, a knowledge of the type of measurement (nominal, ordinal, interval/ratio) that is produced by the operations, a guard against the potential contaminating influence of subjectivity in scoring, demand characteristics and experimenter bias, and a reluctance to replace real measures of behavior with paper chases.

Measures of Central Tendency

Since the concept of average is a descriptive statistic, one needs to know that there are three kinds of averages used in statistics. They are the mean, the median, and the mode. Most statistics refer to the average by using the term measure of central tendency. The mean, median, and the mode are all measures of central tendency (Hinkle, Wiersma, & Jurs, 1994; Dowdy & Wearden, 1991; Blaisdell, 1993; Gravetter & Wallnau, 1996).

The use of central tendency denotes the average performance of a group or individual performance. It does not show the spread of variability or scores, nor does it denote specific characteristics of the group or individual performances. In order to determine the extent to which scores are dispersed around the average, we must employ techniques of variability. Variability allows a range in describing observations, and to make valid decisions concerning the spread of scores in a distribution. The range, quartile deviations, and the standard deviation are the typical techniques to employ.

The Mean

The mean ($\bar{x}$) is the most frequently and commonly used measure of central tendency in scientific research. It is the arithmetic average of a set of scores and is calculated by summing all data values and dividing them by the number of points summed. The formula for the mean is:

$\mu \quad = \varphi X/n$

where:

  μ = the population

  E = to add
  X = data values
  N = the number of items in a sample

or:

  $\bar{x} = \varphi X/n$

When performing a descriptive function, the statistician utilizes rules and procedures for presenting a more usable form where:

  $\bar{x}$ = the sample mean
  X = the data
  N = the number of items in a sample

For Example:

Let's assume that some students conducted a telephone survey over a period of 30 days to gather data about the attitude people have toward candidates running for office in a local political race. There were a total of 1,048 telephone calls made to the local constituents. Using the formula given for the sample mean, we calculate the results as the following:

  $\bar{x} = 1048/30 = = 34.93$

The arithmetic mean or average was 34.93 calls made to constituents per day.

The mean enables the researcher to calculate an average that takes into account the importance of each value to the overall total.

Calculating the Mean From Ungrouped Data

Population Mean   Sum of Values of
                                          all Observations

  $\mu = \dfrac{E x}{N}$

                          number of Elements in
                          the Population

                        and

  Sample Mean   Sum of Values of
all Observations

  $\bar{x} = \mu = \dfrac{E x}{n}$

                        Number of Elements in
                        the Sample

Mean for Group Data

When group measures of data are needed, a frequency distribution table should be constructed, if you do not have exact individual measures to compute a grouped mean.

The formula for a sample mean for group data is:

$$\bar{x} = \frac{\Sigma fx}{N}$$

x = the midpoint of the interval, fx = the sum of the measurement of the interval, Efx = the sum of the measurement, in all class intervals.

In computing the mean for group data the frequency distribution table would follow this format.

Table 8. 2 Data Distribution Table

Class Interval	Frequency (f)	Midpoint (x)	Fx
0-4	8	3	24
5-9	6	8	48
10-14	4	13	52
15-19	2	18	36
20-24	4	23	92
25-29	6	28	168
30-34	2	33	66
	N = 32		$\Sigma fx = 486$

Substituting into the formula:

$$\bar{x} = \frac{\Sigma fx}{n} = \frac{486}{32} = 15.19$$

The average age of 200 visitors was 16.

The Median

The median divides a frequency distribution into two equal parts so that the number of scores below the median equals the number of scores above the median. The median is a positional average, and its value is influenced only by the value of the central observations; extreme values to not greatly influence the value of the median. Therefore, when extreme values are evident, the median generally yields a more representative measure than does the mean.

Calculating the Median From Ungrouped Data

To find the median of a data set, arrange the data in ascending or descending order. If the data set contains an odd number of items, the middle item of the array is the median. If there is an even number of items, the median is the average of the two middle items. The median is:

Mean = the $\frac{(n + 1)}{2}$ item in a data array

Calculating the Median of an Odd Number of Items

To find the median of seven items in a data array, the median is the $\frac{(7 + 1)}{2} = 4^{th}$ item in the array.

Median Group Data

Finding the median in group data is not as concise in finding the mean in group data, because the exact values may not be known using the data in Table 2, the median is between the intervals 25 - 29.

There are a total of 30 measures. The formula is:

Mean = L+ $\underline{W}$ (.5N - EFB)
    f med

L = lower class limit of the interval that contains the median,

N = total number of measures,

W = interval width;

f = frequency of the class containing the median;

EFB = sum of the frequencies for all classes before the median class;

Substituting into the formula:

Mean = L+ $\underline{W}$ (.5N-EFB)
    f Med

$11 + \underline{5}$ (.5 (32) - 14
    5

$11 + \underline{5}$ (16 - 14)
    5

$11 + \underline{5}$ (12)
    5

$11 + 2 = 13$

An Example

If there are seven members of a track team, the fourth element in the array is 4.8 minutes. This is the median for the track team.

Item in Data Array	1	2	3	4	5	6	7
Time in Minutes	4.2	4.3	4.7	4.8	5.0	5.1	9.0

↑

(Median of 4.8)

Calculating the Median of an Even Number of Items

Median = the $\underline{(n + 1)}$ the item in a data array.
        2

$= \underline{8 + 1}$
    2

$= 4.5^{th}$ item

Since the median is the 4.5^{th} element in the array, it is necessary to average the fourth and the fifth elements.

Example:

For patients treated in the emergency room on eight consecutive days:

Item in Day Array	1	2	3	4	5	6	7	8
Number of Patients	85	52	49	43	35	31	30	11

↑

(Median of 39)

The Mode

The mode is that value that is repeated most often in the data set. Whenever the mode is used as a measure of central tendency of a data set, it should be calculated from grouped data. The mode assumes that the value that occurs most frequently than other is most typical. The mode has limited use, especially for quantitative data. Often a data set will not contain any repeated values; therefore, in these cases no mode exists.

Measures of Deviation or Dispersion or Variability

Kerlinger (1979) discussed the concepts of deviation, or dispersion, or variability. These terms are interchangeable. Dispersion may be measured in terms of the difference between two values selected from the data set. Some of the distance measures are: the Range, the Interfractile Range, the Interquartile Range, the Quartile Deviation, and the Standard Deviation.

When examining variability, the more similar the scores, the less variability. The amount of variability differs from group to group.

Table 8. 3 Sample of Scores for 3 Groups of Children (n=15)

	Group A	Group B	Group C
	80	76	85
	80	72	80
	80	80	75
	80	70	70
	80	72	80
Sum	400	370	390
Mean	80	74	78
Median	80	72	80
Mode	80	72	80

In the table above, we can see that there is no variability at all in the set of scores of Group A because all the children in that group received the same exact score on their tests. The children in Group B show some variability within the distribution as do the children in Group C. Although the scores in Group C were relatively higher than those in Group B, there is similar variability between the two.

Students often find nothing unusual in expressing an average in the form of some number. The concept of average is familiar to most of us but because we are not used to thinking of variability in the quantitative terms, students sometimes find it difficult to grasp the conceptual meaning of measures of variability.

The Range

The range (R) considers only the extreme values within a data set. The range of a set of scores is defined by the lowest and the highest score in the set:

R = H-L

For example, in Table 8.3, you can see that Group A has a range that goes from 80 to 80. Using the formula for the range, we can calculate the range for Group A and find that it is "O" (zero). Group B has a range that goes from 70 to 80 and Group C has a range that goes from 70 to 85. This measure of dispersion is meaningful but is of little use because of its instability, particularly when it is based on a small sample. If there is one extreme score in a distribution, the dispersion of scores will appear to be large when in fact the removal of that score may reveal an otherwise compressed or compact distribution.

A good example of that would be to test an adult with autism at a local senior center and find that person has an I.Q. of 120. Using the range calculation, an erroneous impression would be given if the scores of other autistic adults in the same facility were tested and scores ranged from 30 to 120. The numerical range of 90 could be misleading to the statistician. The range actually reflects only the two most extreme scores in a distribution while the remaining scores are disregarded.

The range is computed by subtracting the highest score from the lowest score in a distribution and adding one point. It is less reliable than other measures of variables. The numerical value consists on two extreme scores at both end of the distribution. Extreme scores may not reflect the true spread of scores; thus, making it unreliable from sample to sample. Data in Table 8.3 shows the range computed.

Like the mode, the range is both easier to compute and less stable than any other measure of its kind. It is the one statistic that directly gives information about the highest and lowest scores in the sample.

Normal Distribution Showing Total Range on Baseline

The Interfractile Range

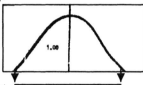

point just below lowest score   point just above highest score

The Interfractile Range is a measure of the spread between two fractiles in a frequency distribution, that is, the difference between the values of two fractiles. Fractiles may have special names, depending on the number of equal parts into which they divide the data. Fractiles that divide the data into ten equal parts are called deciles. Percentiles divide the data into 100 equal parts. It a student scored in the 75th percentile, 3/4 or 75% of the people who took this test did no better than the student did.

Quartiles and Interquartile Range

The lower quartile (Q^1) is defined as the 25th percentile; therefore, 75% of the measures are above the lower quartile. The middle quartile (Q2) is also the median or the 50th percentile. The upper quartile (Q3) is defined as the 75th percentile; therefore, only 25% of the measures are above the upper quartile. The interquartile range (IQR) is the set of measures between the upper and lower quartiles.

The Interquartile Range measures approximately how far from the median the statistician must go either side before he or she can include 1/2 of the values of the data set. To compute the range, the statistician divides the data into four parts, each of which contains 25% of the items in the distribution. The Quartiles are then the highest values in each of these four parts, and the interquartiles range is the difference between the values of the first and third quartiles:

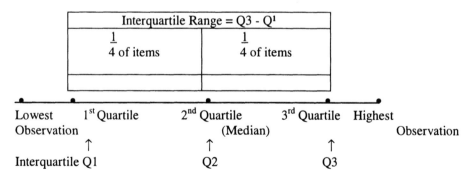

Interquartile Range = Q3 - Q¹	
$\frac{1}{4}$ of items	$\frac{1}{4}$ of items

Lowest   1st Quartile   2nd Quartile   3rd Quartile   Highest
Observation   (Median)   Observation
                    ↑   ↑   ↑
Interquartile Q1   Q2   Q3

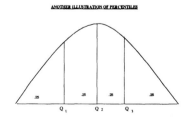

ANOTHER ILLUSTRATION OF PERCENTILES

Range

The concept of the interquartile range shown graphically. The widths of the four quartiles need not be the same.

The quartiles divide the area under the distribution into four equal parts, each containing 25% of the area.

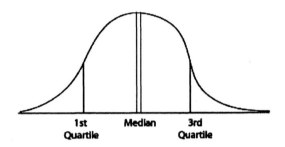

One-half of the interquartile range is a measure called interquartile deviation.
Quartile Deviation = $\dfrac{Q3 - Q1}{2}$

The Quartile Deviation measures the average range of 1/4 of the data. It is representative of the spread of all the data, since it is found by taking the average of the middle half of the items rather than by choosing one of the fourths.

Advantages of Interquartile Range and Quartile Deviation
Like the range, the interquartile range and the quartile deviations are based on only two values from the data set. They are more complicated to calculate than the range, but they avoid extreme values by using only the middle half of the data. Thus, they have a distinct advantage over the range which is affected by the extreme values.

Dispersion: Average Deviation Measures
The variance and the standard deviation are also measures of dispersion. They deal with the average deviation from some measure of central tendency. Variance and standard deviation tell the statistician an average distance of any observation in the data set from the mean of the distribution.

Variance: The population has a variance which is symbolized as $\sigma 2$ (Sigma "squared").

Population variance is the sum of the squared distances between the mean and each item divided by the total number of elements in the population. By squaring each distance, the statistician automatically makes every number positive, and therefore, has no need to take the absolute value of each deviation.

The statistician is finding the average squared distance between the mean and each item in the population. The statistician will square each difference of X - Φ:

$$\Phi 2 = \frac{\Gamma(X - \Phi)2}{N} = \frac{\Gamma X2 - \Phi2}{N}$$

where:

    $\underline{\Phi}$ = the population variance
    X = the item or observation
    Φ = the population mean
    N = total Number of items in the population
    Σ = the sum of all the values (x - Φ), or all the values of X.

Thus, the mean of the squared deviations is called the Variance.

Standard Score: A measure called the standard score gives the number of standard deviations a particular observation lies below or above the mean. If $\underline{X}$ symbolizes the observation, the standard score computed from population data is:

$$\text{Population standard score} = \frac{X - \Phi}{\Phi}$$

Whereas:

X = the observation from the population
Y = the population mean
Φ = the population standard deviation

Variability About the Mean

The topic of measures of variability is also of great interest in descriptive statistics as it is used to describe how a set of scores is distributed about the mean. Such measures take into account the variability exhibited by different groups scores. In other words, these measures can inform us that in Table 8.1, the scores of Group B are distributed relatively close about Group B's mean, but that the scores of Group C are distributed relatively wider about Group C's mean.

The average amount by which each score in Group C differs from its mean is larger than the average amount by which each score in Group B differs from its mean. To make certain that this statement is true; one must determine the average amount by which each s core differs from its respective group mean. The best way to check this is to subtract the groups' mean from each score in the group as shown in the table below:

Table 8. 4 Differences Between Scores and Their Means for Groups B & C

Group B	Difference	Group C	Difference
Scores	Score-Mean	Scores	Score-Mean
80	80-74=6	85	85-78=7
76	76-74=2	80	80-78=2
72	72-74=-2	80	80-78=2
72	72-73=-2	75	75-78=-3
70	70-74=-4	70	70-78=-8
****	Sum of Differences = 0	****	Sum of Differences = 0

The Sum of Differences Equals Zero

When we examine Table 8.4, we can see that the differences in each group were added together and then divided by the number of differences to determine the average. However, when we add up the differences for both groups, the sum turns out to be zero. If we divide zero by five, which is the number of differences in each group, we get zero. If you subtract the mean of the set from each number in the set and add up the differences, the sum is always zero. The mean is defined as that number, which when subtracted from all other numbers found in a set, yields a set of differences that add up to zero. It is at this point that many students begin to have difficulty with statistics. Students often are not told that subtracting the mean from each score in a set and adding up the differences always yields a product of zero.

By knowing this fact, it should be easier for you to grasp conceptually why the computation of variability is not as straightforward as it would appear to be. Take notice in Table 8.4 that the differences between scores and their respective means add up to zero because the negative differences cancel out the positive differences. The sum inevitably must be zero.

The Sum of Squares and Variance

One way to eliminate this dilemma is to get rid of the negative differences. There are a number of possible ways to eliminate negative differences but statisticians do it by squaring the difference scores produce. Multiplying one negative number by another negative number yields a positive number. If we take the different scores shown in Table 8.4 for Groups B and C and square them, you can see the results in Table 8.5. We do this by calculating the Sum of Squares:

$$SS = \Gamma X2 - (\Gamma X)2/N$$

or

$$SS = \Gamma(X - M)2$$

The variance is calculated as follows:

$$(S)2 = SS/(N-1)$$

or

$$\Gamma (X - M)2/N$$

whereas $S2$ = variance. In other words, the arithmetic mean is subtracted from each score; the differences are then squared, summed, and divided by the total number of observations. The variance expresses the average dispersion in the distribution of scores not in the original units of measurement but in squared units.

Table 8.5 Squares of Difference Scores of Groups B and C

Group B Difference Score - Mean	Group B Difference 2 Score - Mean 2	Group C Difference Score – Mean	Group C Difference 2 Score - Mean 2
6	36	7	49
2	4	2	4
-2	+4	-2	+4
-2	+4	-3	+9
4		8	+64
****	Sum of Squares = 64	****	Sum of Squares =130

Table 8.5 reveals that the *Sum of Squares* for Group B is 64 and for Group C is 130. If we divided the sum of squares by the number of scores, the end result is called the *Variance*. The variance for Group B is 64 ÷ 5 = 26. The variance shows how much the average *squared* difference between each score and the mean score is.

The Standard Deviation

Once the sum of squares have been calculated, the next step to consider in the order of statistical operation is the calculation of the *Standard Deviation*: The formula for this is as follows:

$$SD = \sqrt{\Sigma(X - M)2/N}$$

or

$$S = \sqrt{S2}$$

The standard deviation is the most common measure of variability used in statistics (Bogdan & Biklen, 1982). It is the square root of the average squared difference between each score and the mean score. This means that the standard deviation reveals a close approximation of the average amount by which each score differs from the group's mean; basically, how far apart scores deviate from the mean (Blaisdell, 1993; Dowdy & Wearden, 1991; Bruning & Kintz, 1987).

Since the standard deviation is the square root of the variance, the standard deviation for Group B is 3.57 (the square root of 12.8) and the standard deviation for Group C is 5.09 (the square root of 26). This means that the average amount by which each score in Group B differs from Group B's mean is 3.57, and the average amount by which each score in Group C differs from Group C's mean is approximately 5.09. The larger the standard deviation found, the greater the amount of variability (Elmore & Woehlke, 1997). The standard deviation of 5.09 in Group C indicates more variability than the standard deviation of 3.57 of Group B.

The most important thing to remember about the concept of standard deviation is that a standard deviation approximates the amount by which each score in a group differs from the group's mean score. Jacob (1987) said

"...because the sum of the differences between each score ad the mean always equals zero, to calculate the standard deviation it is first necessary to square the differences to eliminate the negative differences and then take the square root to undo the squaring process."

When using descriptive statistics to describe how test scores are distributed among Groups A, B, and C, you should indicate that Group B has a mean (M) of 74 and a standard deviation (SD) of 3.57. Likewise, you should indicate that Group C has a mean (M) of 78 and a standard deviation (SD) of 5.09. The mean (M) for Group A is 80 and has a standard deviation (SD) of "0" (zero). This information indicates that although both groups have means that are close numerically (74 and 78 respectively), the scores in Group C have more variability. There may be occasion when some groups may have different means but have the same standard deviation. In such cases, this indicates that one group on the average, performs at a higher level than the other groups, but the amount of variability at that level within each group is the same.

Finally, the two groups may have both different means and different standard deviations. According to Campbell and Stanley (1963), consider the following example:

One group of students achieves a mean score of 72 points on a spelling test and another group achieves a mean of 80. It is clear that the group with a mean of 80 performed better than the other group. Suppose it turns out that one the same test, one group has a standard deviation of 3 and the other a standard deviation of 10. It should be clear that there is more variability in the scores of the group with the standard deviation of 10 than in the group with the standard deviation of 3.

In this example it does not state which group had which mean nor does it state which group had which standard deviation. The group with the lower mean might have either a lower or a higher standard deviation than the group with the higher mean. There is no consistent relationship between the magnitude of a mean and the magnitude of a standard deviation (Cook & Campbell, 1979).

Table 8.6 provides another example for computing the standard deviation.

Computing the Standard Deviation

The standard deviation provides a more valid measurement of dispersion when compared with other forms previously discussed. The standard deviation is calculated by squaring the deviations from the mean, dividing by the total number of cases, and then taking the square root of the quotient. Table 8.6 provides an example of how data are calculated to find the average and standard deviations.

Table 8.6 Height of Three Fifth Grade Boys in School A

Boy	Height in Inches	Deviation in Inches from the Mean	Squared Deviation
1	62	6	36
2	58	0	0
3	74	6	36
Totals	$\overline{x} = 68$	12	72

AD = Sum of deviations   SD = √ Sum of square deviations
     Total number of cases =   Total number of cases =

$$\frac{12}{3} = 4 \text{ inches} \qquad \sqrt{\frac{72}{3}} = \sqrt{24} = 4.9$$

Normally, the sample used in Table 8.6 for computing the standard deviation would not be used. This simplified example was to demonstrate the process. These small scores have little validity for computing the standard deviation. There is a complex procedure for manually computing the process; however, one can simply use a calculator to determine the standard deviation by dividing the number from the sum of square deviation by the total number of cases and entering it by the $\sqrt{}$ key, or using a table of squares and square roots.

The Standard Error

As a point of study, a researcher may want to study absentee rates of junior high school girls. The researcher would first gather data on boys in 25 randomly selected schools in city X and compute the means for each of the 25 schools. The means would be different ad would disperse themselves around a central point, similar to the bell-shaped curve. The researcher would then plot the means and compute the standard deviation. The computation would be called the standard error of the mean. The major difference between the standard deviation is based upon raw scores, and the standard error is based upon variability among means.

The Normal Distribution

Not all variables are distributed normally, but many are. I.Q. scores are an example of a characteristic that is distributed normally. This means that very few people have very low or very high I.Q. scores that fall somewhere in the middle. A graphic showing of the number of people at each score would be bell-shaped with low and high I.Q. scores placed below and above the mean with the majority of the scores around the mean.

Anyone administering a formal assessment (i.e., Standord-Binet, Peabody Individual Achievement Test [P.I.A.T.], Kaufman Test of Educational Assessment [K.T.E.A.], etc.) will find that the raw scores, when spread about the mean, produce a bell-shape. Two things are needed to construct a normal distribution:

- About 68% of the data falls within 1 SD of the $\overline{X}$.
- About 95% of the data falls within 2 SD of the $\overline{X}$.
- About 100% of the data falls within 3 SD of the $\overline{X}$.

Example:

Suppose we have a collection of 250 numbers that are bell-shaped. If x = 138 and S.D. = 10, the following will be true:

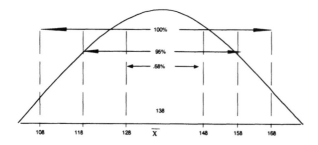

Figure 8.1 Collection of 250 Numbers

68% will fall between 128 and 148
- 95% will fall between 11 and 158
- 100% will fall between 108 and 168

Properties of the Normal Distribution
- The area under the normal distribution is 1.
- The curve is symmetric about the mean.
- The tails of the normal distribution approach the data axis
  but never touch it.

There are infinitely many normal distributions (Dowdy & Wearden, 1991; Hinkle, Wiersma & Jurs, 1994; Gravetter & Wallnau, 1996). The mean score is that score which coincides with the peak of the curve. Since we know that the normal distribution is symmetric about the mean, if we were to start drawing a line at the peak of the bell-shaped cure and continue straight down through the middle of the curve, we would fine that the one-half of the curve is the mirror image of the other half. This means that 50% of the population will score at the mean or higher, and 50% will score at the mean or lower. The closer the curve is, the closer the scores and vice versa.

Example:
>   N.T.E. scores are normally distributed having a mean of 500
>   and a standard deviation of 100. Our score is 620.

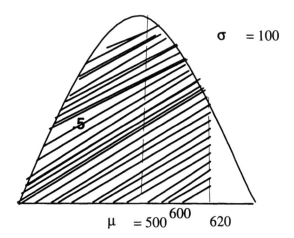

Figure 8.2 NTE Scores

We can transpose this normal distribution to the Standard Normal Distribution by using the following formula:

$$Z = X - \Phi/\Phi$$

This formula converts a score "X" in the normal distribution to a score "X" in the Standard Normal Distribution. A "Z" score measures the number of standard deviation units that the raw (original score falls from its mean). The following example paints a visual picture of raw scores transposed into "Z" scores:

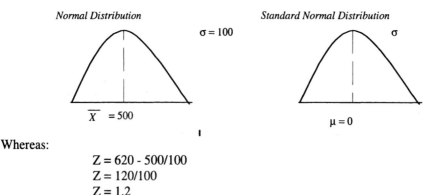

Normal Distribution   *Standard Normal Distribution*

$\sigma = 100$ σ

$\overline{X} = 500$ $\mu = 0$

Whereas:

$$Z = 620 - 500/100$$
$$Z = 120/100$$
$$Z = 1.2$$

Figure 8.3 Standard Normal Distribution

Standardized Scores (Z Scores)

A "Z" score represents the deviation of a specific score from the mean expressed in standard deviation units (Kerlinger, 1979). For example, if the z score value of a raw score is 1.2, we know that the raw score indicates the raw score is greater than the mean and a negative z score indicates the raw score is less than the mean. There are three basic properties of z scores and they are:

1. The sum of the z scores is zero.
2. The mean of the z scores is zero.
3. The standard deviation and the variance of z scores is one.

When any set of scores is expressed in z scores, the resulting distribution has a mean of zero and a standard deviation of one. When anyone refers to the normal curve, that person is referring to a distribution expressed in z scores. Converting raw scores into z scores does not automatically result in a normally distributed set of scores (Gravetter & Wallnau, 1996). A set of z scores will be normally distributed only if the raw scores themselves follow a normal distribution. If the original distribution of scores is non-normal, the distribution of z scores will be non-normal. In other words, the transformation to z's will not convert a non-normal distribution to a normal distribution.

A basic fact to keep in mind is that a distribution can exhibit skewness. A skewed distribution is one that departs from symmetry and tails off at one end. When the mean is higher than the median, the distribution is negatively skewed. The following examples illustrate skewness:

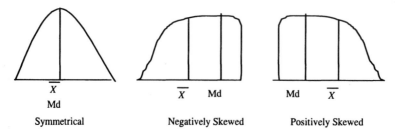

$\overline{X}$ $\overline{X}$ Md   Md $\overline{X}$
Md

Symmetrical   Negatively Skewed   Positively Skewed

Figure 8.4 Skewness

The Normal Curve

The normal curve and its properties are fundamentally essential to understanding statistical analyses of quantitative research data that it is important to grasp thoroughly how a normal curve emerges from a collection of data. It should be pointed out that a normal curve will not emerge from data unless the data are normally distributed (Dowdy & Wearden, 197; Huck & Cormier, 1996; Elmore & Woehike, 1997). Educators are interested in the normal distribution because characteristics such as scores on achievement tests, aptitude tests, etc., are all assumed to be normally distributed.

The normal curve is a mathematical construct which implies if a representative sample is taken for a population, the dispersion when plotted would resemble a bell-shaped curve as indicated in Figure 8.4.

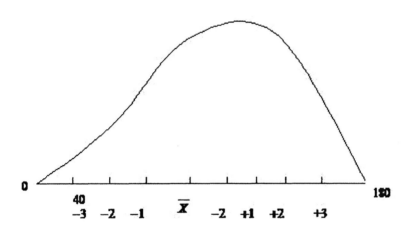

Figure 8.5. Distribution of a Population Mean Score

This approach is recommended because the true zero point may not be known, so one can not start with zero. Second, theoretically the tail of the curve does not touch because there may be higher scores in the population not reflected on the curve. Additionally, the standard deviation is used as a yard stick for sitting points along the baseline of the curve to apply distances above and below the mean. Refer to Figure 8.5.

Assuming that a researcher wanted to know what portions of the curve represented the total number of individuals observed on intelligence, and that data represented the population in which it was drawn. Additionally, she/he knew the mean is 100, and the standard deviation is 15. How will she/he determine what portion of the sample will fall below 115, and what portion of the sample will fall above 115. Look at the bell-shape curve below to answer the question.

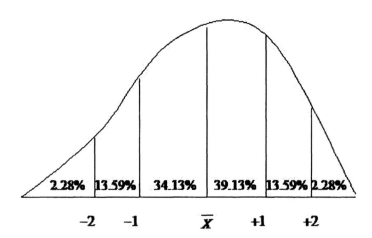

Figure 8.6 Distribution of Intelligence Test Scores

Based on the assumption that this bell-shape curve represent valid data, the researcher would conclude from the curve that 84.13 percent of the sample fell below +1 by adding 34.13 percent, 34.13 percent, 13.59 percent, + 2.28 percent which totaled up to 84.13 percent.

Correlation and Pearson's r

The Pearson Product-Moment Correlation: In order to express a relationship between two variables, one must have some numeral index of the degree of correlation. This index is called correlation coefficient and indicates the degree to which two frequencies distribution are related. There are many different types of correlation analysis available to researchers. It is the nature of the study that determines the one to use. The Pearson product moment is one of the more common correlation techniques. However, in order for this one to be used, the researcher must assume that the variables are linearly related and scores are normally distributed. If these assumptions are not made, then this technique is inappropriate.

The symbol for the Pearson product moment correlation coefficient is r. The Pearson product moment coefficient that indicates a perfect positive correlation is $r = + 1.00$ and a perfect negative is $r = -1.00$. When no correlation exists then $r = .00$. A positive range goes from $-1.00 + 1.00$. A moderate positive is $r = .65$ and a moderate negative is $r = .62$.

EXY indicates that you multiply X by Y and then sum all the products. NEXY indicates that you multiply the sum of the products by N. (EX) (EY) indicates you sum the X and Y scores and then multiply the two sums. (EX) indicates you sum X and the square the sum. The formula goes as follows:

Child	X	Y	X^2	Y^2	XY
A	1	5	1	25	5
B	2	10	4	100	20
C	4	20	16	400	80
D	5	25	25	625	125
E	6	30	36	900	180
F	7	35	49	1225	245

N=6   EX=25 EY=125 EX²=131 EY²=3275 EXY=655

$$\underline{N(EXY) - (EX)\ (EY)}$$

$$r = \sqrt{\quad [NEX^2 - (EX)] [N\,EY^2 - (EY)]}$$
$$= \frac{6(655) - (25)(125)}{\sqrt{\quad [6(9131) - (25)][6(3275) - (125)]}}$$
$$= \frac{805}{\sqrt{(161)(4025)}} \quad \frac{805}{\sqrt{648,025}} \quad \frac{805}{805} = 1.00$$

The researcher must be cognizant of the type of scale of measurement reflected in the data source.

We are frequently interested in two-interval or ratio-scaled variables. For example, high school guidance counselors are often concerned with the relationship between SAT scores and a students' performance in college. Do students who score high on the SAT do well academically in college? Do students who score low perform poorly in college? Is there a relationship between the socioeconomic status and crime or teenage pregnancy? Is there a relationship between binge eating and anorexia? Does income and earning potential influence the amount of control one spouse has over another in a relationship? In order to determine the extent to which two variables are related, it is necessary to compute a measure of association called a correlation coefficient.

According to Henkel (1975) the decision as to which measure of association to use with a specific set of data depends upon such factors as:

- The type of scale of measurement in which each variable is expressed (nominal, ordinal, ratio, interval).
- The nature of the underlying distribution (whether it be continuous or discrete);
- The characteristics of the distribution of scores (linear or nonlinear);

The Pearson correlation coefficient (r) is a measure of the linear or straight-line relationship between two interval-level variables (Snedocor & Cochran, 1956). The form of the relationship between two-interval or ratio-level variable can be presented visually in a scatter diagram. A scatter diagram (as shown in Figure 8.7), is a graphic device used to visually summarize the relationship between two variables. Figure 8.6 displays a chart containing data regarding the actual number of children five different couples had as opposed to the desired number of children the couples had.

Couple	Desired No. of Children	Actual No. of Children
	(X)	(Y)
a	2	2
b	2	3
c	3	3
d	4	2
e	3	1

Figure 8.7

Actual Number of Children

$r = 0.21$

Desired Number of Children

The X-axis (the abscissa) is traditionally the horizontal axis and represents the independent variable. The vertical axis normally represents Y, the dependent variable. The axes are drawn perpendicular to each other, approximately equal in length and marked to accommodate the full range of scores. Each coordinate represents two values: a score on the X-variable and a score on the Y-variable. Figure 7 shows the relationship between the desired number of children five hypothetical couples wanted, and the actual number of children they had. Because of the axes are not always followed by traditional statistical convention, always determine the independent and dependent variable before interpreting data. Couple #1 preferred two children and has two children as did Couple #3; their coordinate has been located at the point at which X and Y both equal 2.

According to Henkel (1975), the scatter diagram allows for a visual inspection of the relationship between two variables and as we can see in Figure 8.7, it is evident that three of the couples do not have the number of children they desired. The Pearson correlation coefficient (*r*) for the data in Figure 8.7 equals +0.21. Since the values of the Pearson correlation coefficient (*r*) vary between +1.00 and -1.00, both extremes represent perfect relationships between variables (Wolcott, 1988). The size of the correlation coefficient indicates the strength of the relationship. The closer the points in the scatter diagram form a straight line, the stronger the relationship between X and Y. The researcher should always disregard the sign of the coefficient when interpreting the strength of a relationship; opposite signs merely indicate positive or negative relationship between variables; nothing more.

Calculation of Pearson's r

$$r = \frac{\Sigma XY - \frac{\Sigma X . \Sigma Y}{N}}{\sqrt{SSX.SSY}}$$

The numerator of the equation is the co-variation of X and Y. It is the numerator that determines the sign of the correlation coefficient. A positive *r* results from high values of X that tend to be paired with high values of Y and, low values of X tending to be paired with high values of Y.

The denominator is always positive because the values are squared. It consists of the square root of the product of the standard deviation of X and Y since the numerator and the denominator are divided by N. It is the denominator that restricts the range of *r* to ± 1 and results in r being independent of the measurement units of X and Y. An example of calculating the Pearson's *r* reported in Table 8.7.

Table 8.7 *Scores of Six Students on Class Attendance and Achievement Test Scores*

Child	Attendance (X)	Achievement (Y)	X2	Y2	XY
A	3	6	9	36	18
B	2	4	4	16	8
C	4	4	16	16	16
D	6	7	36	49	42
E	5	5	25	25	25
F	1	3	1	9	3
	ΣX	Σy = 29	ΣX2 = 91	Σy2=151	ΣXy=112

$$SS = \Sigma X2 - \frac{(\Sigma X)2}{N}$$
$$91 - \frac{441}{6}$$
$$91 - 73.5$$

$$SS = \Sigma y2 - \frac{(\Sigma y)2}{N}$$
$$151 - 841 =$$
$$151 - 140.17$$
$$10.83$$

$$\frac{\Sigma Xy - \Sigma X. \Sigma y}{N}$$
$$r\sqrt{SSX.SSy}$$

$$\frac{112 - \frac{21.29}{N}}{\sqrt{17.5.10.83}}$$

$$\frac{112 - 609}{\sqrt{17.5 \cdot 10.83}}$$

$$\frac{112 - \frac{609}{6}}{\sqrt{189.52}}$$

$$\frac{112 - 101.5}{}$$

$$\frac{112 - 101.5}{\sqrt{13.77}}$$

$$\frac{10.5}{13.77}$$

$r = .76$

Refer to Appendix I for critical values.

Pearson's r and Z Scores

Z scores provide the researcher with an intuitive interpretation that some other methods are unable to offer and the Pearson correlation coefficient can be computed using them. A high positive Pearson's *r* indicates that each individual receives approximately the same Z score on both variables. In a perfect positive correlation (where $r = + 1.00$) each individual obtains the same z score on both variables, but the z scores are opposite in sign.

While remembering that the z score represents a measure of relative position in standard deviation units on a given variable, the researcher can now generalize the meaning of Pearson's *r*. It represents the extent to which the same individuals, events, etc., occupy the same relative position on two variables. The values of X and Y do not need to be the same for the calculation of *r*. This independence permits the researcher to investigate the relationships among an unlimited variety of variables. If the researcher, for example, measures a person's yearly income in dollars or thousands of dollars and separately correlates both measures of income with a second variable such as job satisfaction, the resulting correlation between income and job satisfaction will be the same regardless of which income measure is used. The z scores of each research participant on each variable will be identical in the event of a perfect positive correlation.

Spearman's Rho Rank

Spearman's Rho requires that you obtain the differences in the ranks, square each difference, sum the squared differences, and substitute the resulting values into the following equation:

$$Rho = 1 - \frac{6 \, X \Sigma d2}{N (N2 - 1)}$$

Where: *rho* = correlation between ranked data.
  d = difference between the two ranks for a given
    individual.
  n = number of individuals ranked.

The value of *r* will equal +1.00 when the two sets of ranks are in perfect disagreement, - 1.00 when the two sets of ranks are in perfect disagreement, and 0 when there is no agreement; hence, *r* is a measure of the extent to which the two sets of ranks are in agreement or disagreement. There may be times occasionally when converting scores to ranks that the researcher will find two or more tied scores. In this event, the researcher must assign the mean of the tied ranks to each of the tied scores (Labovitz, 1970). The next score in the array receives the rank normally assigned to it.

Therefore, the ranks of scores 128, 122, 115, 115, 115, 107, 103 would be 1, 2, 4, 4, 4, 6, 7, and the rank of scores 128, 122, 115, 115, 107, 103 would be 1, 2, 3.5, 3.5, 5, 6.

When there are tied ranks on either or both the X and the Y variables, the Spearman Rho Rank equation yields an inflated value, particularly when the number of tied ranks is high (Shaw & Wright, 1967). The Pearson's r equation should be applied to the ranked data when there are numerous ties. The Spearman Rho Rank has been calculated in Table 8.8.

Table 8.8 Ratings Submitted by Two Researchers Concerning Observing a Group of Ten 5th Grade Students on Social Behavior

Child	Observer 1	Observer 2	Rank I	Rank II	d	d2
A	18	15	1	1	-1	1
B	14	16	4	1	3	9
C	15	14	3	3	0	0
D	17	13	1	4	-1	4
E	12	9	6	7	-1	1
F	13	10	5	6	-1	1
G	10	8	7	8	-1	1
H	9	7	8	9	-1	1
I	7	11	9	5	4	16
J	6	6	10	10	0	0
					0	34

$$rho = 1 - \frac{6\,(34)}{10\,(100-1)}$$
$$= 1 - .21$$
$$= .79$$

The correlation index of .79 is significant at the .05 level of confidence, which implies a close relationship between the ratings of the two researchers. Refer to Appendix J for critical values.

Summary

In this chapter we discussed the various types of descriptive statistic, including scales of measurements, central tendency, variability, the normal curve, the concepts of correlation and demonstrated the calculation of the Pearson correlation coefficient (r) using the mean deviation, and z score computational procedures. The scatter diagram was presented as an interpretive and summary device.

Correlation is concerned with determining the extent to which two variables are related or tend to vary together. The quantitative expression of the extent of the relationship is given in terms of the magnitude of the correlation coefficient. Correlation coefficients vary between values of -1.00 and +1.00; both extremes represent perfect relationships. A coefficient of zero indicates the absence of a relationship between two variables. Pearson's r is appropriate only for variables that are linearly related. Spearman's Rho (r) is a measure of the extent to which two sets of ranks are in agreement or disagreement. The value of r, will equal +1.00 when the two sets of rankings are in perfect agreement and -1.00 when the two sets of rankings are in perfect agreement and -1.00 when the two sets of rankings are in perfect disagreement.

Chapter Eight Research Exercise

1.   Using a width of 10 for the X variable and a width of 5 for the Y variable, set up a scatter diagram (bivariate frequency distribution) for the following data:

X	Y	X	Y
24	29	67	48

22	40	58	48
44	36	57	33
72	32	49	47
25	46	87	52
30	47	14	48
38	49	38	46
54	53	32	33
37	51	52	40
61	50	60	49
56	45	76	43
42	48	50	55
30	25	76	43
42	48	40	38
30	25	76	43
28	28	32	56
32	40	61	45
24	37	56	57
42	58	61	42
54	54	17	44
42	44	61	48

2. Compute the Pearson correlation coefficient for the above data.

3. Draw a histogram and a frequency polygon for the following frequency distribution:

X	F	X	F	X	F	X	F
80	1	16	6	73	10	70	7
79	2	74	14	72	17	69	3
78	2	73	22	71	9	68	1

4. Given the following distributions: 15, 14, 14, 13, 11, 10, 10, 10, 8, 5
   a. Calculate the mean
   b. Determine the value of the median
   c. Determine the value of the mode

5. A student's grade on a very difficult examination is 85. What can we say about the merits of the student's performance? Explain.

6. Using the data below, compute Spearman Rho Rank:

X	Y
47	75
71	79
52	85
48	50
35	49
35	59
41	78
82	91
72	102
56	87
59	70
73	92
60	54
55	75
41	68

7.   The Air Force finds a correlation of .73 between extroversion and leadership ability among commissioned officers.   The Air Force finds the two variables to be uncorrelated. Cite come factors that could explain the difference.

8.   Identify the type of measurement scale – nominal, ordinal, interval, or ratio-suggested by each of the following statements:
      a.   Jack speak French, but John does not.
      b.   Jack is taller than John.
      c.   John is 6 feet, 2 inches tall.
      d.   John's I.Q. is 130, while Jack's I.Q. is 110.
      e.   John finished the math test in 35 minutes, while Jack finished the same test in 25 minutes.

9.   In one state, voters register as Republican, Democrat, or Independent and records of the total registrations are kept. Which scale of measurement is used?

10.   Instructor, assistant professor, associate professor, form what kind of scale?

References

Bogdan, R. C., & Biklen, S. K. (1982). *Qualitative research for education: An introduction to theory and methods.* Boston: Allyn and Bacon.

Blaisdell, E. A. (1993). *Statistics in practice.* New York: Sanders College Publishing Company.

Bruning, J. L., & Kintz, B. L. (1987). *Computational Handbook of   Statistics   (3rd   ed.).* Glenview, IL: Scott Foresman.

Campbell, D. T., & Stanley, J. C. (1963). *Experimental and quasi-experimental designs for research.* Chicago: Rand McNally.

Cook, T. D., & Campbell, D. T. (1979*). Quasi-experimentation.* Chicago: Rand McNally.

Dowdy, S., & Wearden, S. (1991). *Statistics for research* (2nd ed.). New York: John Wiley and Sons.

Elmore, P. B., & Woehlke, P. L. (1997). Basic statistics. New York:Longman.

Francisco, B. (1992). Doctoral dissertation. *The effects of whoisticl language versus phonics on students with significant autistic-like behaviors in a level 5 program in the Baltimore City Public Schools.* Baltimore, Maryland.

Gravetter, F. J., & Wallnau, L. B. (1996). *Statistics for the behavioral sciences.*   New York: West Publishing Company.

Harris, M. B. (1995). Basic statistics for behavior science research. Boston: Allyn and Bacon.

Henkel, R. E. (1975). Part-whole correlations and the treatment of ordinal and quasi-interval data as interval data. *Pacific Soc. Review*, 18, 3-26.

Huck, S., W., & Cormier, W. H. (1996). *Reading statistics and research* (2nd ed.). New York: Harper Collins College Publishers.

Jacob, E. (1987). Qualitative research traditions: A review. Review of *Educational Research*, 57, 1-50.

Kerlinger, F. N. (1979). *Behavioral research.* New York: Holt, Rinehart, & Winston.

Labovitz, S. (1970). The assignment of numbers to rank order categories. *American Soc. Review*, 35, 515-524.

Nunnally, J. C. (1967). *Psychometric theory.* New York: McGraw-Hill.

Shaw, M. E., & Wright, J. M. (1967). *Scales for the measurement of   attitudes.*   New York: McGraw-Hill.

Schumacker, R.E. &Akers. A. (2001) *Understanding statistical concepts using S-plus.* Lawrence Erlbaum Associates

Snedecor, G. W., & Cochran, W. G. (1956). *Statistical methods* (6th ed.). Ames, IO: Iowa State University Press.

Wolcott, H. F. (1988). Ethnographic research in education. In R. M. Jaeger (Ed.), *Complimentary methods for research in education* (pp. 187-210). Washington, DC: American Educational Research Association.

Wolf, R. M. (1982). Validity of tests. In H. E. Mitzel (Ed.), *Encyclopedia of Educational Research* (5th ed.), 4, pp. 1991-1998. New York: Free Press.

Chapter Nine
Indicators of Relative Position In a Distribution
Theresa L. Harris, Ph.D.
George R. Taylor, Ph.D.

INTRODUCTION

Percentile ranks, quartiles, and deciles are measures used to bring order and give meaning to data, by identifying the relative position of a given score or set of scores in a distribution. Deciles and quartiles have similar characteristics, as they show the relative positions of scores and cases in a distribution, as well as, show dividing points in the distribution. These methods are employed to bring order and meaning where there is disarray of data, and to helps to identify the relative position of a given score among other scores in a frequency distribution.

Frequency Distribution

Let's examine the following hypothetical situation: Your supervisor has given your department the responsibility of conducting a 90-day feasibility study regarding the expansion of the local zoo. One of the main areas to examine is to determine the number of persons visiting the zoo on a daily basis for 1 year and then showing the relationship between visitations and revenue (Taylor, 2000).

After examining admission rosters from the past 5 years, the data revealed that there were constant increases in attendance; however, financial records reflect a decline in income for the same periods. For example, your team decides to conduct a simple random study that requires you to monitor the attendance and the ages of the park visitors for the next 30 days. You go to the zoo the same time everyday and spend the same amount of hours gathering data. At the end of the 30 days, the data reflects that there were 100 park visitors, the youngest being "0" (zero) in years and the oldest being 74 in years. Table 9.1 below shows the ages of the 100 park visitors selected at random.

Table 9.1 Ages of 110 Park Visitors

40	8	15	29	58	42	49	24	56	5
48	35	33	52	17	35	38	41	42	47
11	22	66	40	34	65	23	49	30	34
16	57	52	53	15	25	31	45	49	51
52	74	47	39	57	48	53	36	48	40
64	13	37	44	44	33	30	26	37	53
21	25	0	60	69	40	52	40	62	44
33	47	24	19	46	52	40	33	73	47
39	27	43	21	23	26	44	39	26	35
69	38	61	37	50	12	25	43	71	42
45	43	35	63	29	65	3	50	45	53

When we examine the ages (x) and the frequency (f) with which that particular aged individual visited the zoo in Table 9.2 (below), we can visually see that some ages visited the zoo more frequently than others, whereas, there were some ages that did not visit the zoo at all. The frequency distribution gives us a clearer, visual perspective of numerical data and the frequency of occurrence at-a-glance. It renders increased definition of the data expressed in both numbers and words (Harris, 1995; Elmore & Woehlke, 1997; Huck & Cormier, 1996).

Table 9.2 Frequency Distribution of Ages of 100 Park Visitors

x	f	x	f	x	f	x	f
0	/	21	//	42	///	63	/
1		22	/	43	///	64	/
2		23	//	44	////	65	//
3	/	24	//	45	///	66	/
4		25	///	46	/	67	
5	/	26	///	47	////	68	
6		27	/	48	///	69	//
7		28		49	///	70	
8	/	29	//	50	//	71	/
9		30	//	51	/	72	
10		31	/	52	/////	73	/
11	/	32		53	////	74	/
12	/	33	////	54			
13	/	34	//	55			
14		35	////	56	/		
15	//	36	/	57	//		
16	/	37	///	58	/		
17	/	38	//	59			
18		39	///	60	/		
19	/	40	/////	61	/		
20		41	/	62	/		

Table 9.2 demonstrates that persons 40 years of age made the most frequent visits (6) with age 52 being the next most frequent age group visiting the zoo. As you can see, the ages spread out with a width stretching from several months in age (0 years) to the age of 74 years.

The frequency distribution allows you to make certain assumptions from the data gathered (Borg & Gall, 1989). In the example given, the frequency distribution allows us to conclude that the group that frequents the zoo most is between 40 to 52 years of age. Depending upon the types of questions found on the survey sheets that were handed out to the zoo visitors, we would possibly be able to ascertain information such as gender, demographic data, occupations of the visitors, income levels, number of children in the family, ages of other children, etc. According to Gronlund and Linn (1990), any and all of this type of data can be presented in the frequency distribution format. Under these conditions, it is necessary to group some scores into what is referred to as class intervals and then obtain a frequency distribution of grouped scores.

Grouped Frequency Distribution

Grouping into class intervals involves "collapsing the scale" and assigning scores to mutually exclusively and exhaustive classes where the classes are defined in terms of the grouping intervals used. The reasons for grouping are threefold:

1. It is uneconomical and unwieldy to deal with a large number of cases spread out over many scores.
2. Some scores have low frequency counts so we are not justified in maintaining these scores as separate entities.
3. Categories provide a concise and meaningful summary of the data.

If you divided the ages of the zoo visitors into two classes, those below 40 and those above 40, practically all the information about the original ages would be lost. On the other hand, class intervals should not be so small that the purposes served by grouping are defeated. Since there is no general solution that can be applied to all data, the choice of the number of class intervals must represent a judgment based upon a consideration of how the data will be utilized (Runyon, 1977). Often the desired interval size determines the number of class intervals used.

If we present the data in 5-year age intervals, examination of the raw scores reveals that 15 class intervals will include all the respondents to the zoo study. Although several different techniques may be used, for the sake of consistency, we shall only use one. The following steps will coincide with Table 9.3:

Table 9.3 Grouped Frequency Distribution of Ages of Zoo Visitors (n=110)

Class Interval	f	Class Interval	f	Class Interval	f
0-4	2	25-29	9	50-54	12
5-9	2	30-34	9	55-59	4
10-14	3	35-39	13	60-64	5
15-19	5	40-44	17	65-69	5
20-24	7	45-49	14	70-74	3

Step 1: Find the difference between the highest and lowest scores contained in the original data. Add 1 to obtain the total number of scores or potential scores. In the present example, this result is (74-0) + = 75.

Step 2: Divide 75 by 15, the number of class intervals, to obtain the number of scores or potential scores in each class interval. If the resulting value is not a whole number, round to the nearest odd number so a whole number will be at the middle of the class interval. In our example, the number of scores for each interval is $75 \div 15$, or 5. The width of the class interval is 5.

Step 3: Take the lowest score in the original data as the minimum value in the lowest class interval. Add this to -1 to obtain the maximum score of the lowest class interval. Therefore, the lowest class interval of the data is 0-4.

Step 4: The next highest class interval begins at the integer following the maximum score of the lower class interval. In our hypothetical example, the next integer is 5. Follow these procedures for each successive higher class interval until all scores are included in their appropriate class intervals.

Step 5: Assign each score to the class interval within which it is included.

Percentile Rank

Percentile ranks may be recorded in a frequency distribution table. An example is provided in Table 9.4. A percentile rank is a score point in a distribution, which reveals the percent of the group that falls below the score. In summary, the percentile rank indicates, in terms of percentage, the relative position of a given in the group in reference of the trait measures. A first step in computing percentiles is to construct a frequency distribution table, showing the cumulative percentage. These percentages may be converted into percentile ranks from the cumulative percentage (Gravetter & Wallnau, 1996).

Table 9.4 Reading Comprehensive Scores of 30 Boys on a Teacher Made Test with a Class
Interval of Three (3)

Reading Scores	f	Cf	Cp
67-69	1	30	100.00
64-65	3	29	96.7
61-63	5	26	86.7
58-60	9	21	70.0
55-57	6	12	40.0
52-54	2	6	20.0
49-51	2	4	13.3
46-48	1	2	6.6
43-45	1	1	3.3

Table 9.4 shows cumulative percentage of reading comprehensive scores for 30 boys. The cumulative percentage shows what proportion of the group fell below a given Interval. At the interval of 58-60, seventy percent (70%) of the boys at the 70th percentile rank.

Deciles and Quartiles

Deciles are points that divide the distribution of raw scores into units of 10% (Elmore & Woehlke, 1997). D1 would represent 10% of the cases, D2 would represent 20% of the case, this order continues to D10 which would represent 100% of the cases. Refer to data in Table 9.4 and locate the intervals that the following deciles will fall 20, 40, 60, and 70.

Quartiles dived raw scores into segments of 25% each. As a result the first quartile Q1 is the point that cuts of the lowest 25%, Q2 the lowest 50% of the group, and Q3 the lowest 75% of the distribution. Using the data in Table9.4 locate the intervals that Q1, Q2, and Q3 are found.

Graphic Representation of Data

Descriptions of descriptive statistics may be displayed or represented by a ban chart, a pie chart, a histogram, or a frequency polygon.

Bar Chart

A bar chart may be used to represent the frequency of observation s by categories of a discrete variable. Some data from Figure 9.1 was used to construct a bar chart for ages of individuals visiting the zoo.

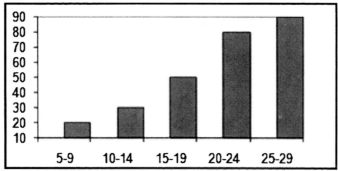

Figure 9.1 - Ages of 200 Visitors

Data clearly show that the 25-29 age groups visited the zoo more frequently.

Pie Chart:

A pie chart is also employed to display discrete data. Each section is allotted a segment of the pie equal to its relative frequency as shown in Figure 9.2 below.

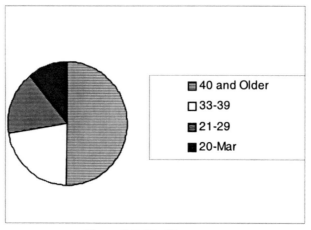

Figure 9.2 Pie Chart

Histogram

A histogram is similar to a bar chart. In a histogram the bar of the frequencies touch each other, they are not separate. Data are used from Figure 9.2 to construct the histogram.

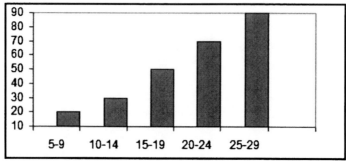

Figure 9.3 - Histogram of Zoo Visitors

Frequency Polygon

A frequency polygon consists of a series of lines connecting dots. These dots are plotted at the intersection of the mid-point of each score interval. Dates were used from Figure 9.3.

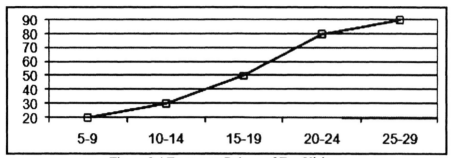

Figure 9.4 Frequency Polgon of Zoo Visitors

Relative Frequencies

These frequencies are defined as the frequency of occurrence of a value divided by the total number of observations (N). On the other hand the relative cumulative is the proportion of data values below the upper real limit of a score interval and is equal to the cumulative frequency divided by (N). An illustration, of computing the relative frequency is shown in Table 9.1.

Table 9.5 Relative Frequencies for Weight of 30 Boys in the Fifth Grade

Weight	F	RF
67-69	1	.033
64-65	3	.003
61-63	5	.166
58-60	9	0.3
55-57	6	0.2
52-54	2	.066
49-51	2	.066
46-48	1	.033
43-45	1 N = 30	.033

Summary

In this chapter we have attempted to demonstrate how meaning can be derived from a collection of data; and how these data can show relative status in a group by indicating portions of the group that fall below give points. Deciles, percentile, and quartiles are used to show relative studies of individuals in a group. They are dividing points in the distribution of scores.

Chapter Nine Research Exercise

1. Fifty graduate students took a statistic test. Their scores were as follows:

    37, 38, 26, 50, 40,   47, 39, 28, 60, 35,
    29, 48, 64, 58, 53,   40, 32, 55, 49, 62,
    43, 56, 59, 44, 37,   43, 49, 30, 42, 50,
    47, 46, 68, 43, 39,   38, 27, 44, 37, 25,
    32, 52, 66, 59, 49,   72, 64, 69, 57, 37

2. Construct a frequency distribution beginning with a score of 26, with an interval width of three points, and compute or locate the following in the distribution:
    a.   The 5th decile.
    b.   The 3rd quartile.

      c.   The following percentiles: P20, P60, and P 80.

3.   Compute the frequency, the cumulative frequency, the relative frequency, and the percentile rank.

4.   Using the data in Number 1 construct the following:

      a.   A bar graph.

      b.   A histogram.

      c.   A frequency polygon.

References

Borg, W. R., & Gall, M. D. (1989). *Educational research* (5th ed.). New York: Longman Publishing Company.

Elmore, P. B., & Woehlke, P. L. (1997). *Basic statistics.* New York: Longman Publishing Company.

Gravetter, F., & Wallnau, L. B. (1996). *Statistics for the behavioral Sciences.* New York: West Publishing Company.

Gronlund, N. E., & Lunn, R. L. (1990). *Measurement and evaluation in teaching* (6th ed.). New York: Macmillan Publishing Company.

Harris, M. B. (1995). Basic *statistics for behavior science research.* Boston: Allyn and Bacon.

Huck, S. W., & Cormier, W. H. (1996). Reading statistics and Research (2nd ed.). New York: Harper Collins College Publishers.

Runyon, R. P. (1977). *Non-parametric statistics.* Reading, MA: Addison-Wesley Publishing Company.

Taylor, G. R. (2000). *Integrating quantitative and qualitative methods in research.* Lanham, MD: University Press of America.

Chapter Ten
Case Study Methodology
Marjorie E. Miles, Ed. D.

George R. Taylor, Ph.D.

INTRODUCTION

Case studies are not a new form of research; naturalistic inquiry was the primary research tool until the development of the scientific method. The fields of sociology and anthropology are credited with the primary shaping of the concept as we know it today. However,, case study research has drawn from a number of other areas as well: the clinical methods of doctors; the casework technique being developed by social science workers; the methods of historians and anthropologists (http://writing colostate.edu/guides/research/case study/com2a 2.cfm).

During the early part of the twentieth century case studies began to be recognized as a viable research technique. It was not before 1950, according to Armisted (1984) that the Harvard Business School launched the movement as a teaching movement. Since the 1950's the method is widely accepted as a research method. Researchers have claimed that students and researchers are instructed to choose selected case study methods and theories to analyze their problem (Boehrer, 1990, Merseth, 1991). Yin (1993); and Stake (1995) asserted that sampling techniques are not required in case study research.

Feagin, Orum and Sjoberg (1991) indicated that the case study is an ideal methodology when a holistic, in-depth investigation is desired. According to Yin (1993) and Stake (1995), case studies have been widely used in the social sciences, employing multiple sources of data and specific types of case studies, which will be summarized later in the chapter.

Case study research tends to assist graduate students and researchers in comprehending complex phenomenon in the social sciences and to validate research findings in other research methods (Gall, Borg, & Gall, 1996). Yin (1984) defines the case study method as an empirical inquiry that investigates a contemporary phenomenon within real life content, when the boundaries between phenomenon and context are not clearly evident; and in which multiple sources of evidence are used (p.23). Multi-method approach is commonly used with additional qualitative methods. See chapter 6 for qualitative methods.

Unlike random sample surveys, case studies are not representative of entire populations, nor do they claim to be. The case study research should take care not to generalize beyond cases similar to the one(s) studied. Provided the researcher refrains from over generalization, case study research is not methodologically invalid simply because selected cases cannot be presumed to be representative of entire populations. Put another way, in statistical analysis one is generalizing to a population based on a sample which is representative of that population. In case studies, in comparison, one is generalizing to a theory based on cases selected to represent dimensions of that theory. This view was supported by Bartlet (1989). His speech at the 70th Annual Meeting of the American Education Research Association held in San Francisco highlight that the effective case records should attempt to connect theory with practice. Yin (2003), p. 47) provided some clarity to the issue by reflecting that case studies should be theory drive. Gall, Borg, and Gall (1996), inferred that case study research involved as a distinctive approach to scientific inquiry partly as a reaction to perceived limitations of quantitative research (p. 544).

Types of Case Studies

There are several types of case studies the graduate student or research can choose; in some instances multiple types may be used. Jensen and Rogers (2001, pp. 237-239) listed the following types:

1. Snapshot case studies: Detailed, objective study of one research entity at one point in time. Hypothesis-testing by comparing patterns across sub-entities (i.e., comparing departments within the case study agency).
2. Longitudinal case studies. Quantitative and/or qualitative study of one research entity at multiple time points.
3. Pre-post case studies. Study of one research entity at two time points separated by a critical event. A critical event is one which on the basis of a theory under study would be expected to impact case observations significantly.
4. Patchwork case studies. A set of multiple case studies of the same research entity, using snapshot, longitudinal, and/or pre-post designs. This multi-design approach is intended to provide a more holistic view of the dynamics of the researcher subject.
5. Comparative case studies. A set of multiple case studies of multiple research entities for the purpose of cross-unit comparison. Both qualitative and quantitative comparisons are generally made.

Case Selection

Graduate students and researchers should select the type of case study based upon the underlying theory to be investigated. Both independent and dependent variables should be identified and observed. When multiple types of case studies are used (Yin, 2003, p. 47) entitled this multiple case study approach designed to replicate findings based upon theoretical principals and expectations. Researchers will need to be apprised on various methods and criticisms in case studies. *For specific case selection methods and patter matching refer to Yin (1984).

Criticism of Case Studies

Beginning in the early part of the twentieth century criticism of the case study method has mounted. Results from case studies were considered not to follow the scientific method; were considered to be subjective in nature; and less rigorous than quantitative methods. Results were assessed as unscientific and were not generalizable (Mertens, 2009; Minnins, 1985; Flyvbjerg, 2006, Yin 1994).

Flyvbjerg's (2006) view is consistent with the above research. It was stated that: "The view that one cannot generalize on the basis of a single case is usually considered to be devastating to the case study as a scientific method" (p. 224). Ruddin (2006) inserted that : "We avoid the problem of trying to generalize inductively from single cases by not confusing case inference with inference. Case study reasoning would be seen as a strong from of hypothetico-deductive theorizing, not as a weak form of statistical inferences" (p. 800). Stake (2005) believes that poor generalizability of case study data is attributed to the researcher or evaluator.

Several critics of the method relate that the study of small number of cases invalidates the reported results. Others believe that case studies are useful only as an exploratory tool.

Methodology

In Mertens (2009) view case studies may employ multifaceted or triangulated strategies to explore a variety of participant's traits using both quantitative and qualitative data. The steps recommended in the procedures outlined for researchers include, selecting participants and location, choosing the intervention, and the time period for conducting the research (p. 169). In order to achieve the goals and objectives of case studies Tellis (1997) and Yin (1984) recommend the following methodology:

1. The study implies that the graduate student or researcher has competencies and skills in developing case studies.
2. Conduct the study, skills are needed in data collection techniques and instrument constructions.
3. Analyze the study, analysis of data is a critical factor which must be given serious attention by the researcher.
4. Conclusions, recommendations, and implications must be based upon data analysis and valid interpretation of findings.

Meta-Analysis

This method may be used to extend ground theory to several case studies by categorizing and summarizing rows and columns which are related to make theoretical generalizations. The following are recommended by graduate students and researchers planning and conducting meta-analysis studies:

1. Select an area of study based upon a theoretical construct.
2. Identify independent and dependent variables and develop methods and techniques to evaluate them.
3. Coder training is essential. It is essential for coders to have similar training in data collection to ensure uniformity of results to be analyzed.
4. Data weighting – when data analyses are used the student or researcher must select appropriate types of statistics to be used to test the research questions and reduce biased results.

Data Analysis

Interpretation of data may proceed in two major ways by graduate students and researchers, holistically or by coding. Holistic analysis is based upon the researcher making inferences and drawing conclusions premised upon the total text (Flowers & Haynes, 1981). On the other hand researchers employ coding to analyze data. This technique involves perusing data to categorize specific characteristics in the data (Berkenkotter, Huckin, & Ackerman, 1988).

We support the view outlined by Merriam (1988) concerning organizing and presenting data from case studies. They are:

1. The role of participants.
2. The network analysis of formal and informal exchanges among groups.
3. Historical.
4. Thematical.
5. Resources
6. Ritual and symbolism.
7. Critical incidents that challenge or reinforce fundamental beliefs, practices, and values.

The major purposes for organizing and presenting data are to discover pattern among the data and seek patterns that attempt to give meaning and validity to the case study. It is recommended that several researchers be involved in the coding process, in order to reduce subjectivity. Standards and agreement should be established among the coders before conducting the study (Berkenkotter, Huckin, & Acherman, 1988).

Validity and Reliability of Case Studies

Both validity and reliability of information in analyzing case studies must be considered by graduate students and researchers, especially when several researchers are involved. Researchers must develop strategies for dealing with validity and reliability of data (Yin, 1994).

Several methods are used by graduate students and researchers to analyze case studies. Some commonly used data sources include, interviews, observations, field studies and protocol analyses, documents, archival records, and artifacts. A combination of methods may be used by researchers to collect data used in completing the case study. Merriam (1985) views are similar to the above researchers. She proposed that cross checking data from multiple sources can assist in verifying and confirming data sources.

Guidelines for Developing Case Studies

As indicated earlier all case studies do not use the identical methodologies, but the selection is based upon thesis committees or publication standards. Case studies developed by graduate students or researchers should reflect scientific researcher standards and be well communicated. Comprehensively written, theoretically based on the literature in the field and show some type of comparison and intervention in private or public institutions.

Case studies are designed to prove or support theories based upon one of selected number of cases. A triangulation approach is recommended which will improve and validate the method. Triangulation infers that a multiple-method design be developed which may include observations, interviews, surveys, rating scales, checklists, focus groups, narrative analysis and archival records (Sabatier, 1993 & 1999; Yin 1984, 1994 & 2002; Goetz & Lecompete, 1984; Morgan, 2001). No specialized training is needed to administer these instruments. In some cases pre and post instruments may be employed to address the research question. Gay, Mills, and Airasian (2009), further offer the following steps and insights for designing case study researcher:

(1) Determine the research questions – considered to be one of the most important steps in the process, one should design questions that address who, what, how, and why – which provide the researcher with a good starting point.

(2) Define the case under study – this step is similar to that in other research approaches where the researcher defines the variables under investigation. In the case research one must take care to define the units of analysis.

(3) Determine the role of theory development in case selection – the researcher must make explicit the theoretical/conceptual framework that supports the choice of participants. Creating a comprehensive list of propositions based on the review of literature is one way determine the role of theory development.

(4) Determine the theoretical and conceptual framework – once again, attending to the literature related to your research interest will help identify the predominant theories and concepts that have emerged over a period of time.

(5) Determine whether a single case study, a multiple case study, or a collective case study is appropriate – researchers are cautioned to resist the temptation to do more unless the use of subcases will strengthen the understanding or even theorizing of the phenomenon under investigation.   (pps. 428 – 429)

Writing the Case Study Report

Bochrer (1990) contended that a case study is generally a story which summarizes the actual details of true events. In summary it has a plot, exposition, characters, and sometimes a dialogue. Generally,graduate students and researchers follow the research process and provides as much context as possible. The researcher may explain his/her scientific explanations or positions and how they assisted in the formation of the researcher questions, data collections procedures, preparation of the coders, and recommendations for further research (Berkenkotter, Huckin & Ackerman (1988); Emig (1971). In preparing the final report (Merrian, 1985) suggested the following:

1. Prepare specialized condensations for appropriate groups.

2. Replace narrative sections with a series of answers to open-ended questions.
3. Present "skimmer's" summaries at the beginning of each section.
   Views reported by Stake (1995) and Yin (1984) suggested the following format for completing the final case study report:
1. Select the case and determine data gathering and analysis techniques, the researcher or the student should decide in advance what data will be analyzed and how the data can tell to what degree the research questions will be achieved.
2. Determining and defining the research question, state one of two questions with "how" or "what". Carefully defining the questions will assist in identifying the method of analysis to be used.
3. Participant selection do not follow the format used in experimental research. One participant or a small group may be selected. A representative sample of the population is not necessary.
4. Prepare to collect the data, graduate students and researchers would be well trained in data collection techniques, anticipate problems, identify physical and mental resources and employ ethical standards. The research design may need to be revised based upon negative information.
5. Collect data in the field, the graduate student and researcher must make a complete analysis of the related literature in the field so that related patterns can be noted between the literature and patters associated with the study.
6. Evaluate and analyze the data, students and researchers must be cognizant of data analysis procedures, including categorizing tabulating, and employing statistical tools to analyze the purpose and research questions of the study.
7. Preparing the report, while preparing the draft report style, grammar, data analysis should be critically examined by the student, research, and individual competent in the area being explored. The final report should reflect all needed changes.

Application

If properly employed case studies can offer graduate students and researchers empirical information to improve teaching, solutions to classroom problems, and state of the art in critical thinking skills. Sudzina (1999), contends that case studies can also offer a window into pre-service, in-service, or graduate students experiences, opinions, perceptions, or misconceptions of educational dilemmas. Case studies also enable researchers, teachers, and students to transfer theoretical concepts into practical applications to solve problems. Multi sources of data could be employed by the graduate student and researcher to insure validity and reliability of results. These sources include using authentic documentation, archival records, interview techniques, observations, and physical artifacts.

Summary

A case study may be defined as a formal collection of evidence presented as an interpretive position of a unique case, and includes discussion of the data collected and evaluated (Hopkins, 1985).

Case studies can assist educators in several ways:
1. To determine current innovation to pre and in-service teachers.
2. To provide examples of how to develop and evaluate case studies.
3. To assist teachers to compare and contrast problems in the classroom.
4. To be used to collectively study school wide problems.
5. To generalize similar case studies to their own problems and experiences.

Case studies assist the researcher in recognizing that using mixed methods provide creative ways to conduct case studies. Today case studies have proven to be a valid research method to employ in finding solutions to problems in the Social and Physical Science.

References

Armistead, C. (1984). How Useful are Case Studies. *Training and Development Journal,* 38 (2), 75-77.

Berkenkotter, C., Huckin, T.N. & Ackerman, J (1988). Conventions, Conversations, and the Writer, Case Study of a Student in a Rhetoric, Ph.D. Program. *Research in the Teaching of English,* 22, 9-44.

Boehrer, J (1990). Teaching With Cases: Learning to Question. *New Directions for Teaching and Learning,* 42, 41-57.

Emig, J. (1971). *The Composing Processes of Twelfth Graders.* Urbana: NTCE.

Feagin, J., Orum, A., & Sjoberg, G. (Eds.) (1991). A Case for Case Study. Chapel Hill, NC: University of North Carolina Press.

Flower, L., & Hayes, J.R. (1984). Images Plans and Prose: The Representation of Meaning in Writing. Written Communication, 1, 120-160.

Flyvbjerg, B. (2006). Five Misunderstanding About Case Study Researcher. Qualitative Inquiry, 12 (2), 219-245.

Gall, M.D., Borg, W.R., & Gall, J.P. (1996). Educational Research: An Introduction (6th ed). White Plains, NY: Longman Publishers.

Gay, L.R., Mills, G.E., & Airasian, P. (2009). Educational Research: Competencies for Analysis (9th Ed). Upper Saddle River, NJ: Merrill Publishers.

http://faculty.chass.ncsu.edu/garson/PA765/cases.htm

http://writing colostate.edu/guides/research/casestudy/com2a2.cfm

Jensen, J. L., & Rogers, R. (2001). Cummulating the Intellectual Goal of Case Study Research. Public Administrator Review, 61 (2), 236-246.

Merriam, S.B. (1985). The Case Study in Educational Research: A Review of Selected Literature. Journal of Educational Thought, 19 (3), 204-217.

Merseth, K.K. (1991). The Case for Cases in Teacher Education. RIE. 42p. (ERIC).

Mertens, D. M. (2009). Transformative Research and Evaluation. New York: The Guilford Press.

Minnis, J.R. (1985, September). Ethnography, Case Study, Grounded Theory and Distance Education Research. Distance Education, 6, 2.

Ruddin, L. P. (2006). You Can Generalize Stupid: Social Scientist, Bent Flyvbjerg, and Case Study Methdology. Qualitative Inquiry, 12 (4), 792-812.

Selfe, C. L. (1985). An Apprehensive Writer Composes. When a Writer Can't Write: Studies in Writer's Block and Other Composing-Process Problems (pp.83-95). ED. Mike Rose.NY: Guilford Press.

Sjoberg, G., Williams, N., Vaughan, T., & Sjoberg, A. (1991). The Case Study Approach in Social Researcher. In Feagin, J., Orum, A., & Sjoberg, G. (Eds). (1991) A Case for Case Study (pp.27-29). Chapel Hill, NC: University of North Carolina Press.

Stake: R. (1995). The Art of Case Research. Newbury Park, CA: Sage Publications.

Stake, R. E. (2005). Qualitative Case Studies. In US. L. Lincoln &N.K. Denzin (Eds.). The Sage Handbook of Qualitative Research (3rd ed., p. 443-446). Thousand Oaks, CA: Sage.

Sudzina, M.R. (1999). Case Applications for Teacher Education. Needham Heights, MA: Allyn & Bacon.

Tellis, W. (1997). Introduction to Case Study. The Qualitative Report. http://www.nova.edu/sss/or/or3_2/tellisI.html.

Yin, R. (1984). Case Study Research: Design and Methods (1st ed).Beverly Hills, CA: Sage Publishing.

Yin, R. (1993). Applications of Case Study Research, Newbury Park, CA: Sage Publishing.

Yin, R. (1994). Case Study Research: Design and Methods (2st ed).Thousand Oaks, CA: Sage Publishing.

Yin, R. (2003). Case Study Research: Design and Methods (3st ed).Thousand Oaks, CA: Sage Publishing.

Chapter Eleven
Major Parametric Statistical Tests
George R. Taylor, Ph.D.

INTRODUCTION

There are parametric tests designed to measure the results on research studies involving the use of statistical procedures to draw certain assumptions about a population that is normally distributed. One of the most important assumptions of parametric tests is that the data are measured on an interval or ratio scale. If the data are nominal or ordinal so that it makes sense to talk about a mean or average scale, then parametric tests cannot be used. With the exception of some highly sophisticated procedures such as log-linear analysis, parametric tests can't be used to compare people's favorite brand of jeans; their ownership of IBM, IBM-clone or Macintosh computers; or their choice of colleges to attend. We will summarize the major parametric tests in use by social researchers today. We have listed those procedures which have occurred with the greatest frequencies in the professional literature.

The T-Test

When testing the null hypotheses of two groups that have the same means, the t-test is frequently the parametric test used. It is also employed to determine if a correlation coefficient is significantly different from no correlation as well as to compare a mean to a set of values when computing a t-value, the researcher compares two means, the two sample means from the experiment and the control groups. This t-value is used to obtain a level of significance of the same population. It can then be looked up in a table, usually located in the appendix to determine the *p* value (Brase & Brase, 1991; Dowdy & Wearden, 1985; Elmore & Woehlke, 1977).

The df column in the t-test table is referred to as the *degree of freedom* (N-1), or it refers to the number of subjects in the study to calculate the level of significance. The researcher may choose from two types of t-tests. The *independent* sample test is used when there are different subjects in each group. When the subjects in the two groups are matched to the *dependent* samples, a correlated t-test is used. The design is usually a pre-post one where subjects are given a pretest, exposed to a treatment, and given a posttest. The means from both tests are used to compute a t-test value (McMillan, 1996).

As indicated, one of the most useful inferential tests in the t-test, which relies upon probability distribution to test hypotheses. Interval/ratio data sources are used to provide data to test null and alternate hypotheses to determine if differences between two population means exist. Samples drawn from the population may be independent or dependent, matched or equal. Standard selection procedures should be followed as outlined in Chapter 6. Calculated t-values for the t-test are based upon the means of the two groups, the standard deviation, and "N." The researcher may elect to use a BS design (two different groups) or a WS design (the same group measured twice). Regardless of the design selected, the researcher must be aware of the assumptions of the t-test (Harris, 1995).

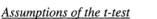

<u>*Assumptions of the t-test*</u>

BS form (different groups)	*WS form (repeated)*
Interval/ratio data	Interval/ratio data
Normally distributed population	Normally distributed population
Random sampling	Random sampling
Homogeneity of variance	Correlated measures

If the stated assumptions are not met, the researcher should employ other ways of testing his/her hypotheses through using non-parametric techniques. We have reserved Chapter 11 for summarizing the major non-parametric tests in use.

When designing studies using the t-test, researchers must consider the hypotheses being tested, and the type of data sources being used in selecting the type of t-test to be used: single, independent, or dependent sample (Hinkle, Wiersma & Jurs, 1994; Borg, Gall & Gall, 1935; Blaisdell, 1993).

Single Sample t-test

This test is designed to compare the means of a single sample with a hypothesis. The formula is:

$$t = \frac{\overline{x} - \Phi}{S\overline{(x)}} \qquad S\overline{x} = \frac{S}{\sqrt{N}}$$

Listed below is an example of a single *t*-test:

A researcher wants to determine whether or not selected scores are greater than some well known standard.

Example:

A researcher is attempting to determine the average number of miles a computer salesperson drives a month (1,200 is typical for other sales persons). A random sample of 50 salespersons' mileage ranged from 700-1,500 miles a month with a mean of 1,100 and a standard deviation of 200 miles. The researchers' question or hypotheses is to determine if the salespersons' average monthly mileage is significantly below the 1,200 miles.

Method for solving the problem or answering the question:

1. Compute $S\overline{x}$. The sample consisted of 50 salespersons.

$$S\overline{x} \frac{200}{\sqrt{50}}$$
$$= \frac{200}{28.28}$$
$$= 7.071$$

2. Compute *t*.

$$t = \frac{\overline{x} - \Phi}{S\overline{(x)}}$$
$$= \frac{1,100 - 1,200}{1.071}$$
$$= \frac{100}{7.071}$$
$$= \sqrt{14.142}$$
$$= 3.76$$

Referring to a table of t-values the researcher looks up a two-tailed t-value with 49 df (degrees of freedom) and finds that a t-value of 0 + 3.53 is significant at the .01 level of confidence. In analyzing the data, it would appear that the salespersons as a group drove fewer miles than the 1,200 miles driven by the computer salespersons over a period of a month.

T-test for Independent Samples

This test is used more frequently than another type of t-test. The researcher attempts to compare the means of two independent groups, when random samples are taken from both groups or when subjects are randomly assigned to an experimental or control group.

The independent samples t-test may be employed with samples having equal N's. The formula for the independent samples t-test is:

The difference in the population means. The standard error of the difference in the means.

The following hypothetical example is given to demonstrate how the independent samples t-test may be used:

> Assuming that a researcher wanted to determine if parental involvement in the school would increase the number of homework assignments completed and turned in. After discussing the problem with fellow researchers, a pilot study was implemented with 12 parents participating; 6 were randomly assigned to the experimental group and 6 were assigned to the control group. After two weeks of structured involvement in the school, the number of homework assignments completed were compared. The 8 children of parents in the experimental group completed 5, 3, 4, 6, 3, 4, 2, 3 (N=30) assignments. The eight children of parents who were not involved completed, 3, 2, 1, 0, 4, 0, 3, 4 (N=17) assignments. Was parental involvement in the school successful?
>
> Using the formula below, we will be able to answer the question:

1. Compute raw scores based on the formula below:
    Experimental Group
    $\Sigma x_E = 30$, $\Sigma x^2 = 124$, $\bar{x} E = 3.75$ $(\Sigma x E)^2 = 900$
    Control Group
    $\Sigma x_c = 17$, $\Sigma x E^2 = 55$, $\bar{x} c = 2.12$ $(\Sigma x_c)^2 = 289$

2. Compute the independent samples *t*-test:

$$t = \frac{\bar{x}_1 \qquad \bar{x}_2}{\sqrt{[\Sigma x_1^2 - (\Sigma x_1)^2/N_1 + \Sigma x_2^2 - (\Sigma x_2)^2/N_2]\,(1/N_1 + 1\,N_2)}}$$
$$(N_1 + 1\,N_2)$$

$$t = \frac{3.75 - 2.12}{\sqrt{[124 - (900/8) + 55 - (289/8)]\,(1/8 + 1/8)}}$$
$$(8+8) - 2$$

$$t = \frac{1.63}{\dfrac{\sqrt{(124 - 112.5) + 55 - 36.12]\,(2/8)}}{16-2}}$$

$$t = \frac{1.63}{\dfrac{\sqrt{(11.5) + (55 - 36.12)\,(2/8)}}{14}}$$

$$t = \frac{1.63}{\dfrac{\sqrt{[(11.5) + (18.9)]\,(.25)}}{14}}$$

$$t = \frac{1.63}{\dfrac{\sqrt{11.5 + 18.9}\,(.25)}{14}}$$

$$t = \frac{1.63}{\dfrac{\sqrt{30.4}\,(.25)}{14}}$$

$$t = \frac{1.63}{}$$

$$\frac{\sqrt{2.17}\,(.25)}{14}$$

$$t = \frac{1.63}{\sqrt{(.16)\,(.25)}}$$

$$t = \frac{1.63}{\sqrt{.04}}$$

$$t = \frac{1.63}{.20}$$

$$t = 8.15$$

$N_1 + N_2 = (8 + 8) - 2 = 14;$

the critical value of 8.15 with 14 degrees of freedom is 2.9771 which is greater than the .01 level of confidence. We may sum up the problem by stating that parents of children who participated in the school's involvement program did significantly more homework assignments than those who did not which implies that the null hypotheses was rejected. Refer to Appendix D for critical values.

Dependent Samples t-test

This test is sometimes called a *correlated* or *paired-samples* t-test. It is used to compare the means of two groups by pairing one group's scores with another group. Some examples would include *natural pairing*, where the researcher simply chooses individuals based upon some pre-determined trait or criteria. The commonly used pre-post test design is another use. The same individual is tested twice; once before intervention, and once after intervention. Measures from the two testing conditions are compared. Pairing may be done by equating individuals on some trait, such as, some physical or mental trait. By using this approach, the researcher hopes to reduce errors by selecting subjects with similar traits.

Suppose a researcher wanted to find out if reading novels have more impact upon college students than viewing the video tapes. Students are assigned a novel to read and a video to review. The researcher sets up a matched pair design in which a novel is read by participants and the video tape is reviewed. Ten subjects are randomly assigned to read one of five novels and to review the comparable video tapes. Each subject is asked to rate how the novel and the video tape changed his/her attitude on a 7-point scale from 0-7. The researcher tabulates the results of his/her research in the following table:

Table 11.1 Researcher's Tabulations

Subject	Novel	Video	D	D²
A	3	6	-3	9
B	2	7	-5	25
C	4	5	-1	1
D	0	6	-6	36
E	4	5	-1	1

The formula used by the researcher is:

$\Sigma D = 13$, $\Sigma D^2 = 72$, $(\Sigma D)^2 = 169$, $(\Sigma D)^2/N = 33.8$, $\overline{D} = .32$.

The Standard Deviation is:

$$\sqrt{\frac{72 - 169}{4}} = \sqrt{24.25} = 4.924$$

The Standard Error is:

$$\overline{}\quad 4.924 \quad \underline{4.924}$$

$S D = \sqrt{5} = 2.236 = 2.202$
The t-value is:
$$t = \frac{3.2}{2.202} = 1.453$$

The t-value reported (1.453) with 4 degrees of freedom, is not significant at the .05 level of confidence. The researcher, based upon the t-value, may conclude that the participants reading novels and viewing comparable videos do not significantly change students' attitudes. Some final observations relevant to using the t-test:

1. The t-test is a statistical test of the equality of means. It can be used to test the equality of two means from two different groups or two means from the same group taken under different conditions. Computer software packages for t-tests provide all the basic information necessary for an interpretation of the data, namely the means themselves, group standard deviations, degrees of freedom, the t-value, its associated *p* value, and a test of important assumptions. Refer to Chapter 7 for additional use of computers in research.

2. The t-test assumes interval/ratio data and normally distributed data. What would a researcher do with the same type of question if data were skewed, or if measurement were really ordinal rather than interval/ratio? In this case, he/she would use what are called non-parametric equivalents of the t-test, namely the Kruskal-Wallis test, or the Mann-Whitney "U"test.

3.

Simple Analysis of Variance (ANOVA)

This powerful test is frequently abbreviated as ANOVA. This parametric test basically serves the same purpose of the t-test discussed earlier. The chief differences in the two tests is that the t-test is used to compare two means and the ANOVA is used to compare two or more means. A simple type of ANOVA is frequently called a one-way ANOVA. In this case, the researcher is analyzing a single independent variable with a single dependent variable (Cochran & Cox, 1957). An example may be that a researcher wants to compare three ways of teaching reading; the traditional text, phonics, and computerized instruction reading achievement. The three reading approaches would be the independent variables. Analysis of variance would test the null hypothesis that there is no difference among the means of all three reading methods. This type of experiment would be referred to as a 1 x 3 ANOVA which would translate to teaching reading on three levels.

The ANOVA formula uses the variances of the groups to calculate a value called the *F* statistic. The *F* statistic is similar to the t-value in that it is a three- or four-digit number used to obtain the level of significance that the researcher uses to reject or accept the null hypothesis. If the *F* value is significant, the null hypothesis can be rejected with assurance that at least two of the population means are not the same (Hays, 1994; Glass & Hopkins, 1996).

Calculating the Variance

Variance is a measure of spread. It is the square of the standard deviation. Two types of spreads in data are discussed below relevant to the research problem outlined above:

1. V*ariance or spread among means*. The computer group had a mean of 77, the textbook group had a mean of 81. These means are different, and the more different they are, the higher the variance among means becomes. If the means were all equal, there would be no variance among means. If the researcher wants to compare means, and if he/she hopes to reject the null for the analysis of variance, he/she would like to be able to report strong differences among means or a large *variance between groups*. Variance between groups is the statistical name for differences among means.

2. *Variance inside (within) a single group*. Even within a single group there are differences between scores. When the researcher is comparing groups, he/she are assuming that study method contributes to the differences among means. What contributes to the

differences among means. What contributes to the differences within a single group? The answer is factors which cannot be controlled which are called error factors. Error factors are also possible in differences among means, but the are the only possible explanation for differences within a single group. By recognizing factor such as skill, luck, anxiety, and so on, "error factors," we are not implying that these factors affected the scoring. Consequently, variance within groups is also called error variance. Another name for this same variance is residual or written cells variance. The two variances are compared by means of an *F* ratio; a test which divides variance among means by error variance as follows:

Variance Among Means (or Between Groups Variance)
F = Variance Within Cells (or Within Groups Variance)

As the value of *F* increases, the researcher is more and more likely to reject the null hypothesis of equality of means. Because differences among means are sufficiently larger than differences due to error, the researcher may begin to take them seriously. The analysis of variance, which is designed to compare any number of means from two up involves the use of the null and alternate hypotheses.

Null: All means being compared are equal (there is no variance among means).

Alternate: There is some difference (or some variance) among the means being compared.

The *F* distribution is the probability distribution used to decide if the null may be rejected. The larger the ratio, the better chance of rejecting the null. Each *F* ratio also has two degrees of freedom. Degrees of freedom are based upon the number of scores used to calculate each variance, and are used in order to decide exactly which *F* distribution should be consulted in rejecting the null.

Assumptions for the Analysis of Variance (Cochran & Cox, 1957; Hinkle, Wiersma & Jurs, 1994; McMillan, 1996):

Interval/Ratio data
Normally distributed data
Random samples
Independent samples (different groups)
Homogeneity of Variance

Analysis of Variance Problem

Assuming that a researcher wants to determine whether male and female college students are equally majoring in physical science and math, it is generally known that women have not significantly majored in those fields for several reasons; most of the majors have been males. A small pilot sample was selected. The researcher divided the sample into three groups: lower class females (Group 1), lower class males (Group 2), and upper class males (Group 3). Each student is then asked to list the number of hours per week devoted to studying physical science and math. Table 11.2 reflects the results.

Table 11.2 Number of Hours Male and Female Students Devoted to Studying Math and Physical Science

Group 1		Group 2		Group 3	
X_1	X_2	X_1	X_2	X_1	X_2
2	4	6	3 6	9	8 1
4	1 6	4	1 6	8	6 4
5	2 5	5	2 5	8	6 4
Σ : 11	4 5	1 5	7 7	2 5	2 09

Step 1. Sum the raw scores and then square the raw scores.

$$N_1 = 3, N_2 = 3, N_3 = 3 \ [N = 9]$$
$$\Sigma X = 11 + 15 + 25 = 51 = T$$
$$\Sigma X^2 = 121 + 225 + 625 = 971$$
$$T^2 = (\Sigma X)^2 = 51^2 = 2601$$
$$T^2/N = 2601/9 = 289$$

Step 2. Compute the total Sum of Squares.

$$SS = \Sigma X^2 - T^2/N$$
$$= 971 - 2601/9$$
$$= 971 - 289$$
$$= 682$$

Step 3. Compute the Sum of Squares Between:

$$SS_B = \Sigma T_1/N_1 = (11^2/_3 + 15^2/_3 = 2^2/_3) - 289$$
$$= 121/_3 + 225/_3 + 625/_3) - 289$$
$$= 323 - 289$$
$$= 24$$

Step 4. Compute the Mean Square Between. The degrees of freedom re N-1=2:

$$MS_B = SS_B/df_B = 34/2 = 17$$

Step 5. Compute the Sum of Squares Within.

$$SS_w = \Sigma X^2 - \Sigma(T^2/N) = 311 \ (121/_3 + 225/_3) = (971 - 323 = 648$$

- Find the degrees of freedom for Within.

$$MS_w = (N - 9) - 3 = 6$$

- Compute *F*:

$$F = MS_B/MS_w = 17/_2 = 8.5$$

Significance Level

Look up (8.5) value in the Critical Values for *F* with 2 and 6 degrees of freedom, $p < .05$ level. (Refer to Appendix K for critical values.) Findings may be interpreted as *male students spent more hours studying physical science and math than females* (lower class females [M=3.66] and lower class males [M=5.00] and upper class males [M=8.33]).

Step 6. Construct an Analysis of Variance Summary Table.

Table 11.3 ANOVA Summary Table

Source	SS	Df	Ms	F(2, 6)	*p*
Between	34	2	17	8.5	.05
Within	648	6	2		
Total	682				

The results in the Summary Table above indicate that the means do not represent random samples from the same population. The main effect for sex was rejected ($p<.05$) while for upper or lower class was not. Data show that males spent more hours per week than females in studying physical science and math ($p<.05$).

Factorial Analysis of Variance

According to McMillan (1996), factorial designs have more than one independent variable (IV) and one dependent variable (DV) to enable the investigation of interaction among the independent variables. Factorial analysis of variance is the statistical tool to employ to determine the degree of interaction. Most factorial designs have two independent variables and is commonly called a *two-way ANOVA*. The researcher is attempting to test three null hypotheses, the two independent variables and the interaction between and among them.

Suppose the researcher wanted to study the influence of gender (m/f) and race (Black, Hispanic, and White) on fairness of employment in the country. There are 2 genders and 3 racial groups. This is a 2 x 3 factorial design which gives 6 groups total. Factorial designs are so named because they multiply the *factors*, the numbers of each type of group together.

The means from cross-combinations of at least two sets of groups in terms of main effects and interactions, with all groups measured only once. This is a BG factorial ANOVA. (Note: Main effects are equivalent to doing a one-way ANOVA for a single IV; each IV has its own main effect.) An interaction occurs when the combination of two (or more) independent variables is the cause for the observed magnitude in the dependent variable. For instance, the marks obtained by students in a math course might be determined by the experience of the students (freshman, junior, senior) and the number of hours spent studying per week (3, 5, 8, 12, >20). One possible interaction is that seniors who studied more than 20 hours per week got significantly higher marks than any other group combination. Examples of the two possible main effects here are:

a. More experienced students score higher in math,

b. Students who studied longer did better in math.

An *F* ratio is given for each null hypothesis, which may be converted to a *p* value. A factorial design may include a variable with multiple levels.

Example:

> A 4 x 4 x 5 ANOVA may be interpreted as a design that has 4 independent variables, 4 with four levels, and 1 with five levels. Caution and consultation is advised when multiple variables and levels are attempted (Harris, 1995; Hays, 1994; Elmore, 1997).

Factorial ANOVA Examples:

a. Does reading skill in children depend on grade (3, 5, 6) or (m/f) or a combination of both? [IV's = grade, sex; DV = vocabulary skill.

b. Does memory for names depend on their familiarity (high, low) or their length (high, medium, low) or their emotionality (active, passive)? [IV = familiarity, length, emotionality; DV = recall).

Means from cross-combinations of at least two sets of categories with the same group being measured under all conditions is a fully repeated design (WS factorial ANOVA). It is called *repeated* because the observations are made again and again on the same group of subjects. WS factorial ANOVA has two or more repeated factors and one IV.

Example:

a. A single group of automobile workers tries out combinations of two types of shifts (day/afternoon), three pay schedule (daily/weekly/bi-monthly), and three types of breaks (1 hour/½ hour/¼ hour/or four 5-min.). Does this effect productivity? [IV= shift type, pay schedule, break type; DV=productivity].

b. The same group of subjects is used to test some itching relief medication. Each subject tries out three different doses (2mg/25mg/30mg) injected in one of two different locations (home/clinic). Does dose and location affect itching? [IV=dose/location; DV=sleep].

Mixed Designs (Partial repeated ANOVA)

Not all designs are BG or WS, rather, some designs are mixed. They have some BG variables and some WS variables. The Mixed Designs have means from cross-combinations of at least two sets of categories with at least two different groups involved. This is called a *partially repeated* ANOVA. Partially repeated ANOVA has some combination of grouping and repeated factors as IV's and one DV:

Example:

a. Boys and girls are measured for weight in both October and May. Are month and gender associated with height differences? (IV=gender/month; DV=height).
b. A group of city workers and a group of medical interns each undergo a training session for sensitivity training.
c. Measures of sensitivity are taken prior to the program and after completion. How is their sensitivity level affected, and how do the groups compare to each other? (IV=group/before-after; DV=sensitivity).
d. The city workers and the medical interns are independent groups. However, each of these groups is tested before and after the running of the program.

Proliferation of tests. A two-way analysis of variance contains three statistical tests; two main effects and one interaction. A three-way analysis has seven tests: three main effects and four interactions. A four-way analysis has fifteen tests: four main effects and eleven interactions. A seven-way analysis of variance would have more than forty tests in it; seven main effects and a plethora of interactions.

Interpreting interactions. Interactions are never interpreted solo. Their impact is always deduced by a comparison to simpler results from previous tests. An interaction of seven factors would be interpreted only in comparison to all other tests in the analysis.

Chapter 11 Research Exercise

1. Using the following data, perform an ANOVA analysis. Is there a significant difference between the way 60 students perform in target practice as a function of variability in target size and choice of machine utilized? Think reflectively about the experimental procedures used to come up with the diagram indicated below. Think reflectively about the criteria one needs to consider in determining than an ANOVA is appropriate for the design indicated below.

Table 11.4 Target Practice

Target Size	Machine # 1	Machine #2	Machine #3
A	6	4	4
	4	1	2
	2	5	2
	6	2	1
	2	3	1
B	8	6	3
	3	6	1
	7	2	1
	5	3	2
	2	8	3
C	7	9	6
	6	4	4
	9	8	3
	8	4	8
	5	5	4
D	9	7	6
	6	8	5
	8	4	7
	8	7	9
	9	4	8

2. An undergraduate student in a psychology laboratory wanted to test the hypothesis that adolescent boys are brighter than their fathers. He collected IQ's on 15 year-old boys and their fathers. Compute a *t*-test from the data below:

Table 11.5 Boys Brighter Than Their Fathers

Fathers	Sons	Fathers	Sons
120	115	95	107
117	114	107	105
112	114	106	100
118	110	93	97
102	108	99	95

3. Using the following data, perform an ANOVA analysis. Is there a significant difference between the mean score among the four sets of data? Write a statement that describes the procedures used in arriving at your interpretation of the findings?

Table 11.6 ANOVA Analysis

Set 1	Set 2	Set 3	Set 4
114	119	112	117
115	120	116	117
111	119	116	114
110	116	115	112
112	116	112	117

4. A local research agency was contracted to assess the achievement of children for the 1997-98 school year. The researcher conducted a pilot study on 12 fifth-grade students, assessing science and social study skills. The teacher was instructed to rank each student

in these areas. The Spearman Rho Rank order correlation was used to analyze the data. The researcher was pleased with the results and wanted to include a larger sample (N=85) using the same statistics as last year but adding reading and the sixth-grade. Answer the following questions:

a.   Was the correct statistics used last year? Explain and justify.
b.   Is the Spearman rank correlation an appropriate statistical formula to use for the new school year? Defend your position.

5.   From a group of students enrolled in science in a high school, a researcher randomly selected 60 of them and divided them into two groups by random assignment of 30 to a group A (traditional science curriculum) and 30 to group B (a new program designed to deal with the history of two ethnic groups). The two groups were compared at the end of the semester on a scale designed to measure attitudes towards the two ethnic groups. In this study identify the following:

1.   Independent variable
2.   Dependent variable
3.   Control group
4.   Experimental group
5.   Method(s) used to control for differences between the groups
6.   Research design used

References

Blaisdell, E. A. (1993). *Statistics in practice.* New York: Sanders College Publishing Company.

Borg, W. R., Gall, J. P., & Gall, M. D. (1993). *Applying Educational Research: A Practical Guide* (3rd ed.). New York: Longman Publishing Company.

Brase, C.H., & Brase, C.P. (1991). *Understandable statistics: concepts and methods* (4th ed.). Massachusetts: D.C. Heath and Company.

Cochran, W. G., & Cox, G. (1957). *Experimental designs.* New York: John Wiley & Sons, Inc.

Elmore, P., & Woehlke, P. L. (1997). *Basic statistics.* New York: Longman Publishing Company.

Glass, G.V. & Hopkins, K.D. (1996). *Statistical methods in education and psychology* (3rd ed.) Boston: Allyn and Bacon.

Harris, M. B. (1995). *Basic statistics for behavioral science research.* Boston: Allyn and Bacon.

Hays, W.L. (1994). *Statistics* (5th ed.). New York: Harcourt-Brace College Publishers.

Hinkle, D. L., Wiersma, W., & Jurs, S. G. (1994). *Applied statistics for the behavioral sciences* (3rd ed.). Boston: Houghton-Mifflin Company.

McMillan, J. H. (1996). *Educational research: Fundamentals for the consumer* (2nd ed.). New York: Harper Collins College Publishers.

Chapter Twelve
Sampling Method
George R. Taylor, Ph.D.

INTRODUCTION

Scientific research cannot be based upon   sound judgment without adequate samples. Much of our data in the public domain is based upon this premise, good samples and selected to make general comments about the population being studied. The average deviation will not do for purposes of generalization. It ceases to be valid as soon as we try to draw generalizations from any measured group to the larger population of which it is a sample. To understand this better, it is necessary to discuss briefly theory which is involved in sampling When we set out to secure information about a certain trait or quality, it is hardly ever possible to measure all of the persons or things in the universe which posses that trait or quality. We must therefore content ourselves with the measurement of a segment or sampling of the total universe. From our findings about this sample, we may then perhaps draw certain conclusions as to the existence of this trait or quality in the total universe. Thus, for example, if we wish to know the average height of all men, it would be a super-human as well as unnecessary task to set out to measure every man in the world. It is far more feasible to take a representative sample of men and try to draw all justifiable conclusions as to the height of the total population from this sample.

Needless to say, it is very important how we select our samples. If we should go to universities alone to select our cases, the average would be too low since we would undoubtedly include a high proportion of men who had not yet stopped growing. On the other hand, if we selected eases only from the army, our average would undoubtedly be too high since the army does not admit men who are shorter than a specified minimum height, thus, excluding from our table allot this group of short men.

To secure an average that would truly serve as an index to the height of all men who are short, men who are young and men who are old, men living in cities and men living in the country, men who are healthy and men who are sick, and so on. In order to avoid the extent to which our sample is representative of the total population from which it is drawn depends not only on the care which we take in choosing our cases but also on the number of cases included in the sample. Thus, in our example about the average height of all men, it would be folly to draw conclusions from the measurement of 100 men, no matter how carefully we may have picked the hundred. The sample would still be too small a fraction of the total population to give an adequate picture. If, however, we measured 10,000 men or 100,000 men, our sample would be much more likely to approximate the true facts about all men. This would be verified by the fact that measuring additional samples of the same size would be likely to give us very similar findings. As the total sample grows larger, the average changes less and less. Thus, the second million men would show much less variation from the first million than the second hundred from the first hundred.

Since perfect truth about a total population can be achieved only when the sampling includes every case in that total population, the smaller the proportion of the total population which the sample includes, the less reliable the generalization which we can make from measurement of any single sample. Here the laws of chance come to our assistance - they indicate how reliable the conclusions we draw from a sample are apt to prove.

Students conducting or planning to conduct research according to Charles, (1988); Gall, Borg, and Gall (1996), Drew (1990); Mertens (2005); Grissom and Kim (2005) and Mertens (2005) should consider the following factors when selecting samples. Sample size and type of sampling techniques to employ.

Sample Size

The sample size is very important if it is to reflect adequately the characteristics of the population. The smaller the sample the more bias toward reflecting the true population. Large samples tend to reduce bias. If a sample size of 30 is chosen, reflecting characteristic in the population, it is <u>usually</u> adequate if parametric statistics are used, sample less than 30 the research should use non-parametric statistics. Refer to chapters 13 and 14 for additional information in choosing appropriate statistics (Gall, Borg, Gall, 1996; Kline, 2005; Dyba, Kanpenes, Sjoberg, 2006).

SampleMethods

Sampling is a process of selecting a representative part of a population by the researcher in order to estimate the subject's performance, without collecting data from the entire population (Creswell, 2009; Keppel, 1991). Using a valid sample, a researcher measure performance in an effective and scientific manner. Sampling is a particularly useful technique for performance measures that require primary data collection from a source. Sampling should not be used unless the researcher has a large number of cases in the measurement set population because a fairly large number of sample cases is needed to achieve a representative sample of the population.

Researchers have classified sampling methods as probability or non-probability Kline, 2009). Probability samples denotes <u>that</u> each person has an equal change of being selected. This method includes random systematic, and stratified sampling. On the other hand, no probability sampling includes convenience sampling, questa sampling, and snowball sampling (hiww. Statp accomi suiveys/sampling.htm)Mertens, 2009). Judgment sampling is a common nonprobability method. The researcher selects the sample based on judgment. This is usually an extension of convenience sampling. For example, a researcher may decide to draw the entire sample from one ¨representative¨ city, even though the population includes all cities. When using this method, the researcher must be confident that the chosen sample is truly representative of the entire population.

Quota sampling is the nonprobability equivalent of stratified sampling. Like stratified sampling, the researcher first identifies the stratums ad their proportions as they are represented in the population. Then convenience or judgment sampling is used to select the required number of subjects from each stratum. This differs from stratified sampling, where the stratums are filled by random sampling.

Snowball sampling is a special nonprobability method used when the desired sample characteristic is rare. It may be extremely difficult or cost prohibitive to locate respondents in these situations. Snowball sampling relies on referrals from initial subjects to generate additional subjects. While this technique can dramatically lower search costs, it comes at the expense of introducing bias because the technique itself reduces the likelihood that the sample will represent a good cross section from the population.

When using probability sampling the research can calculate sampling error. This optional is not provided to the researcher who employs non-probability sampling. It is highly recommended that the researchers choose valid sampling techniques through using random techniques to validate their sample selections.

Random Sampling

Several researchers have voiced their concerns relevant to random sampling (Grewell, 2009; Dyba, Kampenus, & Sjoberg, 2006; Kline, 2009; & Mertens, 2009), it is universally agreed by these authors that randoming imply that the population must be identified and that everyone has an equal chance of being selected. Based upon the research, the following procedures are recommended.

Gathering data about a certain number of people and assuming that these data are representative of a larger group to which those people belong is a risky undertaking. If the selection of persons to be interviewed or tested is peculiar, the results will be peculiar and not generally applicable to other groups. The question then is: When can a sample be trusted?

There are two ways to proceed. If a polling organization is trying to obtain a sampling of public opinion about an issue, it does not pick people at random. It carefully selects some 1500 persons who are believed to be a cross section of the whole population of the country-so many of each race or ethnic background, so many from each political party, so many from each major religious group, and so on, according to the percentages of those groups in the country. The answers given by this sample arc then assumed to be typical of what would be obtained if one questioned everybody. This is basically the **approach** also of the Nielson rating and other schemes for the collection of data on television viewing.

The second procedure is to use random numbers. This means that numbers have been listed in such a way that there is no known pattern in them except that each digit will occur approximately as often as every other digit. This is the kind of procedure that could be used when one wants the results to be governed by pure chance, as in a lottery. This could have been used to pick persons to be drafted for military service instead of the birthday system used for the Vietnam war draft.

There are occasions when teachers want to pick students at random. The accompanying table can be used for this purpose.
1. Assign a number to each individual in the group.
2. Use a table of random numbers to select the required number of individuals from the group to make up the sample you need.

How to Use the Table of Random Numbers
1. Start by chance, anywhere in the table. Drop a pin and begin with the number closet to the point of the pain, or close your eyes and put a pencil point on a number.
2. Read the numbers in any direction-right, left, up, or down.
3. Read the numbers as single digits or pairs or triplets, as needed.
4. Ignore numbers that exceed the number in your parent group. For example, if you combine four classes and have 122 students in your parent group, any number above that is ignored, go on to the next number.

Let's take an example, using the table here.

Assume that you want to choose 10 students out of 31 for some purpose and you want the choice to be purely random, not selective. Assign each student a number from 1 to 31. Then randomly pick a starting place in the table and randomly determine what direction you will move in. Then read from the table.

Assume that we are starting with row 13, column 2, and moving right.

The first number is 41 - discarded as being to high for our group. The next number is 08, so we have our first selected student.

The third number is 88 - also discarded because it is too high. The fourth number is 22, so we have our second selected student.

And so on, until we have our 10 students. This process insures that every individual has an equal chance of being selected.

Stratified Sampling

Frequently, random sampling does not meet the needs of researchers. When special traits of the sample is needed, such as age, sex, income, or education. Employing random numbers will not give samples with these different traits. Stratification will permit researchers to classify the population into sub-populations based upon some of the above characteristics. Stratified sampling maybe proportionate or disproportionate. In proportionate sampling stra sample are proportional to the strate population. In disproportionate sampling higher proportions are selective from some groups and not others. The 50% rules does not apply as in proportionate sampling (Kline, 2009).

Cluster and Systematic Sampling

This technique is used when group of individuals are selected to participate in a study from a specific population. Cluster sampling involves the random selection of groups or areas. Examples of naturally occurring groups may include, school districts, schools, universities, classrooms, etc. The research list clusters and take samples from the list. Instead of sampling individual members, a random sample clusters are selected by the researcher. All subjects in the clusters may be used or the research an select to use samples from selected clusters (Drew, 1980; Mertens, 2009),

Convenience Sampling

Convenience samples are often biased. They do not represent everybody equally and may omit significant groups of people from the study (Kline, 2009). This approach is taken when the sample is convenient for the researcher to use, because of location, administrative endorsement, place and type of employment. A convenience sample is a group of subjects selected because of availability. There is not scientific way of generalizing findings from this sample to the population. Researchers using this sampling technique may yield different results. Convenience sampling is used in exploratory research where the researcher implies, the sample is selected because they are convenient. This non-probability method is often used during preliminary research efforts to get a gross estimate of the results, without incurring the cost or time required to select a random sample. (See Appendix I for additional sampling techniques).

Summary

According to Mertens (2009) choosing a sample depends upon characteristics of the population. Sampling strategies for quantitative research may take several forms, such probability, random, stratified, cluster or convenient, depending on the purpose of the research. These strategies will enable the researcher to select samples free of bias and representative of the population.

Choosing sampling strategies for qualitative research follow a non-probability approach in that no strategies are used to relate samples characteristics of the population. Qualitative sampling strategies may involve convenience, quota, judgment and snowball sampling. For a detail analysis of these qualitative sampling strategies refer to Gall, Borg & Gall (1996).

Research Exercise

1. Distinguish between a sample and a population.
2. Why is it important to define the population?
3. Specify and give examples of probability and nonprobability sampling.
4. Give an example of stratified random sampling.
5. Discuss cluster sampling.
6. What are some disadvantages of using convenience sampling techniques?
7. Discuss ways that sampling may be biased.
S. Give examples of a research project using random and stratified sampling.

References

Crewell, *J. W. (2009). Research design: Qualitative, quantitative, and mixed methods approaches.* Los Angeles, CA: Sage.

Drew, C. J. (1980). *Introduction to designing and conducting research.*St. Louis: The Mosby Company.

Dyba, T., Kampenes, V.B., & Sjoberg, D. I.K. (2006). A systematic *Review of* statistical power in software engineering experiments. *Information andSoftware Technology, 48, 745*755.

Gall, M. D., Borg, W. It., & Gall, J. P. (1996). *Educational research: An Introduction.* White Plains, NY: Longman.

Grisson, R. J., & Kim, J. J. (2005). *Effect sizes for research: A broad practical approach.* Mahwah, NJ: Erbaum.

Keppel, G. (1991). *Design and analysis: A researcher's handbook (3^{d} ed.).*Englewood Cliffs, NJ: Prentice Hal.

Kline, R. B. (2009). *Becoming a behavioral science researcher.* New York: The Guilford Press.

Mertens, D, M. (2009). *Transformative research and evaluation.* New York: The Guilford Press.

Taylor, G. R. (2005). *Integrating quantitative and qualitative methods* in research. (2nd ed.). Lanham, MD: University Press of America.

Chapter Thirteen
Inferential Statistics
George R. Taylor, Ph.D.
Theresa L. Harris, Ph.D.
Kriesta L. Watson, Ed.D.

INTRODUCTION

When using inferential statistics, the researchers are attempting to draw conclusions from data yielded by the sample which characterizes the population. Additionally, data generated is used to make judgments about the probability that an observed difference between groups may have occurred, by chance. The purpose of this chapter is to give an overview of commonly used statistical tools and to provide directions for the researcher to complete some simple inferential statistical procedures. For the more advanced researcher seeking detailed information on inferential statistical procedures, we have listed some comprehensive references to consult at the end of this chapter. McMillan (1996) has summarized some excellent strategies to employ in evaluating inferential statistics.

Inferential statistics are designed to estimate from a sample what is true for a population and whether or not the obtained results are different from chance occurrences. Appropriate sampling techniques are critical if we are to make valid judgments about the population in which the sample is drawn (Drew, 1980; McMillan, 1996, Healy 2009). There are adequate textbooks devoted to sampling techniques to employ.

Sample selection is essential in conducting research. Many studies do not meet significant levels because of inadequate or poor sampling techniques. Samples should be matched as closely as possible on all traits and as closely representative of the population to ensure that its measurement or analysis produces the same results we would get if we measured or analyzed the total population (Guilford, 1965). According to Elmore and Woehlka (1997) "Representativeness is the idea goal in sampling, but we now know if we have attained it if we knew what the population looked like, so that we could recognize a representative sample, we would not need to draw a sample in the first place" (p. 125). The various types of sampling technique are summarized below.

Convenience Samples

The research has no control over the number and types of samples used. Frequently, researchers are told that a select group by an institution or agency is all that they may be involved, either the research accepts or must seek sample elsewhere (Minimum, 1993). This type of sample selection cannot be used to make probability statements or generalize about the study, because random or stratified techniques cannot be used.

Probability Samples

Probability samples include several basic types, simple random, stratified, cluster, and systematic. Each type denotes that every individual in the population has an equal chance of being selected, as well as making valid decisions relative to the investigation.

Simple Random Samples

This is one of the basic samples used in research. Frequently a list is obtained from all individuals in a population. A number is assigned to each individual or a table of random numbers and physical and a physical mixing process may be used (Harris, 1995). The researcher randomly selects a sample from the population, thus each individual has an equal chance of being selected. A list of the total population is needed.

Stratified Random Samples

In a stratified sample, all individuals of the population are grouped or categorized into groups based upon common characteristics. When individuals are selected from each group or stratum the process is referred to as disproportional stratified random sampling, when samples are selected based upon their frequencies in the population, the process is referred to as proportional stratified random sampling.

The research must use extreme caution in selecting sample size (Jaeger, 1984). Samples that are too small may fail to detect true differences in the population means; samples that are too large may detect differences in population means that are so small that they are of no practical significance. For example, suppose a researcher wants to study how a preparatory course for 1st and 2nd year teachers impacts their test scores on the PRAXIS (National Teacher's Examination). If the researcher is trying to determine course effectiveness, the teachers should first be stratified into at least three to four groups; 1st year/1st-time test takers as opposed to 1st year/2nd-time test takers, etc. From each group, a number of teachers would be selected that reflects the proportion of the total population of new teachers. In other words, if a total sample size of 100 is to be used, 25 would be randomly selected from each group. If stratified sampling is not used in such a case, the result might be that the samples do not reflect accurately the proportion of teachers in the total new teacher population.

Cluster Samples

When employing this sampling technique, the researcher divides the population into heterogeneous clusters or groups such as universities, elementary grades, community programs, polling places, and police precincts are but a few examples. From selected clusters in the population, the researcher draws samples. A population is not necessary when using clusters; however, the researcher has limited control over sample size.

Systematic Samples

This sampling technique is similar to the strategies employed in cluster sampling. All individuals in the population are arranged in some logical order, such as age, weight, height, intelligence, or achievement levels. A list of random numbers may be used to select the samples needed as well as the sample size. The researcher has close control over the sample type, size, and design.

Sample Design

The type of sampling technique chosen will depend upon certain factors such as the objectives, purposes, design of the study, hypotheses to be tested, and the use of the findings. In all cases, the researcher should:

1.   Carefully consider the characteristics of the total population.
2.   Select some attribute or characteristic of the population to observe.
3.   Objectively select a sample based upon one of the standard techniques.
4.   Avoid biased sampling techniques.

Appropriate sample techniques assist in assuring that results obtained are reflective of the population-at-large, and indicate results from the study may be generated to the population. The results also point out that chance could not be reasonable for the results. Most researchers are attempting to show in their research that treatment, not chance, was responsible for the results (Drew, 1980).

Several types of sampling designs may be employed by the researcher to random select a sample from the population. Figure 13.1 display how a simple randomized design would look.

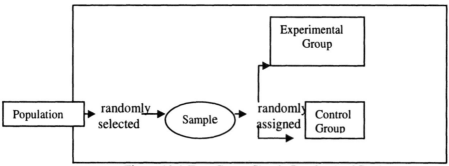

Figure 13:1 *Two-Group Simple Randomized Design*

It is clear from Figure 13.1 that the sample was randomly drawn from the population and randomly assigned to the experimental and control group. This process ensures that both groups have the sample characteristics, and that any differences in the groups can not be attributed to the selection process, but rather to the intervention imposed.

Difference Between Samples and Populations

1. Statisticians gather data from a sample. They use this information to make inferences about the population that the sample represents. Thus, sample and population are relative terms.
2. A population is a whole, and a sample is a fraction or segment of that whole.
3. A population is a collection of all the elements that are being studied and about which the researcher is trying to draw conclusions.
4. A sample is a collection of some, but not all, of the elements of the population; therefore, sampling means drawing from the target population.
5. A representative sample contains the relevant characteristics of the population in the same proportion as they are included in that population.

Conventional Symbols

Characteristics of a sample are called *statistics*. A sample of a population consists of n

observations with a mean of X (read X-bar). The measures that are computed for a sample are called statistics.

Characteristics of a population are called *parameters*. The mean of a population is symbolized by Φ, which is the Greek letter "mu." The number of elements in a population is denoted by the capital italic letter "N." Generally in statistics, Roman letters are used to symbolize sample information and Greek letters to symbolize population information. The role of probability is sampling is an integral part of the process.

The Role of Probability in Decision-Making

Statistics are used to objectively determine the change that sample phenomena will occur so that reasonable predictions based upon probability can be made. The probability of an event is the proportions of times that the event would occur if the changes for occurrence were infinite. In essence, if one had a coin with a head and tail side, what is the probability that we will get 50% for each side of the coin if we toss it 20 times? Each time we toss the coin the most like event 50% heads and tails, will not occur every time as expected. Data from this experiment can be placed in a frequency distribution table to determine where the cluster occurs and a means and standard deviation can be computed to statistically show the proportion of occurrences. (Refer to Appendix F for details in computing probabilities.)

The sample discussed clearly indicates that successive sample of observations will not necessary produce or give us the same proportion of a given observation. Solving problems in the social sciences following the strategies outlined for tossing coins. In the social sciences, outcomes are based on samples randomly drawn from the population in the hope of determining the likelihood of getting a particular sample outcome from the population. Probability deals with the prediction of a given events occurrence when using random selection criteria, the outcome of events can not be adequately predicted, however, probability statements will indicate what proportion of events will have given outcome.

Probability tests aid us in answering many questions, including those posed above, scientifically, rather than intuitively (Blaisdell, 1993). Other examples may include those posed above, flipping a coin and coming up heads 9 times out of 10; the coin came up 6 times heads, or 60 times out of 100. The researcher should attempt to ascertain whether or not chance is responsible for the results. In analyzing the data, the researcher should conclude that the coin with 6/10 heads when compared with 60/100 had a better chance of being fair. The coin with 6/10 had appeared 10% more frequently, thus it may be concluded that the 6/10 heads occurred more often than one would expect by chance. Intuition may provide some estimating of the coin fairness, but by applying the laws of probability, the researcher can come up with valid and reliable results.

Suppose a researcher wanted to determine if Native Americans are less intelligent than Hispanic Americans. He/she secures the IQ scores of 165 for 20 Native Americans and 106 for 25 Hispanic Americans. In analyzing the data, it appeared that any noted differences are due to *chance* because IQ tests do not give an accurate assessment of intelligence; especially when cultural factors are not considered. In order to reduce chance, a probability test should be employed.

If the probability of the results being caused by chance is low (95th confidence level or less), the difference will be statistically significant. In this case, the researcher is relatively safe to conclude that the differences obtained are results of the effectiveness of the treatment or intervention. In order to determine what the probability of chance is, a statistical tool must be applied. There are numerous statistical tools which the researcher can use in research. This is based upon the nature of the research, the research questions posed, the testable hypotheses, and the purpose and utility of the statistical tools (Dowdy & Wearden, 1991). We indicated in Chapter 4, the value of the review of the literature in this aspect.

Purpose of Inferential Statistics

The major purpose of inferential statistics is to test the null hypothesis by indicating the probability of rejecting or accepting the process for accepting or rejecting the null hypothesis is frequently referred to as the level of significance, which is presented with P (probability) or A (alpha). A $P<.05$ or greater is considered significant for the social sciences although $P<.01$ and $P<.001$ are frequently reported in the professional literature. Once the researcher states the criterion for rejecting the null hypothesis, he/she must also state how large the statistical test must be for rejection. In making a decision to accept or reject the null hypothesis, the researcher takes some risk of being incorrect. The lower the value, the greater the likelihood that the null hypothesis is false. Borg and Gall (1993) and Gail and Borg and Gall (1996) clarified the issue by stating that a P value of .001 indicates that it is much more likely that the null hypothesis is false than would a P value of .01. A P value of .001 indicates that a mean score difference as large as the obtained mean score difference would occur only once in 1,000 drawings of two samples from identical populations. A P value of .01 indicates that a mean score difference as large as the obtained mean score difference would occur only once in 100 drawings. If a researcher rejects the null hypothesis when, in fact, it is true, he has made what is called, a TYPE I error. On the other hand, if a researcher fails to reject the null hypothesis when it is in fact, *not* true, he has made a TYPE II error (Dowdy & Wearden, 1985). A parametric or non-parametric statistical test must be computed in order to arrive at a critical value to test hypotheses. The critical values from the statistical tests may result in the researcher making a TYPE I or TYPE II error as projected above.

Locate the Critical Value of the Statistical Test

Levels of significance must be set for the statistical test used to assess the hypothesis, as well as the degree of freedom associated with the test. The chosen level of significance is called the critical value. Critical value of a statistical test may be found in the appendices of most statistical texts.

Parametric and Non-Parametric Statistics

The major types of statistics used in inferential studies are parametric and non-parametric tests. Both techniques assist in determining whether the results obtained from the study are likely to be due to chance or to variables identified in the study. The techniques are frequently used in research that is conducted to investigate different questions or to determine if relationship exists among the variables. As indicated, there are numerous statistical tools the researcher may choose to test his/her research question or hypotheses. Selection depends upon many factors such as:

1. The Type of Instrument Being Used To Collect The Data;
2. The Size of the Sample Selected To Participate In the Study;
3. The Characteristics of the Population in Which the Sample Is Drawn;
4. The Classification of Data (Nominal, Ordinal, Interval/Ratio).

The selection of parametric or non-parametric statistics requires that the researcher make some assumptions relevant to the population in which the sample is drawn. If the assumptions are in correctly determined, the analyses will be in error. If assumptions cannot be accurately make about the population, then non-parametric statistics should be used. Non-parametric statistical procedures require fewer assumptions about the population than parametric statistics. We have summarized some selective criteria to use in selecting parametric or non-parametric statistical tests.

Non-parametric tests are often called "distribution-free," because they do not assume that the scores under analysis were drawn from normally distributed population. Consequently, many non-parametric are identified as "ranking tests." Test may be used with scores which yield no numerical value, are simply ranks- the median is used with non-parametric tests. In parametric tests, the mean is used and scores must be numerical. We have summarized below some selective criteria to use in selecting parametric or non-parametric tests.

Criteria for Choosing Parametric Statistical Tests (Dowdy & Wearden, 1985; Minimum, 1993; Harris, 1995):

1. The observations must be independent.(Selection of subjects and assigned scores must not be biased in the study or data.)
2. The observations must be drawn from normally distributed populations.
3. These populations must have the same variance.
4. The variables involved must have been measured in at least an interval scale.
5. The means of these normal (and homocedastic) populations must be linear combinations.
6. The effects must be addictive.

Criteria for Choosing Non-Parametric Statistical Tests (Siegel, 1956):

1. Probability statements obtained from most non-parametric statistical tests are exact probabilities. The accuracy of the probability statement does not depend upon the shape of the population.
2. If the sample size as small as N=6 are used, then there is no alternative to using a non-parametric statistical test.
3. There are suitable non-parametric statistical tests for treating samples made up of observations from several populations.
4. Non-parametric statistical tests are available to treat data which are in ranks.

Disadvantages of Non-Parametric Statistical Tests:

1. Wasteful if the requirements for parametric tests are met.
2. There are non-parametric tests for testing interactions.

Research Exercise 9

1. If one investigator uses a .05 level of significance in investigating this question and another investigator uses a .001 level of significance, which would be more likely to make a TYPE II error?
2. Distinguish between research hypotheses and a null hypothesis.
3. How does one determine the level of significance to use in an experiment?
   A cigar manufacturer employed a group of researchers to compare the rate of occurrence of lung cancer among smokers and non-smokers. Considering the results of previous research on this question, the manufacturer would probable urge the researchers to be especially careful to avoid making a:
   a.   TYPE I error.
   b.   TYPE II error.
4. If a researcher tosses a group of five pennies, what is the probability of him getting:
   a. Five tails.
   b. Three heads, two tails.
   c. Two heads, three tails.
5. What factors should be considered when selecting a Parametric or a non-parametric statistical test. Justify your choice.
6. How would a researcher select an appropriate sample technique?

References

Blaisdell, E. A. (1993). *Statistics In Practice.* New York: Sanders College Publishing.

Borg, W. R., Gall, J., & Gall, M. D. (1993). *Applying Educational Research: A practical guide(3rd ed.).* New York: Longman Publishing Company.

Dowdy, S., & Wearden, S. (1985). *Statistics for Research.* New York: John Wiley & Sons.

Drew, C. J. (1980). *Introduction to Designing and Conducting Research.* St. Louis: The C.V. Mosby Company.

Gall, M. D., Borg, W. R., Gall, & J. P. (1996). *Educational Research: An Introduction (6th ed.).* New York: Longman Publishing Company.

Gravetter, F., & Wallnau, L. B. (1996). *Statistics for the Behavioral Sciences (4th ed.)* New York: West Publishing Company.

Guilford, J.P. (1965). *Fundamental Statistics in Psychology and Education.* New York: McGraw Hill Book Company.

Harris, M. B. (1995). *Basic Statistics for Behavioral Science Research.* Boston: Allyn and Bacon.

Healey, Joseph F. (2009) *The Essentials of Statistics: A Tool for Social Research.* Macmillan Publishing Company.

Hinkle, Denise E., Wiersma, William, & Jurs, Stephen G. (1994). *Applied Statistics for the Behavioral Sciences (3rd ed.).* Boston: Houghton Mifflin Company.

Jaeger, R. M. (1984). Sampling in education and the social sciences. New York: Longman Publishing Company.

McMillan, J. H. (1996). Educational research: Fundamentals for the consumer (2nd ed.). New York: Harper Collins College Publishers.

Minimum, E. W. et al. (1993). *Statistical Reasoning in Psychology and Education.* New York: John Wiley & Sons.

Siegel, S. (1956). *Non-Parametric Statistics for the Behavioral Sciences.* New York: McGraw-Hill Book Company.

Chapter Fourteen
Major Similarities and Differences Between Two Paradigms
George R. Taylor, Ph.D.
Michael Trumbull, Ph.D.
Kriesta L. Watson, Ed.D.

INTRODUCTION

Both quantitative and qualitative research have similarities and differences. However, they are more similar than different in that problems are defined in both approaches; research questions or hypotheses are stated, methods and procedures and analysis of data are developed. Theory is used in both approaches although different strategies are employed. Quantitative research *tests* theories whereas qualitative research *develops* theories. The deductive method is used in quantitative research while the inductive method is used in qualitative research (Taylor, 2002, 2005).

Generally, quantitative methods are *ob*jective and reliable and can be generalized to a large population. Conversely, qualitative methods are *sub*jective and generate rich, detailed and valid data (Steckler, 1992). Qualitative procedures generally include personality variables such as, attitudes, feelings, and emotions. In quantitative research, these factors are frequently missing (Dereshiwsky, 1992).

Similarities and Differences

Quantitative research is designed to provide objective descriptions of phenomena and to demonstrate how phenomena can be controlled through specific treatments. On the other hand, qualitative research is designed to develop understanding of individuals in their natural environments that cannot be objectively verified. Researchers using quantitative research methods make assumptions that findings will be based upon existing laws and principles. It is believed that these assumptions will lead to accurate predications. In contrast, researchers employing qualitative methods also draw certain assumptions, however, their assumptions are based upon the individuals uniqueness and cultures. No value judgment is formed until all data have been analyzed. Findings may be replicated, but they may lose validity from study to study.

In quantitative research, the researcher is objective measurements are taken through instrumentations rather than through human judgment. Attempts are made to keep personal values and philosophies from influencing the process. They have minimum contacts with the subjects. Qualitative research is different in that this method endores using human judgment in coding, rating interventions, and observations. Procedures are designed so that the researcher will have direct contact with the subjects. The researcher may become a participant in the study. Subjectivity is practiced and encouraged, values are perceived differently in the two methods. Quantitative researchers attempts to keep their personal values out of the experiment and reject making value judgments about subjects participating in the study. Qualitative researchers' opinions are opposite to this view. They support the notion that all research is value-laden, and attempts to incorporate values that often include their own into the research (Barbour, 2007; Creswell, 2002).

Another issue involving the two designs is in the area of context. Quantitative researchers prefer to study phenomena by dividing the variables into parts, examining and analyzing selected variables, and determine the interrelationships among them. Qualitative researchers prefer to look at phenomena as a total and complete context; the whole, rather than the part method is advocated. In the area of data analysis, quantitative research relies upon numerical data which is used to perform various statistical procedures to analyze data. In contrast, qualitative research relies upon narrative descriptions which are categorized to analyze data (Borg, Gall & Gall, 1993; Guba, 1991). Refer to Figure 13.1 for additional details as well as Chapters 5 and 6 for basic understanding and information on the two methods.

Either or both research method outlined may be employed by the researcher depending upon the following use:

1. Quantitative methods if clarity , reliability, and validity are sought.
2. Qualitative methods, if richness, complexity, and data which can not be translated into numerical scales.

The   researcher   should   not   conclude   that   one method is
superior to the other, that quantitative methods are more scientific than qualitative methods, or that qualitative methods are easy to apply. This issue is reflected through the chapter.

Quantitative	Qualitative
1. Representative sample. Based on central limit theorem.	1. Small sample; not representative, idiosyncratic.
2. Literature review at the beginning of the study.	2. Literature review at the end of the study.
3. Data collected through instruments based upon precisely defined variables.	3. Emphasizes organizing, coordinating, and synthesizing large quantities of data.
4. Objective control for bias replicable and reliable.	4. Subjective strive for personal data, value laden.
5. Deductive in nature.	5. Inductive in nature.
6. Test theories.	6. Develop theories.
7. Develop conclusion based upon data outcome oriented.	7. Develop values and judgment based upon data-process oriented.
8. Clarity based upon interpreting numerical data.	8. Complex and rich experiences; void of most numerical data.
9. Known reliability and validity.	9. Unknown reliability and validity.
10. Standardized measuring devices.	10. Non-standard measuring devices.
11. Intervention; no participant involvement.	11. Participant involvement.
12. Adhere to the scientific method used HO + HA to accept, reject, prove, or disprove hypotheses.	12. Does not follow the scientific method step-by-step, seeks meaning or essence.
13. Numerical data.	13. Narrative data - words to describe the complexity.
14. Controlled - laboratory setting.	14. Conducted in the natural environment - 90 to the co-researcher's world.
Quantitative	Qualitative
15. Various instruments are used.	15. Principally use observations and interviews.

16. Based upon facts , causes and relation shifts.	16. Based upon understanding, meanings and essences of the human experience.
17. Short duration.	17. Long duration.
18. Separate, a study component parts (reductionistic).	18. Together , tries to understanding the whole.
19. Descriptions based upon numerical data.	19. Rich narrative descriptions.
20. Subjects.	20. Participants, co-researchers.
21. Conducted using known measurements, techniques, and formulas.	21. Measurements frequently not known, researcher
22. Descriptions of human behavior cannot always be expressed in numbers.	22. Human behaviors can be accurately described in words.
23. Assumes stable reality (static).	23. Assumes a dynamic reality.
24. Verification oriented.	24. Discovery oriented.
25. Validate themes and relationships.	25. Discover themes and relationships.
26. Assume an objective reality.	26. Assume that social reality is constructed by participants.
27. Analyze social reality through variables.	27. Make holistic observations of the total context within which social action occurs.
28. Use statistical methods to analyze data.	28. Use analytic induction to analyze data.
29. Use statistical inferences procedures to generalize findings from a sample to a defined population.	29. Generalize case findings by searching for other similarities.
30. Study populations or samples that represent populations.	30. Study cases.

Figure 14.1: Similarities and Differences Between Quantitative and Qualitative Research Methods

Date in Figure 14.1 were derived from viewing the following sources: (1) Meredith D. Gall, Walter R. Borg, & Joyce, P. Gall (1996). Educational Research (6th ed.). White Plan, NY: Longman Publishers, (2) B. J. Biddle & D. S. Anderson. (1986). Theory, Methods, Knowledge, and Research on Teaching. In M. C. Wittrock (Ed.). J. W. Creswell (2002). Research design: Qualitative Qnantitative, and Mixed methods Approaches (2nd ed.) Thousand Oaks, CA: Sage Publishers, P. D. Leedy and J. E. Ormrod (2000). Practical research planning and design (8th ed.). upper Saddle River, NJ: Prentice-Hall, L. R. Gay & P. Airasianp. (2003). Educational research: Competencies for analysis and applications (7h ed.) Upper Saddle River, NJ: Prentice hall, c. L. Jackson and G. R. Taylor (2007). Demystifying research: A primer for novice researchers. The Netherlands, Sense Publishers,Handbook of Research on Teaching (3rd ed.). New York, Macmillan, and (3) Michael A. Patton. (2002). Qualitative Research and Evaluation Methods. New York: Sage Publishers., (4) G. Shank. (1993). Qualitative Research? Quantitative Research? What's the Problem? Resolving the Dilemma via a Post Constructivist Approach. Presented at the Association for Educational Communication and Technology Convention. ED 362202.

Part vs Whole Approach

Quantitative researchers employ the part method. Their views are premised upon the concept that complex factors or questions can be broken down into component parts or variables and be studied, by the researcher selecting the variables he/she wishes to study. A research design is usually developed with an experimental and a control group. The experimental group under study are exposed to the identified variables. Outcomes are based upon the comparison of the group involved.

In using qualitative research methods, the reverse is evident when compared to quantitative research methods. In qualitative study the whole method is employed, all attributes of the subjects are of interest to the researcher. Data gathering procedures are expedited through observations, interviews, and tape recordings. Those data sources constitute the information needed to analyze the data by identifying categories and themes, which will provide detail information on subjects studied.

Value Laden

The quantitative researcher views values differently than the qualitative researcher in that he/she place little weight on values. Whatever values are reflected in investigations are reflected in instruments constructed by researchers. Strategies for determining perceptions toward subjects values are not deemed important (Taylor 2000, 2005).

The above view is not supported by qualitative researchers. They support the notion that all research is value-laden and attempt to incorporate their personal values concern the phenomena under study, as well as controlling making value judgments, about subjects in the study.

Subject Selection

When using quantitative research methods, the researcher assumes that he/she can discover laws that can control social and educational condition in society. It is believed that appropriate and random sample technique and assigning subjects to the experimental and control group will ensure that phenomena are control and that valid predictions can be made.

In using qualitative research methods, the researcher does not employ random selection techniques. It is assumed that each individual is unique. Rather than study groups, as required in quantitative research, the qualitative researcher studies the uniqueness of the individual through techniques such as observations, interviews, and case studies.

Contact with Subjects

The major intent of quantitative research is to be objective by not permitting their personal bias to influence how they will analyze data. Instruments and data gathering procedures are designed to limit the amount of personal contacts with subjects. Attempts are made to standardized all data gathering instruments. Subjects are not required to give their personal reactions concerning the instruments. All procedures associated with the above procedures are designed to limited personal contact between subjects and researchers.

Techniques in qualitative research permits the researcher to interacts directly with each individual in the study. Data are modified, adapted, and change based upon the reactions of the subjects. The research has the flexible to change or modify data sources based upon his/her judgment. Subjects are encouraged to provide ideas and participate in all aspects of the investigation, including data analysis. In quantitative research, interaction with subjects, modifying instruments, and having subjects to participate in data analysis are not practiced (Spradley, 1980).

Data Gathering Procedures

Most data in quantitative research is numerical and can be statistically treated. Data may be analyzed by the use of hand and calculator as well as computers. There are several computer software programs which may be used to analyze the data. We have addressed this issue in Chapter 3.

Instruments used in quantitative research are usually administered under standardized conditions. Procedures for scoring instruments are also uniformed. The step reduces and minimize the researcher's bias in selecting, administering, and scoring instruments.

Procedures using in gathering data for qualitative research methods are conducted differently than those used in qualitative research methods. Data sources comprise mostly of observations and interviews, which are converted to verbal and narrative descriptions.
These descriptions are transferred to categories and themes, and used to analyze the data.

Choosing Between the Two Paradigms

Researchers should carefully consider the types of research they wish to conduct. (Refer to Figure 14.1 for various types of qualitative research methods.) If they are seeking to show the richness and complexity of the human condition, they may want to employ qualitative measures. Consequently, if reliability and validity are sought in analyzing the human condition, quantitative methods may be used (see Chapter 5). We support the notion that a skilled researcher should combine the two methods to further provide data to accept or reject their research findings. The following research project demonstrates how both quantitative and qualitative methods may be used:

> A researcher at University "X" designed a study to investigate the reasons for high suicide rates among adolescents. A survey was constructed and administrated. Data were tabulated and analyzed (quantitative methods). Although data yielded from both methods were revealing, quantitative data simply could not show the deep emotions projected by the adolescents. In this case, qualitative methods would be the better choice.

Again, the reader should exercise caution and examine both methods and choose the method which will best meet the purpose and objectives of the study. In many cases, both methods may be combined. We have addressed this issue in greater detail in Chapter 18.

Action Research	Focus Group Research
Case Study	Grounded Theory
Clinical Research	Hermeneutics
Cognitive Anthropology	Heuristic Research
Collaborative Inquiry	Holistic Ethnography
Content Analysis	Imaginal Psychology
Dialogical Research	Intensive Research
Conversation Analysis	Interpretive Evaluation
Delphi Study	Interpretive Interaction
Descriptive Research	Interpretive Human Studies
Direct Research	Life History Study
Discourse Analysis	Naturalistic Inquiry
Document Study	Oral History
Ecological Psychology	Panel Research
Educational Connoisseurship	Participative Observation
& Criticism	
Educational Ethnography	Participative Research
Ethnographic Content Analysis	Phenomenography
Ethnography	Phenomenolog
Ethnography of Communication	Qualitative Evaluation
Ethnomethodolgy	Structural Ethnography
Ethnoscience	Symbolic Interaction
Experimental Psychology	Transcendental Realism
Field Study	Transformative Research

Figure 14.2 *Quantitative and Qualitative Research Methods and Inquiry*
Source: Adapted from Tesch (1990). Qualitative Research: Analysis, types, and software tools. Bristol, PA: Falmer

Examples of four of the above:

A.   Ethnographies - studying culture.

B.   Ground Theory - generating and building theory.

C.   Case Studies - collecting, organizing, analyzing in-depth information or a phenomena.

D.   Phenomenological Studies - studying lived experiences.

Each qualitative study is individually designed. Methods and procedures are developed by the researcher that will best elucidate the research question.

Many of these qualitative methods are outside of the scope of this text. The reader is referred to: Michael Q. Patton. (2002). Qualitative Research and Evaluation Method (3rd. ed.). Thousand Oaks, CA: Sage Publications. For specific applications of qualitative strategies, see George R. Taylor. (2000, 2005). Quantitative and Qualitative Research Methods. Laurel, MD: University Press.

Both paradigms use the review of the literature extensively. The qualitative researcher usually places research at the end of the study. This approach is used in order to not influence the researcher with the interpretation of the data and the development of theory. The quantitative researcher is concerned with testing theory, therefore, the review of the literature precedes the experimental conditions. The review of the literature is extensive and an integral part of the study in quantitative research. In qualitative research, the review of the literature may have little impact upon the study's outcome, and is usually completed at the end of the investigation.

Researchers in qualitative research collect large amounts of data using non-standardized instruments. These data are classified and synthesized based upon themes and categories. Data collection are more intense and continuous. The quantitative researcher validates theme and categories and develops or uses standardized instruments to collect data on narrowly defined variables (Biddler & Anderson, 1986). The amount of data collected is limited by the number of instruments developed to collect data on pre-determined variables.

The absences of experiments' conditions tend to make qualitative research more subjective than quantitative research. The inductive method is an essential in qualitative research; the research is value-laden. On the other hand, quantitative research employs the deductive method and is value-free. Qualitative research develops theories based upon research findings, whereas quantitative research tests theory. Validity and reliability are not essential in qualitative research. In quantitative research, validity and reliability must be established prior to the study. The qualitative researcher is involved with participants in the study as a co-researcher or an active participant. This approach is not condoned in quantitative research. The researcher remains independent of participants' involvement. It is not commonly agreed that both quantitative and qualitative data can be successfully employed and used equally in research. Quantitative methods may be used to support qualitative studies and qualitative data may be used to verify quantitative data using a process called the multi-method approach (Cook, 1995; Patton, 1990; Dennis, 1994; Steckler, 1992; Dereshiwsky & Packard, 1992). (Refer to Chapter 18 for specifics in using the above approach.)

The type of approach selected will largely depend upon what the researcher is attempting to discover. Both approaches will yield data that may be used to validate hypotheses or research questions. In both approaches, the research must be well designed to yield significant results (Kitoa, 1991; Cooper, 1993). Systematical procedures must be employed in the collection and analysis of data regardless of the method used. Qualitative research may be used to develop theory for quantitative research, and believed to be incompatible to quantitative research because it is based on different theoretical assumptions and models (Stoynoff, 1990; Gall, Borg, & Gall, 1996).

Criteria for Choosing An Appropriate Research Design/Paradigm

Creswell (1994, 2002) outlined five criteria to consider when selecting a quantitative or a qualitative design/paradigm:

1	Researcher's world view;
2	Training and experience of the researcher;
3	Researcher's psychological attributes;
4.	Nature of the problem; and
5.	Audience for the study.

He stated that "...the researchers world view deals with how an individual views reality; subjectively or objectively." Subjective researchers would endorse the qualitative design, while objective researchers would accept the quantitative design. The nature and type of training received by researchers are important. Qualitative researchers need excellent communications and analytical skills.

Quantitative researchers will need to be versed in instrument selection and construction, data analysis, and statistical techniques. Psychological attributes are important for both designs, however, the qualitative researcher must frequently work in the absence of structure and guidelines; procedures are systematically outlined for the quantitative researcher. Nature of the problem must be carefully considered by both researchers. The qualitative researcher is concerned with building theory; the quantitative researcher is concerned with testing theory. The audience for the study will greatly impact the method employed. Determination of the audience's view, objective or subjective, will need to be assessed (Taylor, 2005).

Summary

Similarities and differences can be readily seen when reviewing the two paradigms. Quantitative and qualitative research methods have different purposes for sample selection, data collection, procedures, intervention, and analyzing data. The qualitative researcher studies participants in their natural habitat. His/her view is subjective due to the small number of subjects selected. On the other hand, the quantitative researcher is objective and attempts to control phenomena through intervention. Individuals are studied in all environments (Cary, 1988).

Both methods have advantages and disadvantages as articulated throughout this chapter. There is a move to combine the two approaches by using and collecting both types of data. Qualitative data may be combined and integrated with quantitative data. This process is referred to as triangulation. A survey, questionnaire, interview schedule, or observation form may be modified to be used with quantitative or qualitative methods or procedures. The two approaches may complement each other, or they may not be based upon what phenomenon is being assessed (Shapiro, 1973; Tashakkori & Teddler, 1998). Qualitative data are used for generating hypotheses, or describing process, on the other hand quantitative data are used to analyze outcomes, or verify hypotheses. We have indicated the value of using this approach earlier in the chapter. In essence, our view is that the human condition is too complex to be regulated to one approach and in some instances, the qualitative approach will best serve the purpose; on the other hand, quantitative approaches will best serve the purpose. The skilled researcher can draw the best from both approaches and combine them. Researchers should not assume that one approach is superior to the other, or that qualitative data are easier to use. If the two approaches are scientifically conducted, they are equally difficult to construct and administer.

Research Exercise for Chapter 17

1. Using the data in Figure 14.1, develop your own table of similarities and differences between quantitative and qualitative research methods based upon a research project you wish to conduct. Be sure to summarize the research project you wish to investigate.

2.   Using the same research project outlined in #1 above, indicate how you would combine quantitative and qualitative methods in conducting the research. You may also refer to Chapters 8 and 10 for additional information to assist you.

3.   Develop a research design employing both quantitative and qualitative methods.

4.   What strategies would you employ in selecting a research method. Consider both quantitative and qualitative approaches.

References

Barbour, R. *(2007). Introduction qualitative research: A student's guide to the craft of doing qualitative research.* Thousand Oaks, CA: Sage

Biddle, B. J., & Anderson, D. S. (1986). Theory, methods, knowledge, and research on teaching. In M. C. Wittrock (Ed.). *Handbook on research on teaching* (3rd ed.). New York: MacMillan.

Borg,W.R., Gall, J., & Gall, M. (1993). *Applying Educational Research: A Practical Guide* (3rd ed.). New York: Longman Publishing Company.

Cary, R. (1988). *A general survey of qualitative research methodology.* ERIC Publication ED 30448.

Cook, T. D. (1995). *Evaluation Lessons Learned.* Plenary keynote address of the International Evaluation Conference. Vancouver, British Columbia.

Cooper, P. W. (1993). *Field relations and the problem of authenticity in researching participants perceptions of teaching and learning in classrooms.* British Educational Research Journal, *19,* 4, 323-338.

Creswell, J. W. (2002). *Research design: Qualitative, Quantitative, and Mixed methods approaches* (2nd ed.). Thousand Oaks, CA: Sage.

Dennis, M. L. (1994). *Integrating qualitative and Quantitative evaluation methods in substance abuse research.* Evaluation and Program Planning, *17,* 4, 419-427.

Dereshiwsky, M. I., & Packard, R. D. (1992). *When words are worth more than a thousand number: The power of qualitative research procedures in evaluating the impact of educational programs and practices.* Paper presented at the annual meeting of the National Council of States, San Diego, CA:ED 362499.

Gay, L. R., & Airsian, P. (2003). *Educational research: Comparencies for analysis and applications.* (7th ed.). Upper Saddle, NJ: Merrill Prentice Hall.

Guba, E. G. (1981). Criteria for assessing the trustworthiness of naturalistic inquiries. *Educational Communication and Technology Journal, 29,* 75-91, as cited in Owens (1982). Methodological perspective: Methodological rigor in natuarlistic inquiry: Some issues and answers. *Educational Administartive Quarterly, 18* (2), 1-21.

Jackson, C. L., & Taylor, G. R. (2007). *Demystfying research: A primer for novice researchers.* The Netherlands, Sense publishers.

Kitao, K. S. (1991). *Principles of quantitative research.* RIEN.ED 333755, pp.1-22.

Leedy, P. D., & Ormrod, J. E. (2004). Practical research planning and desing (8th ed.). Upper Saddle River NJ: Prentice hall.

Patton, M. Q. (1990). *Qualitative evaluations and research methods.* Newbury Park, CA: Sage Publications.

Patton, M. Q. (2002). *Qualitative research and evaluation methods.* Thousand Oaks, CA: Sage Publications.

Shank, G. (1993). *Qualitative research? Quantitative research? What's the problem? Resolving the dilemma via a post constructivist approach approach.* Presented at the Association for Educational Communication and Technology Convention. ED 362202.

Spradley, J. P. (1980). *Participant observation.* Fort Worth, TX: Harcourt Brace.

Steckler, A. (1992). Toward integrating qualitative and quantitative methods: An introduction. *Health Education Quarterly, 19*, 1, 1-8.

Stoynoff, S. J. (1990). English language proficiency and study strategies as determinants of academic success for international studies in U. S. universities. *Dissertation Abstracts International, 52* (01), 97A.

Taylor, G. R. (2000). *Integrating quantitative and qualitative methods in research*. Lanham, MD: University Press of America, Inc.

Taylor, G. R. (2005). *Integrating quantitative and qualitative methods in research*. Lanham, MD: University Press of America, Inc.

Tesch, R. (1990). Qualitative research: Analysis, types, and softwaretools. Bristol, PA: Falmer.

Weber, R. P. (1990). Basic content analysis. Newbury Park, CA:Sage Publications.

Chapter Fifteen
Developing A Multi-Faced Research Design/Paradigm
George R. Taylor, Ph.D.
Charity Welchi, Ph.D.

INTRODUCTION

The many unique research studies developed by students often do not meet research design/paradigms that have frequently been already constructed. This necessitates that the researcher develop his/her own design/paradigm for conducting research (Ary, 1995; Borg, Gall & Gall, 993; Leedy, 1993). Generally, research designs are constructed to give directions for conducting both quantitative and qualitative research. The design provides a framework for directing the research by indicating the breadth and limitations of the research. Research designs provide the blueprint for testing the study hypotheses. As with all blueprints, research designs do not specify exactly what to do, rather, indicate possible directions to take to successfully conduct the research.

All research starts and ends with observations. Some research is purely observational and others are both observational and manipulative. In observational research, the investigator systematically observes existing conditions. Manipulative data are associated with experimental designs. Some research designs emphasize the use of numerical data. They are called *quantitative* designs because they focus on quantities (numbers). Other research designs emphasize the analysis of complex data in terms of its content. Such designs are called *qualitative* research designs because they focus on the important qualifies and attributes of the materials being investigated (Patton, 2002).

The research design/paradigm developed in Figure 14.1 is descriptive/causal. The reader is referred to Chapter 14 to note the similarities and differences between Figures 14.1 and 15.1. The major difference is that Figure 14.1 is more theoretical in nature whereas, Figure 15.1 is the application of the theoretical concepts reflected in Figure 14.1. The research design/paradigm may provide some orderly and cohesive manner for conducting scientific and empirical research; whether the research is qualitative or quantitative is not an issue. Most designs/paradigms can be adapted for use with either type of research because all research follows a basic strategy designed to seek solutions to problems. A single research paradigm may be combined with both quantitative and qualitative methods. Creswell (1994) advocated three approaches that researchers may combine and they are as follows:

1. *The Two-Phase Design.* A quantitative and qualitative phase of the study is conducted separately. No attempt is made to connect the two phases.
2. *Dominant/Less-Dominant Design.* One of the designs (qualitative or quantitative) is chosen as the dominant approach. The other approach

is merely a small component. Procedures for choosing a dominant approach may raise questions for advocates of the less dominant design.

3. *Mixed-Methodology Design.* This is the most complex of all the designs. All of many aspects of methodological steps in both paradigms may be mixed.

Creswell and Clark (2007), indicated that researchers should consider the following factors in developing mixed-methods designs:

1. Comparability: Match the purpose, research focus, questions, and design.
2. Timing: Determine the temporal relationship between data collection for the two methods.
3. Weight: Establish priority of the qualitative and quantitative research in the study.
4. Mixing: Determine when quantitative and qualitative data will be mixed in the process of research.

This design represents the highest degree of mixing the two paradigms. The researcher would mix aspects of both designs as reflected in Figure 15.1. Additionally, Figure 15.1 reflects both the deductive (quantitative research) and inductive (qualitative research).

In using combined methods, the researcher has the options of using multiple data sources from both quantitative and qualitative methods. (Refer to Chapters 5 and 6, the process for combining data sources is referred to as triangulation. The term implies that any bias in data sources in either paradigm is reduced when used in conjunction with each other (Swanson, 1992; Jick, 1979; Patton, 2002; Creswell, 1994; Taylor, 2000). Data analyses, from both paradigms, can support the research process by showing the relationship of a principle being experimented.

For a comprehensive view of implementing the above strategies, the readers are referred to Creswell. We have attempted to emphasize the mixed-methodology design in Figure 15.1, however, the design in Figure 15.1 may be adapted to be used with the other two designs.

Quantitative	Qualitative
Observation	
Review of the Literature	
Selection of Problems	
Developing Research Questions and Hypotheses	
Validating Instruments	
Experimental Conditions	
	Narrative/Descriptive Analyses
Statistical Analyses	
	Constructing Theory
Testing Theory	
Results	

Figure 15.1: *Developing a Multi-Faced Research Design/Paradigm*

The research design/paradigm in Figure 15.1 reflects the mixed-methodology design. Lines connecting the two paradigms denote where the various methodology steps may be combined, infused, or integrated in the research process. As noted, the experimental conditions, validating instruments, statistical analysis, and testing theory, are not part of the qualitative method but are reserved for the quantitative method. Additionally, Figure 15.1 shows that narrative descriptions and analyses and constructing theories are not factors in the quantitative method. Data reflected in Figure 15.1 clearly show that most components in the paradigm can be interfaced or integrated. Methodology steps, observations, review of the literature, selection of problems, developing research questions (and sometimes hypotheses) and reporting results and findings, can be combined in a research project.

We also noted that the researchers may employ the two-phase design or the dominant/less-dominant design in using the paradigm projected in Figure 4. Again, our view is that the ;mixed-methodology design is the better design; premised upon the fact that we believe that using both methods can give support and validation to the research findings by using both deductive and inductive methods (Creswell,1994, 2003, 2007, and Onwuegbuzie (2003) recommended the following procedures to use in evaluating mixed methods research:

1. Select the research design.
2. Collect data.
3. Analyze the data.
4. Validate the data.
5. Interpret the data
6. Write the research report.

It is incumbent that the researcher clearly articulate in the beginning of the study how methods in the two paradigms will be used. Methods employed in this design may be labeled and reported separately under each of the paradigms. Interpretations from the two methods can be analyzed and conclusions drawn relevant to how findings from the two methods support or oppose each other.

Throughout the text, we have attempted to emphasize the similarities and differences between quantitative and qualitative research methods. Figure 15.1 clearly shows this relationship. Both methods employ observations. The review of the literature is used differently. Usually in qualitative research, the review of the literature comes at the end of the study so that the results will not be biased. Conversely, in quantitative research, the review is completed at the beginning of the study to determine if similar results can be found, and to test the theory as reflected in the professional literature. Selection and identification of the problem is necessary in both paradigms. Qualitative research does not have to employ the same rigor as quantitative research.

Generally, qualitative research methods do not include hypotheses. They frequently use research questions. Quantitative research may also use research questions and hypotheses, however, if methods nor procedures are being validated, hypotheses are recommended. Experimental conditions such as samples selection, treatment or intervention and statistical treatment of data are not required in qualitative research since numerical data are not needed.

Both methods use theory. There are differences in the use of theory as reflected in Figure 15.1 and the narrative description. Both research methods report on results and findings. The model is designed to show the importance of the review of literature for using either the quantitative or qualitative research method. Differences have been highlighted in the following narrative description.

Observations. The research design/paradigm begins with observations. Observations provide the initial approach to begin scientific inquiry in both quantitative and qualitative research design/paradigms. Mertens (2009) contends that observations can be conducted formally and informally. They can be made by using field notes or checklists based upon specific criteria outlined to collect information. Patton (2002) has provided an elaborated list to observe in observations. They include:

1. Program settings.
2. Human and social environments
3. Program activities and human or subjects behaviors
4. Informal or formal interactions.
5. Native language.
6. No verbal communications.
7. Unobstrusive measures.
8. Observing what does not happen

For a detailed of the listed activities, refer to Patton (2002).

Review of the Literature. Reviewing the literature is important in both quantitative and qualitative research. The use of the review of the literature have different purposes when using the two methods. In quantitative research, the review precedes the experimental conditions; in qualitative research, the review is conducted after the study has been completed. The researcher using the qualitative method may find minimal use of the review since he/she will be constructing theories; there may not be current research on the topic. The quantitative researcher would use the review liberally, since he/she will be testing theory based upon current models and research findings. In quantitative research, the review of literature will enable the researcher to use it inductively so that the researcher's review will not have a significant impact upon the question(s) being posed. In quantitative research, the review of the literature is used deductively, where the researcher is drawing from general principles and theories in the field in developing and conducting his/her research. We have reserved Chapters 2 and 3 to discuss various techniques for reviewing the literature.

Identification, Selection, and Statement of the Problem. Identification, selection, and statement of the problem are frequently minimized by the researcher in both quantitative and qualitative research. These areas must be carefully considered and weighted against such factors as:

1. Values and needs of the study;
2. Prospects of making a contribution to the field;
3. Training and experience of the researcher;
4. Availability of human and physical resources to conduct the study;
5. Interest and motivation in the study;
6. Use of expert advice in identifying and selecting the problem; and
7. Attended audiences for the study.

A systematical and detailed investigation of the above factors will assist the researcher in determining the feasibility of pursuing the problem in greater depth, or to change and modify procedures.

Development of Testable Hypotheses and Research Questions

Once the research topic has been selected and the problem formulated, the next step is to develop testable research questions or hypotheses to scientifically guide the study (Gonzalez, 2009). In quantitative research, questions and hypotheses are *developed* to test theory whereas in qualitative research, questions and hypotheses are *designed* to test theory. Researchers may employ a variety of techniques in developing research questions or hypotheses for the two paradigms. In quantitative methods, various types of hypotheses may be used. The null and alternative hypotheses are frequently used. In qualitative methods, research questions are most frequently used (Taylor 2005).

Validating and Establishing Reliability of Instruments

The use of validated instruments are required and necessary in conducting quantitative research. It is not a prerequisite for conducting qualitative research. In conducting quantitative research, many researchers choose standardized instruments in which validity and reliability have already been established. When a researcher constructs his/her own instrument, validity and reliability will need to be established. Creswell (1994, 2003 & Creswell & Plano, 2007) provides an excellent approach to validating and establishing reliability for instruments.

Experimental Conditions

An essential part of quantitative research is the experimental conditions, sometimes referred to as the *intervention* or *treatment*. This aspect closely follows the scientific method. Variables are systematically identified and controlled. Subjects are randomly selected and matched in the experimental and control groups, and performances of the two groups are compared at the end of the experiment. In qualitative research, experimental conditions are not employed. As indicated in Figure 17, the experimental conditions are not required. By deleting the experimental conditions, researchers may readily use the research design to conduct qualitative research.

Statistical Analysis

Various statistical tools to test data quantitatively may be explored. Both parametric, and non-parametric statistics may be used to test hypotheses. Various methods and procedures for testing different types of experimental designs may be selected based upon sampling, instruments and experimental conditions. Statistical analysis is limited in qualitative research. Some descriptive statistics may be used, i.e., graphs, charts, percentages, and measures of central tendency; however, descriptive analysis (as shown below) is the most frequently used technique.

Descriptive Analysis

Descriptive analysis may be used in both designs such as graphs, mean scores, percentiles, and correlations. Generally, researchers categorize and develop themes when using qualitative methods. The themes provide narrative descriptions of the behaviors. The process can be completely void of numerical data. Numerical data may add to the understanding and the interpretation of the research questions or hypotheses under study. Quantitative research has more structure and narrative interpretations are limited. Observations and interviews are used in both designs. In quantitative research, descriptive and inferential statistics are used to analyze data. In qualitative research, analysis is continuous and infrequently employ the use of the statistics. Additional details concerning the two methods are located in Chapters 5 and 6.

Constructing Theory

Qualitative research attempts to construct theory using observational and interviewing techniques to define human behavior. Experiences are documented, identified, and described. Patterns and categories are developed in an attempt to provide theoretical explanations to human behavior. Theory is used inductively and is developed at the end of the study. Data are collected and analyzed before the theory is developed (Patton, 2002).

Testing Theory

Quantitative research attempts to test theory deductively. The theory provides the framework for conducting the study and is usually placed before the experimental conditions. In essence, the theory guide the type of research conducted. The major emphasis is to test or verify a theory. Instruments are developed or selected and data are analyzed to test hypotheses. Hypotheses are used to accept or reject the variables in the study (Creswell & Plano, 2007).

Findings/Results

Data are analyzed in both quantitative and qualitative research. In quantitative research, statistics are employed to determine to what degree the hypotheses have been accepted or rejected. Some degree of objectivity is inherited in the process. Findings in qualitative research are usually reported in narrative form. Data must be coded, classified, and categories formed in order to be appropriately analyzed. Findings are subjective and are frequently not considered obsolete (Taylor, 2005).

Summary

Today attempts are underway to combine the two paradigms in the collection and analysis of data. Green, Caracelli, & Graham, 1989 & Denzin, 1978B summarized the purposes of mixed designs in five major areas:

1.   Triangulation. Tests the consistency of findings obtained through different instruments. In the case study, triangulation will increase changes to control, or at least assess, some of the threats or multiple causes influencing our results.
2.   Complementary. Clarifies and illustrates results from one method with the use of another method. In our case, in-class observation will add information about learning process and will qualify the scores and statistics.
3.   Development. Results from one method shape subsequent methods or steps in the research process. In our case partial results from the preprogram measures might suggest that other assessments should be incorporated.

4.   Initiation. Stimulates new research questions or challenges results obtained through one method. In our case, in-depth interviews with teachers and principals will provide new insights on how the program has been perceived and valued across sites.

5.   Expansion. Provides richness and detail to the study exploring specific features of each method.

Integration of procedures mentioned above will expand the breadth of the study. The process is referred to as *triangulation* (Denzin, 1978b).The trend is to objectify techniques by combining the two approaches in research activities. Computer programs have been developed to assist in the interpretation of the massive amounts of data generated through the qualitative method. Computer programs can assist greatly in using the two paradigms in evaluating research. Refer to Chapter 7 and Appendix M for additional details for additional usage of computers in research. Using maps are another technique that may be employed by making diagrams of the relationships among data through the use of computerized hypertext techniques. Descriptive types of statistics may be employed to assist in analyzing data from the two paradigms. Data sources such as interviews and demographic information may yield qualitative data which may be analyzed through descriptive statistics. These data can enhance quantitative data reported in the research.

The research paradigm outlined can assist the researcher in conducting either qualitative or quantitative research. The research design/paradigm provides a mechanism by which both qualitative and quantitative approaches can be used employing the scientific method in both paradigms. One of the most promising computer software programs for analyzing qualitative date is QSR NUD 1st 4: Qualitative

Data Analysis Software. Method begins with observations and proceed through analysis of data and reporting results. The Research/Paradigms design can serve as a blueprint for guiding both types of research.

Reporting data using the two approaches may be accomplished by reporting qualitative and quantitative data separately in the report; or using qualitative data to support quantitative data. An example may be that quantitative research may reveal through a survey or questionnaire, that computers are not being effectively used in instruction. Interviews with subjects using qualitative measures may reveal that computers were effectively used in instruction but negative results were reported using quantitative measures because (1) teachers were not adequately trained; (2) inappropriate software was used, or (3) outdated hardware was used. Qualitative data may reveal the true essence of the experience as reflected above. If the hypothetical example reported above had shown using quantitative methods that computers were effectively being used and qualitative methods supported that view, this would be an example of the two processes validating each other.

As researchers become better trained in the use of qualitative research methods in the social sciences, it will emerge as a prime technique in analyzing human reactions. Personality attributes which are vital in assessing the human experience, can be scientifically evaluated using qualitative methods. This trend will not replace quantitative research, but rather, it will aid in merging the two paradigms in conducting research in the social and behavioral sciences (Taylor, 2002).

Chapter Fifteen Research Exercise

Refer to Figure 15.1 and complete the following:
1.   Develop a real or hypothetical research design in which you have an interest or wish to investigate.
2.   Modify and adopt the research design to show one or three phases of a research design outlined in the chapter.
3.   Justify and defend your use for using the phase you have selected.

References

Ary, D., Jacobs, & L.C., Razaviech, A. (1995). *Introduction to research in education* (5th ed.). Fort Worth, TX: Harcourt Brace.

Borg, W. R., Gall, J. P., & Gall, M. D. (1993). *Applying educational research.* New York: Longman Publishing Company.

Creswell, John W. (1994). *Research Design: Qualitative and Quantitative Approaches.* Thousand Oaks, CA: Sage Publishing Company.

Denzin, N. K. (1978b). *The research act: A theoretical introduction to sociological method* (2nd ed.). New York: McGraw Hill.

Jick, T. D. (1979). Mixing qualitative and qualitative methods: Triangulation in action. Administrative *Science Quarterly, 24,* 602-611.

Leedy, P. D. (1993). *Practical research: Planning and design* (3rd ed.). New York: MacMillan Publishing Company.

Patton, M. Q. (2002). *Integrating quantitative and qualitative methods in research.* Lanham, MD: University Press of America.

Swanson, S. (1992). *Mixed-method triangulation: Theory and practice compared.* Paper presented at the Annual Meeting of the American Educational Research Association, San Francisco.

Taylor, G. R. (2000). *Integrating quantitative and qualitative methods in research.* Lanham, MD: University Press of America.

Taylor, G. R. (2005). *Integrating quantitative and qualitative methods in research* (2nd ed.). Lanham, MD: University Press of America.

Chapter Sixteen
Major Non-Parametric Statistical Tests
George R. Taylor Ph.D.
Jacqueline H. Williams, Ed.D.

INTRODUCTION

Major Non-Parametric Statistical Tests

Non-parametric statistics is a branch of statistics concerned *with non*parametric statistical models and non-parametric statistical tests. Nonparametric statistics are statistics that do not estimate population parameters. In contrast, see parametric statistics.

Non-parametric models differ from parametric models in that the model structure is not specified is instead determined from data. The term *nonparametric is not* meant to imply that such models completely lack parameters but that the number and nature of *.the* parameters are flexible and not fixed advance. Nonparametrric models are therefore also called *distribution free.*

Non-parametric *(or distribution-free)* inferential statistical methods are mathematical procedures for statistical hypothesis testing which; unlike parametric statistics, make no assumptions about the frequency distributions of the, variables being assessed.

Non-parametric tests: have less power than the appropriate parametric tests, but are more robust when the assumptions underlying the parametric test are not satisfied;

Parametric and nonparametric methods. Nonparametric methods were developed to be used in cases when the researcher knows nothing about the parameters of the variable of interest in the population (hence the name *nonparametric).* In more technical terms, nonparametric methods do not rely on the estimation of parameters (such as the mean or the standard deviation) describing the distribution of the variable of interest in the population. Therefore, these methods are also sometimes (and more appropriately) called *parameter free* methods or *distribution-free* methods.

Non parametric Methods

Basically, there is at least one nonparametric equivalent for each parametric general type of test. In general, these tests fall into the following categories:
- Tests of differences between groups (independent samples);Tests of differences between variables (dependent samples);

- Tests of relationships between variables.

Non-parametric Statistics. Nonparametric statistics requires a basic understanding of parametric statistics (Wolfowitz, 1942). If we have a basic knowledge of the underlying distribution of a variable, then we can make predictions about *how, in* repeated samples of equal size, this particular statistic will "behave," that is, how it is distributed The runs test (also called \ Wald-Woffowitz test) is a non-parametric statistical test that checks a randomness hypothesis for a two-valued data sequence. More precisely, it can be used to test the hypothesis that the elements of the sequence are mutually independent.

A "run" of a sequence is a maximal non-empty segment of the sequence consisting of adjacent equal elements. For e x a m p l e, the sequence"....................." consists of six runs, three of which consist of +'s and the others of-'s. If +Fs and -s alternate randomly, the number of runs in a sequence *of length N for which it is* given that there are N+ occurrences of+ and N-occurrences of $-(so N = N+N-)$ is a random variable whose conditional distribution_ given the observation of N+ and N- - is approximately normal with[1]: These parameters do not depend on the "fairness" of the process generating the elements of *the* sequence in the sense that + 's and −"s most have equal probabilities, but only on the assumption that the elements are independent and identically distributed, If there are too many runs more or less than expected, the hypothesis of statistical independence of the elements may be rejected.

Runs test can be used to test:

1. the randomness of a distribution, by taking the data. in the given order and marking with + the data greater than the median, and with the data less than the median; (Numbers equaling the median are omitted)
2. whether a function fits well to a data set, by marking the data exceeding the function value with -' and the other data with -. For this use, the runs test, which takes into account the signs but not the distances, is complementary to *the chi square test*, which takes into account the distances but not the signs.

Descriptive statistics. When data are not normally distributed, and the measurements at best contain rank order information, then computing the standard descriptive statistics (e.g., mean, standard, deviation) is sometimes not the most informative way to summarize the data, In the area of psychometrics it is well known that the *rated* intensity of a stimulus (e.g., perceived brightness of a light) is often a logarithmic function of the actual intensity of the stimulus (brightness as measured in objective units *of Lux),* In this example, the simple mean rating (sum of ratings divided by the number of stimuli) is not an adequate summary of the average actual intensity of the stimuli. (In this example, one would probably rather compute the geometric mean). Nonparametrics and Distributions will compute a wide variety of measures of location (mean, median, mode, etc.) and dispersion (variance, average deviation, quartile range, etc.) to provide the "complete picture" of the data.

Sample size. We can assume that the sampling distribution is normal even if we are not sure that the distribution of the variable in the population is normal, as long as our sample is large enough (e.g., 100 or more observations). However, if our sample is very small, then those tests can be used only if we are sure that the variable is normally distributed, and there is no way to test this assumption if the sample is small,

When to Use Which Method

The Kolmogorov-Smirnov two-sample test is not only sensitive to differences in the location of distributions but is also affected by differences in their shapes. Large data sets and nonparametric methods. Nonparametric methods are most useful when the sample sizes are small. When the data set is large, you should. not use nonparametric statistics. When the samples are large, the sample means will follow the normal distribution even if the respective variable is not normally distributed In the population, or is not measured very well. Parametric methods, which. are usually much more sensitive (i.e., have more *statistical power)* are in most cases appropriate for large samples. However, the tests of significance of many of the nonparametric statistics described here are based on asymptotic (large sample) theory; therefore, meaningful tests can often not be performed if the sample sizes become too small. Please refer to the descriptions of the specific tests to learn more about their power and efficiency.

To Index

Another type of data researchers are concerned about is frequency data with which an event takes place, for instance the number of people who conclude that hypnosis helps them to determine the meaning of their drawings or the number of people who conclude that drawing while in a waking state, helps them to determine the meaning of their drawing. There are a variety of non-parametric tests at the disposal of the researcher. As indicated in the previous chapter on Parametric Statistics, our aim is to summarize the major nonparametric tests in existence. In determining the major non-parametric tests in use, we perused the literature and conversed with researchers who have used the tests (Harris, 1995; Huck, 1996; McMillan, 1996). Premised upon the above, we summarized the use of the following nonparametric statistical tests:

The Chi-Square.
The Chi-Square-Goodness-of-Fit.
The Chi-Square Test of Independence.
The Mann-Whitney U-Test.
The Wilcoxon Matched-Pairs Signed Rank Test.
The Kruskal-Wallis Test.

The Chi-Square Test

A chi-square test is any statistical hypothesis test in which the sampling distribution of the test statistic is a chi-square distribution when the null hypothesis is true; 'I7ie sampling distribution (if-the null hypothesis is true) can be made to approximate a chi-square distribution as closely as desired by making the sample size large enough.

Some examples of chi-squared tests where the chi-square distribution is only approximately valid:

- Pearsonn's chi-square test, also known as the chi-square goodness-of-fit test or chi-square test for independence. When mentioned without any modifiers or without other precluding context, this test is usually understood (for an exact test used in place $x2$, see Fisher's exact test).

- Mantel-Haensxel chi-square; test.

- Linear-by-linear association chi-square test.

- The portmanteau test in time-series analysis, testing for the presence of autocorrelation.

- Likelihood-ratio tests in general statistical modeling, for testing whether there is evidence of the need to *move* from a simple model to a more complicated one *(where the* simple model is nested within the complicated one).

One case where the distribution of the test statistic is. an exact chi-square distribution is the test that the variance of a normally-distributed population has a given value based on a sample variance. Such a test is uncommonly in practice because values of variances to tent against are seldom known exactly.

Pearsori's chi-square (X2) test is the best-known of several chi-square tests -- statistical procedures whose results are evaluated by reverence to the chi-square distribution. Its properties were first investigated by Karl Pearson. In contexts where *it is* important to make a distinction between the, test statistic and its distribution, names similar to Pearson
X-squared test or statistic are used.

It tests a null hypothesis that the frequency distribution of certain events observed in a sample is consistent with a particular theoretical distribution. The events considered must be mutually exclusive and have total probability . A common case for this is where the events each cover an outcome of a categorical variable. A simple example is the hypothesis that an ordinary six-sided die is "fair", i.e., all six outcomes are equally likely to occur; Pearson's chi-square is the original and most widely-used chi-square test.

The Chi-Square-test was found to be an effective tool for examining frequencies. It was commonly used with comparative studies where the observed and expected frequencies were sought. Chi-squares may be used when there are two variables from independent samples which are categorized in at least two ways. Additionally, Chi-squares appear to be an appropriate statistical tool when data are expressed as frequencies, rather than measurements (Borg, Gall & Gall, 1993).

The Chi-Square-tests-of-goodness-of-fit are also called one-sample chi-square tests. These statistical tests are used to determine if the observed frequency of various categories are different from expected frequencies of these categories. The expected frequencies are usually determined from some hypothesized distribution. The hypothesized distribution may be uniform (rectangular), normal, or some distribution determined from previous scientific work or theory. For the examples discussed in this chapter, the hypothesized distribution will be uniform. The two requirements for this statistical test are:

1.   The categories are mutually exclusive nominal
         Classifications for the variable and,
2.   The number of observations in each category can
         be counted.

The formula for a one-sample chi-square is:
         The formula for a one-sample chi-square is:

$$X^2 = E \; \frac{k}{j=1 E_j} \; 10_j - E_j^2)$$

where:
         O_j = observed frequency for the jth cell
         E_j = expected frequency for the jth cell
         k = number of cells
         $df = k-1$ = number of cells-1

The number of degrees of freedom for a chi-square goodness-of-fit- test is equal to the number of categories (cells) minus one. The loss of one degree of freedom is due to the restriction that the sum of the observed and expected frequencies must be equal (Elmore & Woehlke, 1997).
Example;

A researcher designs a study to determine the number of novels read by girls and boys. The null hypothesis stated that there would be no significant difference. Using the critical value of $x2$ (6.66) with two degrees of freedom, the null hypothesis was rejected at the .05 level. (Refer to Appendix D for critical values.)

Table 16.1 *Calculation of Chi-Square-Goodness-of-Fit*

	Boys	Girls	
Novels Read	Fe 513	Fe 412	R5
No Novels Read	Fe 113	Fe 412	R5
	6c	4c	10

$$X2 = Ex(Fe, - F,)^{2\backslash}$$
$$Fe$$

To find expected frequencies, multiply the rows by the columns and divide by the total (R/C):

$$\frac{5 \times 6}{10} + \frac{30 = 3}{10}$$

$$\frac{5 \times 4}{10} = \frac{20 = 2}{10}$$

$$\frac{(5 - 3)^2 + (4 - 2)^2}{3} + \frac{(1 - 3)^2}{3} + \frac{(4 - 2)^2 =}{2}$$

$$1.33 + 2.00 + 1.33 + 2.00 =$$

$$x2 = 6.66 \; p > .05$$

Refer to Appendix K for critical values.

Using the Yates Correction Factor when frequencies fall below 5 in any cell:

$$x2 = {}^E(F0. \; Fe \, 2$$
$$F2$$

The degrees of freedom (df) for the above table value is: (rows -1) x (columns -1).

Chi-Square Test of Independence

The chi-square test of independence, also called the *chi-square test of association,* answers the question: Are the two factors or dimensions independent, or is there some degree of association between them? It is used when the expected frequencies are estimated *from the* data to be analyzed. The formula for the chi-square test of independence is:

$$x2 = E \quad \frac{r \; c \; (Q_j\_E_k f}{Ejj}$$
$$J=1 \; j=1$$

where:

Oij = observed frequency for the ijth cell Eij= expected frequency
for the if ijth cell *r* - number of rows
c = number of columns
df (r- 1)(c-1)

The chi-square test of independence is used when subjects are classified on two characteristics. Each characteristic has two or more mutually exclusive categories (Elmore & Woehlke, 1997). For example, a researcher may wish to consider comparing males with females on their feeling toward adequate housing on campus. He/she develops a contingency table to record their responses. The researcher hypothesized that there will be no significant difference in agreement vs. disagreement:

Table 16.2 *Extent of Agreement or Disagreement Toward Housing as Perceived by Males and Females*

	Agree	Disagree	Total
Males	30	20	50
Females	50	20	70
Totals	80	40	120

Fe for Male students who agree: $\frac{50 \times 80 = 33.33}{120}$

Fe for Male students who disagree: $\frac{50 \times 40 = 16.67}{120}$

Fe for Female students who agree: $\frac{70 \times 80 = 46.67}{120}$

Fe for Female students who disagree: $\frac{70 \times 40 = 23.3}{120}$

$$\frac{(Fo - Fe)^2}{}$$

fo	fe	fe
30	33.3	3.33
20	16.67	.66
50	46.67	.24
20	23.33	.48

$x^2 = 1.71$ $p < .05$

The x^2 value of 1.71 was not significant at the .05 level, thus, the null hypothesis was accepted. Refer to Appendix K.

The following example is showing the chi-square test of independence. A question is posed: Do you prefer chocolate ice cream over vanilla ice cream?

	f
Yes	20
No	60
N =	80

Out of 80 people 20 said yes and 60 said no. The 20 and 60 are the frequencies and the yes and no answers are called categories.

The next question is are the frequencies of the individuals in the two categories significantly different? The null hypothesis test is: There is no difference between the two frequencies. If there is no difference between the frequencies you would expect 50% of the answers to fall into each category. The frequencies obtained in the two categories are commonly called observed frequencies. The 0 represents the observed frequencies and the E represents the expected frequencies.

	0	E	O-E- .5	$\frac{(0-E-.5)}{(0-E-.5)}$	E
Yes	20	40	19.5	380.25	9.5
No	60	40	19.5	380.25 9.5 $\underline{(0-E-.5)} = 19$	
	X =		E		

The 0 - E - .5 indicates that you obtain the absolute difference between the 0 and E for each category and then subtract .5 from the difference. By subtracting .5 from the absolute difference between 0 and E you are reducing this difference and this is called the Yates correction for continuity. In order to determine if the frequencies in the two cells (i.e., the yes and no cells) you must determine the degrees of freedom. This is determined by how many raw scores are free to vary. When the frequency of the yes is known the frequency for the no cell is fixed because the sum of the frequencies must equal 80. Thus the cells are not free to vary. The df associated with X is the number of cells that are free to vary. When your data are divided into two cells, the for one cell is free to vary; but once the f of the other cell is determined, the f of the other cell is fixed. In the above sample the df = 1. Once this is determined one refers to a table which gives the values of Chi Square (X) at the .05 and .01 levels of significance. Because the obtained 19 is larger then either of the two X values listed in the table, you can conclude that the difference between the frequencies is significantly beyond the .01 level which means you can reject the hypothesis that there is no significant difference between the two frequencies. Since you've rejected the null hypothesis at the .01 level, you can conclude that in this population most people prefer vanilla over chocolate ice cream. In cases where you have more then one degree of freedom, it is not necessary to apply the Yates correction for continuity. For example, Which flavor of ice cream do you prefer.

	0	E	0-B	(0-E)	$\frac{(0-E)}{E}$
Flavor A	35	32	3	9	.28
Flavor B	28	32	4	16	**.50**
Flavor C	30	32	2	4	.12
Flavor D	35	32	3	9	.28
	N = 128				

   In order to determine X you must sum the above values. X = ,28 + ,50 + ,12 + .28 = 1.18. There are four cells and if the frequencies in three cells are known then the frequency of the fourth cell is fixed. Therefore for this data the df is c. Once the three frequencies are known, the frequency of the fourth cell is fixed because the sum of the frequencies must = N. for the df of 3 the table tells us at .05 the level is 7.82 and at .01 the level is 11,34. Because 1.18 is not as large as either of the two X values you concluded that the observed difference among the four cells are non-significance, Since the obtained X is less then what is required for significance, you accept the null hypothesis. Therefore you conclude that any differences in the frequencies among the cells is due to sampling error. Another type of Chi-Square analysis is the 2 x 2 contingency table.

2 x 2 Contingency Table

When the *contingency table* has only two categories on each factor, the formula is:

$$X2 = \underline{\qquad} \frac{N(AD-BC)}{(A+B)(C+D)(A+C)(B+D)}$$

where *df* = 1 and the *contingency table* which has two rows and two columns. An example follows:

Major Non-Parametric Statistical Tests

A+B	A	B
C+D	C	D
N	A+C	B+D

Example: Suppose a researcher was attempting to see how many male and female high school seniors in Central High School were accepted into colleges. The hypothesis stated that there will not be a significant difference between the number of males and females accepted into college. The alternate hypothesis stated that there will be a significant difference between the number of males and females accepted into college. The level of significance was set at .05 with I degree of freedom.

Table 16.3 Number of Central High School Seniors Accepted into College

	Yes	No	Row Marginals
Male Seniors	35	15	50
Female Seniors	20	15	35
Column Marginals	55	30	85

The expected frequencies for each cell are calculated by multiplying the row marginals times the column marginals and dividing that product by N.

Computing the Chi-Square is as follows:

$$X2 \quad \frac{N(AD - BC)^2}{(A+B)(C+D)(A+C)(B+D)}$$

$$\frac{(85)(35)(15) - (15)(20)^2}{(35+15)+(20+15)+(35+20)+(15+15)}$$

$$\frac{(85)(525 - 300)^2}{(50)+(35)+(55)+(30)}$$

$$= \frac{4303,125}{1,925,000}$$

$$= 2.24$$

Refer to Appendix L for critical values.

The calculated $X^2 = 2.24$ is less than the 3,84 needed for $p = .05$. Therefore, the null hypothesis was accepted and the alternative hypothesis was rejected. There was no significant difference between males and females in being accepted into college.

Nonparametric Correlations

The following are three types of commonly used nonparametric correlation coefficients (Spearman R, Kendall Tau, and Gamma coefficients). Note that the chi-square statistic computed for two-way frequency tables, also provides a careful measure of a relation between the two (tabulated) variables, and unlike the correlation measures listed below, it can be used for variables that are measured on a simple nominal scale.

Spearman R. Spearman R (Siegel & Castellan, 1988) assumes that the variables wider consideration were measured on at least an ordinal (rank order) scale, that is, that the individual observations can be ranked into two ordered series. Spearman R can be thought of as the regular Pearson product moment correlation coefficient, that is, in terms of proportion of variability accounted for, except that Spearman R is computed from ranks.

Kendall tau. Kendall tau is equivalent to Spearman R with regard to the underlying assumptions. It is also comparable in terms of its statistical power. However, Spearman R and Kendall tau are usually not identical in magnitude because their underlying logic as well as their computational formulas are very different. Siegel and Castellan (1988) express the relationship of the two measures in terms of the inequality:

-1 < 3 * Kendall tau - 2 * Spearman R < 1

Kendall tau and Spearman R imply different interpretations: Spearman R can be thought of as the regular Pearson product moment correlation coefficient, that is, in terms of proportion of variability accounted for, except that Spearman R. is computed from ranks. Kendall tau represents a probability, that is, it is the difference between the probability that in the observed data the two variables are in the same order versus the probability that the two variables are in different orders.

Gamma. The Gamma statistic is preferable to Spearman R or Kendall tau when the data contain many tied observations (Siegel & Castellan, 1988). In terms of the underlying assumptions, Gamma is equivalent to Spearman R or Kendall tau; in terms of its interpretation and computation it is more similar to Kendall tau than Spearman R. In short, Gamma is also a probability; specifically, it is computed as the difference between the probability that the rank ordering of the two variables agree minus the probability that they disagree, divided by 1 minus the probability of ties. Thus, Gamma is basically equivalent to Kendall, tau, except that ties are explicitly taken into account.

The Mann-Whitney U -Test

This test may be used when the conditions for using the t-test are not met (Stafford, 1965). It also is used to determine if the median from two independent samples are statistically different. Data must at least be on the ordinal level (Siegel, 1956). The Mann-Whitney is sometimes called the *rank sum* test and is used to compare the medians of two groups of unpaired scores (Brase &Brase,1991). Refer to Appendix N for critical values.

The Wilcoxon Matched-Pairs, Signed Rank Test

The Wilcoxon matched pairs test assumes that you can rank order the magnitude of differences in matched observations in a meaningful manner. If this is not the case, you would use the Sign test. If the result of a study is important, you should run different nonparametric tests; should discrepancies in the results occur contingent upon which test is used, you should try to understand why some tests give different results. It gives more weight significantly to a pair which shows a greater difference between the two conditions than to a pair which shows a small difference. The test is very useful in the behavioral sciences and aids the researcher in (a) determining which member of a pair is greater and indicates the sign of the differences and (b) ranking the differences in order of size. Nonparametric statistics are less statistically powerful than their parametric statistics.

The Kruskal-Wallis Test

The Kruskal-Wallis test compares medians for three or more groups. It is similar to the t-test but can be used even when data are skewed or simply ordinal. It is an extremely useful test for determining whether independent samples are from different populations (Siegel, 1956). The test purports that the variables being studied are continuous and requires at least ordinal measurement of the variables. Assumptions for the Kruskal-Wallis test are:

- Ordinal data
- Random samples

Integrating Quantitative and Qualitative Methods in Research 290
Chapter Eleven Research Exercise

1   Using the following data:

Obtained Frequencies

Response	L	H	Both
Yes	20	10	30
No	4	9	13
Both	24	19	43

We have discussed four non-parametric tests that we felt were relevant for use in the social sciences. These tests do not represent all of the non-parametric tests in use. For a detailed analysis and methods for computing non-parametric tests, the reader is referred to Siegel (1956). Additionally, there are references at the end of this chapter which may be consulted. A non-parametric test does not make assumptions about the distribution as in non-parametric tests.

shape of the data distribution. Parametric tests do not require a normal Computer the Chi-Square for the above data; interpret your results clearly and concisely.

a. Calculate the median.

b. Write a statement that compares/contrasts the uses of parametric vs. nonparametric statistical procedures.

c. Use a bar graph to plot the data.

2. Given the information below about the life of three types of automobile batteries, express in years, graph the data and complete the Kruskal-Wallis test to analyze the data.

Brands

A	B	C
3.6	5.6	5.4
4.8	5.0	4.8
4.4	4.9	3.9
5.1	5.8	3.0
Total: 17.1	21.3	17.1

a. Why would a researcher want to use a nonparametric test on the above data?

b. State the null and alternative hypothesis.

c, What is the critical value for the Kruskal-Wallis test?

3. List and give examples of nominal and ordinal levels of measures. Why do we use these measures in non-parametric statistics? Explain.

References

Borg, W.R., Gall, J., & Gall, M. (1993). *Applying Educational Research: A Practical Guide* (3[1-d] ed.). New York: Longman Publishing Company.

Brace, C.H., & Brace, C.P. (1991). *Understandable Statistics: Concepts and Methods* (46 ed.). MA: D.C. Heath and Company.

Elmore, P., & Woehlke, P.L. (1997). *Basic Statistics.* New York: Longman Publishing Company.

Harris, M. B. (1995). *Basic Statistics for Behavioral Science Research.* Boston: Allyn & Bacon.

Huck, S. W., & Cormier, W. H. (1996). *Reading Statistics and Research* (2rd ed.). New York: Harper Collins College Publishers.

McMillan, J. H. (1996). *Educational Research: Fundamentals for the Consumer* (2rd ed.). New York: Harper Collins College Publishers.

Ohman, M.L. (1994). Aspects of Analysis of Small Sample Right Censored Data Using Generalized Wilcox on Rank Tests. University of UMEA.

Siegel, S and Castellan Jr., N. J. (1988). Nonparametric Statistics for Behavioral Sciences. New York: McGraw- Hill Book Co.

Stafford, :R..E (1965). Nonparametric analysis of twin data with the Mann-Whitney U test Research report from the Louisville twin study).

C h a p t e r Seventeen
Practical Applications for Developing Research Paradigms in Quantitative and
Qualitative Research
Charity Welch, PhD.

INTRODUCTION

Research is responsible for many of the improvements made in society during the present century. It is responsible for providing information to increase our life span, improved child rearing practices, educational reforms, parenting skills, and computer technology, are to name but a few improvements. The research process is too complex to be regulated to one type of research. Both *quantitative* and *qualitative* research methods may be employed depending upon the type of research under investigation. Prior to this century, qualitative research received little attention (Taylor, 2000, 2005).

Historically, there was little support or no comparison between quantitative and qualitative research. Research scholars Guba (1990), Maxwell and Delaney (2004) articulated that for more than a century, the advocates of qualitative and quantitative research paradigms have engaged in ardent dispute. Qualitative research methods were viewed too subjective to yield objective results. Only quantitative research methods were believed to provide objective research. Qualitative research has come of age during this century and has done much to dispel the aforementioned myth. Qualitative methods have been endorsed by several authorities, agencies, and institutions of higher learning. Today, the method is considered to be equal with quantitative methods (Dereshiwshy, *1992;* Hashman, *1989;* Marshall & Rossman, 1989; Morse, 1995; Patton, 1990, 2002; Taylor, 2005). Mertens (2009) provided some clarity to the research process b' proclaiming that depending on circumstances, the researcher may decide to give equal weight to both quantitative or qualitative or greater weight to a selective method (p. 166).

All research, quantitative and qualitative, is guided by relevant methods and procedures (Dzurec & Abraham, 1973). The continuum of research on one hand, is quantitative (assigning numerical values and utilizing descriptive or inferential statistics to mathematically calculate relationships of the sample under investigation and then generalizing to a population). At the other end of the continuum is qualitative, through individual personal interviews, collecting data on live human experiences and through a variety of methodological procedures, attempting to uncover/discover the essential meaning of the experience under investigation. Qualitative research involves some of the same procedures employed in quantitative research.' Data sources and materials used must be authenticated and as much as possible data should be primary rather than secondary. The researcher will also need to know to draw meaning from the data. The uses of data sources in qualitative research differ from quantitative research when the researcher analyze the data. In quantitative research data are arranged to yield numerical data which can be statistically treated. In qualitative research, data to be analyzed frequently, are designed to yield narrative data (Lodge, D., & Dianne, S., 1988; Patton, 2002; Taylor, 2000; Jackson & Taylor, 2007).

Quantitative methods permits the researcher to make generalizations to the larger population, while the inverse is true for qualitative research methods. Several research studies in quantitative methods have been shown to be poorly constructed, having inaccurate sample sizes, inappropriate statistical procedures applied, and results being misinterpreted (Patton, 2002). Trochin and Donnelly (2007) provided a format for improving poorly constructed quantitative designs. They include

1.   Selecting appropriate samples.
2.   Specify conditions and treatments.
3.   Identify the sampling technique used.
4.   Conduct systematic observations.
5.   Set appropriate timing for results.

The above examples of quantitative methods can be applied to qualitative methods with the exceptions of sample size and statistical procedures. Additionally, the scientific method is not rigidly applied in qualitative research. Refer to Chapter 6 for specific strategies.

The major issues facing researchers in selecting one research paradigm over another one should not be deciding which one is best, rather which method will provide valid and reliable data to scientifically answer the research question and hypotheses posed. Experiences and a basic understanding of human behavior will assist the researcher in determining which type of design will best represent his/her study.

The sharp separation often seen in the literature between qualitative and quantitative methods is a spurious one. The separation is an unfortunate artifact of power relations and time constraints in graduate training, it is not a logical consequence of what graduates and scholars need to know to do their studies and do them well. In my interpretation, good social sciences is opposed to an either/or and stands for a both/and on the question of qualitative versus quantitative methods. Good social science is problem driven and not methodology driven in the sense that its employs those methods that for a given problematic, best help answer the research questions at hand. More often than not, a combination of qualitative and quantitative methods will do the task best. Fortunately, there seems currently to be a general relaxation in the old and unproductive separation of qualitative and quantitative methods (Flyvbjerg, 2006).

This chapter is not designed to cover qualitative or quantitative research in lengthy detail, but rather to provide enough information for the researcher to understand the construction of the research/paradigm outlined later in this chapter. Adequate sources where detailed information may be found on each method is discussed in Chapters 5 and 6. Other factors which will impact upon the researcher's choice will be time, money, resources, methodology, knowledge, and philosophical beliefs concerning the two paradigms (Anderson & West, 1995; Hathaway, 1995).

Qualitative Research

Qualitative research methods are designed to give real and stimulating meaning to the phenomenon by involving the researcher directly or indirectly in the process. According to Gilquin (1992) qualitative research is not represented by numbers, rather, it is focused on meaning and the involvement of the researcher in the process. The research is usually conducted in a natural setting. A high level of communication and analytical skills are needed to accurately report the full essence of the experience, reflecting holistic and detailed views of the participants. Observations, interviewing and collection of specific documents constitute the major data sources (Creswell, 1994; Marshall & Rosman, 1989; Morse, 1995; Miles, Hubeerman, 1984; Lofland & Lofland, 1995).

As with all empirical research, qualitative research begins with the observation of the phenomenon. Data are then collected classified. Themes are developed to organize the massive amount of data generated (Refer to Appendixes H and I for a computer program to analysis data).

Often times there is no theoretical framework to base the research. Consequently, most qualitative research is designed to develop theory (Miller & Fredericks, 1994) for future studies. Qualitative research may be classified as deliberative, integrative, and historical purposes of research design (Creswell, 2003).

Two research studies conducted by Fetterman (1987) and Dreher (1994) overviewed the various types of qualitative research methods available for the researcher's use. They discussed the various formats used in conducting qualitative research. The usefulness of the methods as well as safeguard and cautions were highlighted for researchers to follows.

Constructing Research Designs

Some research designs emphasize the gathering and manipulation of numerical data; these designs are frequently referred to as quantitative. Other research designs involve the analysis of complex data collected by observations, interviews, or actual participation by the researcher. These designs are frequently referred to as qualitative. Qualitative methods may be employed when the research question addressed cannot be solve by using conventional methods, rather they are design to provide in-depth insight into the human condition.

Research designs are constructed plans and strategies developed to seek, explore and discover answers to quantitative and qualitative research questions. For example, that the researcher wanted to compare the dieting habits of adolescents to those of adults. A questionnaire could be constructed to collect data on the sample (Taylor, 2002, 2005). The type selection, and treatment of the sample should be important. Factors such as gender and age may influence dieting habits. Without considering true factors, any differences found cannot be attributed to gender and age. This is an example of poor quantitative research design. Using the above information, instead of using a questionnaire, the researcher decided to interview the sample concerning their dieting habits. If race and gender are not employed in analyzing the interviews, the researcher's questions cannot be appropriately answered. This is an example of a poorly constructed qualitative design (Taylor, 2000, 2005).

We have attempted to provide information so that the researcher can avoid some of the pitfalls articulated above in designing research designs/paradigms for conducting quantitative or qualitative research methods. The plan should include a blue print for conducting the research, outlining all of the major steps in the process, including stating the hypotheses and their implications for analyzing the data. The following research paradigm summarizes the major components which should be included. The design is similar to the *Conceptual Framework* presented in Chapter 7. Several of the components have been reflected in the research design presented below. The major difference being that Figure 17.1 is the practical application of the conceptual framework and provides a step-by-step process in conducting research.

→Observations	→Assumptions	→Select a possible topic
Develop a testable research question hypotheses ↓	Define primary and Secondary ←	Review the Literature
Consult the review of the literature and expert opinion → on crossing quantitative or qualitative design	Field test or pilot Test program if Needed →	↓ Conduct the research

Summarize, draw conclusion(s) and ← recommendations	Present findings and Discussion ←	Choose an Appropriate ← Inferential Statistic

Figure 17.1 *A Research Design/Paradigm for Conducting Quantitative and Qualitative Research*

Recycling may take place at any point in the design if desired results have not been accomplished.

The research design begins with observations. The researcher must observe a need to conduct the proposed research. Observations may be formal or informal; complex or simple, but sonic organizations or observations should be evident. Some type of data gathering instrument is recommended such as check lists, rating scales, or summary notes in order to see common patterns, as well as organize the observations. Once observations have been confirmed, the researcher should have an unbiased reason for conducting the research.

Assumptions are hunches and guesses. They are frequently based upon observations and are frequently assumed to be true, based upon some standard criterion. This is a pitfall that beginning researchers must avoid since assumptions cannot be scientifically accepted or rejected. Assumptions have value in aiding the researcher by focusing and controlling his/her research. They may also be made based upon one's philosophy and beliefs. Assumptions are necessary in formulating the research and constructing testable hypotheses. Quantitative research begins with a review of literature addressed fully in Chapter 12.

We have attempted throughout this text to articulate the importance of selecting a topic. Typically, topics are too broad and - midst be delimited. In selecting topics, the following are recommended for researchers:

1.　　Have an interest in the topic.
2.　　Justify a need for the topic.
3.　　Make sure that the necessary human and physical resources have been identified, including the competency of the researcher.
4.　　Consult with professionals in the field concerning the need and value of the topic.
5.　　Change proposed topic in the light of additional or new data generated from current research.

We have outlined specific reasons and values for using the review of research in the Conceptual Framework presented in Chapter 4. It will suffice at this point to say that the researcher will need to address both the pros and the cons of the research as they relate to the topics; in essence, the researcher should know the controversies.

Both primary and secondary problems must be identified and strategies indicated for answering them. Most primary problems will have secondary problems which will aid in answering the primary problem. Once the problem has been clarified, specific procedures for conducting the research should be outlined. Procedures chosen will depend upon the type of research being conducted, quantitative or qualitative.

Research questions and hypotheses are designed to assist the researcher in finding solutions to the problem, Previous steps outlined in the model are necessary in formulating testable research questions or hypotheses. The various types of hypotheses are discussed in Chapter 13 under *Inferential Statistics.* Testable research questions and hypotheses should have at least two variables which are measurable. Both the independent and dependent variables should be identified and the process for evaluating them stated.

In choosing an appropriate research design or paradigm, the researcher may consult with experts practitioners in the field to ascertain their perceptions. Figure 12 provides a guide for researchers to follow when implementing quantitative and qualitative research. Additionally, the researcher may pursue a review of the literature to examine samples of quantitative and qualitative research designs. In Chapters 5 and 6 we have discussed additional information to aid the researcher in choosing an appropriate design to conduct his/her research.

Figure 17.2 *Paradigm Selection for Quantitative and Qualitative Research Methods*

I. Quantitative
   A. Test a theory/hypothesis.
   B. Select variables that have been quantified to numbers.
   C. Select statistical procedures to analyze data.
   D. Determine if the theory/hypothesis is accepted or rejected.
II. Qualitative
   A. A process of inquiry in a naturalistic setting.
   B. In-depth person-to-person interviews to understand a lived experience or social or human problems.
   C. Qualitative procedures to analyze data.
   D. Developing complex, holistic, descriptions derived from co-researchers.
III. Five Criteria for Selecting Quantitative or Qualitative Paradigm
   A. Researcher's Worldview.
   B. Training or Experience of the Researcher.
   C. Researcher's Psychological Attributes.
   D. The Nature of the Problem.

Criteria	Quantitative	Qualitative
A. Researcher's	Researcher's comfort with the ontological epistemological, axiological, rhetorical, and methodological assumptions of the paradigm.	Researcher's comfort with the ontological epistemological, axiological, rhetorical, and methodological assumptions of the paradigm.
B. Training and/or experience of the researcher	Technical writing skills; computer statistical skills; library skills.	Literary writing skills; computer text analysis skills, or cut-
C. Researcher's Psychological Attributes	Comfort with rules and guidelines for conducting research; low tolerance for ambiguity, time relatively short	Comfort with lack of specific rules and procedures for conducting research, high tolerance for ambiguity, time relatively long
D. Nature of the Problem.	Previously studied by other researchers so that the body of Literature exists; known variables; existing theories.	Exploratory research; Variables unknown; context important; may lack theory base for study.
E. Audience for the Study (graduate committees, journal editors, and readers.	Individuals accustomed to/supportive of quantitative studies and readers.	Individuals accustomed to/supportive of qualitative studies.

Audience for the Study (Committee members, journal editors, *Information in Figure 17.2 was compiled from the following sources: Michael Patton, 1990, 2002; John Creswell, 1994, 2002; Catherine Marshall & Gretchen, Rossman, 1989; Diane Pounder, 1993; R. Hathaway, 1995. Refer to the Reference List at the end of the chapter.

Ontological Assumption: What is real?
Epistemological Assumption: What is the relationship of the researcher to that being researched? What is the role of values? What language is used? What are the methods, procedures, and processes of research?
Axiological Assumption:
Rhetorical Assumption:
Methodological Assumption:

Assumption	Question	Quantitative	Qualitative
Ontological Assumption	What is the nature of reality?	Reality is objective, singular, and separate from the researcher.	Reality is subjective, multiple as known by the participants in the study.
Epistemological Assumption	What is the Relationship of the researcher to that is being researched?	Researcher is independent from that being researched,	Researcher is
Axiological Assumption	What is the role of values?	Most take precautions to be value-free and unbiased.	Takes measures to fully acknowledge values and biases.
Rhetorical Assumption	What is the process of research?	1. Formal 2. Based on set definitions 3. Impersonal voice 4. Use of accepted Quantitative words	1. Informal 2. Evolving decisions 3. Personal voice 4. Use of accepted qualitative works

Assumption	Question	Quantitative	Qualitative
Methodological Assumptions	What is the process of research?	1. Deductive process 2. Cause and effect Correlations 3. Static design-categories isolated before study 4. Context free 5. Generalized bonds leading to predictions, explanation, and understanding 6. Accurate and reliable through validity and reliability	1. Inductive process 2. Mutual simultaneous shaping of factors. 3. Emerging design-categories are identified during the process 4. Context free 5. Themes, categoric, emerge for greater understanding 6. Accurate and reliable through verification and triangulation

Data presented in Figure 17.2 will provide the researcher with purposes, characteristics, and competencies needed by to conduct either quantitative or qualitative research methods. These selection strategies are essential in developing research designs articulated in this chapter and Chapter 16. Information in Figure 17.2 may also be employed to assist the researcher in validating instruments, experimenting with new intervention techniques, field test or validate an instrument or program, or develop or refine a research design in either paradigm. Additionally, data in Figure 14 will assist the researcher in specifying the type of research that he/she is best equipped to conduct.

Summary

The major purpose of research designs are to assist researchers to: (1) provide answers to assumptions, research questions, and hypotheses, and (2) control variance. They are constructed to enable the researcher to answer questions posed by the research, as well as to make inferences from the data. Design also aids the researcher in determining the types of observations to make, how to make them, and the type of research to employ (quantitative or qualitative). Specific procedures are outlined to guide the researcher in manipulating and categorizing the variables. Research designs should also indicate appropriate type of statistical analysis to use, as well as anticipated or projected conclusions to be drawn from the statistical analysis; this includes both descriptive and inferential statistics. In quantitative research methods, the researcher must choose appropriate descriptive or inferential statistics. Many research projects will employ both. In qualitative research, emphasis is not placed on numerical data, however, some descriptive statistics may be used (Barbour, R., 2007). The review of the literature and expert opinion can facilitate the researcher's selection of appropriate statistics to use in either quantitative or qualitative research. It is commonly agreed by researchers that qualitative and quantitative research design have different goals, which usually require different designs (Dever & Frankel, 2000; Creswell, 2003; Taylor, 2005; Mertens, 2009). This division is clearly articulated by Creswell, 1994).

In presenting findings in quantitative research, tables, graphs, and other forms of numerical data are used. Qualitative researchers use generally words to present findings. Refer to Chapter 16 for similarities and differences in presenting findings. In both quantitative and qualitative methods, data are summarized, conclusions, and recommendations are drawn. A systematic plan for conducting research using either paradigm will follow a similar pattern. In choosing one approach over another, the issue should be to assess which approach will best serve the research under investigation. We have attempted to reflect how this can be accomplished in this chapter and Chapter 16.

For specific guidelines for developing qualitative research designs refer to R. Barbour (2007) *Introducing qualitative research: A student's guide to the craft of doing qualitative research.* Thousand Oaks, CA: Sage Publishing Company.

Research Exercise Thirteen

1. Develop a checklist for evaluating a problem selected by you. Have three other researchers to evaluate the problem using the checklist. Conduct an item analysis on all checklists. Summarize the results with a rationale for any differences

2. Consider the following research question. Does teaching reading to children using the computer rather than the traditional textbook method alter children's performance on a standardized test on reading? Complete both a quantitative and qualitative research design using the following instructions:

   a. Design the ideal research design to answer the above question assuming that there are no administrative or other restrictions (Refer to Figure 14 as a guide).

   b. Design the research design that would most likely be required in the typical high school setting.

   c. State the relative advantages of the ideal research design in question (a) as compared with the design in question (b).

   d. Choose a quantitative or a qualitative research method and develop a research design. Justify your choice.

References

Barbour, R. *(2007). Introducing qualitative research: A student's guide to the Craft of doing qualitative research.* Thousand Oaks, CA: Sage Publishing Company.

Campbell, D., & Stanley, J. (1963). Experimental and quaisexperimental designs for *research on teaching.* In. N. Gage (Ed.). *Handbook of research on teaching.* Chicago: McGraw-Hill.

Creswell, J. W. (1994). *Research Design: Qualitative and Quantitative Approaches.* Thousand Oaks, CA: Sage Publications.

Creswell, J. W. (2003). *Research design: Qualitative, Quantitative, and Mixed Methods* Approaches (2nd ed). Thousand Oaks, CA: Sage Publishing Company.

Denzin, N. K. (1978b). *The research act: A theoretical introduction To sociological methods (2nd ed.).* New York: McGraw- Hill.

Dereshiwsky, M. 1.4 Packard, R D. (1992). *"When words are worth more than a thousand* number: The power of qualitative research procedures in evaluating the impact of educational programs and practices". Paper presented at the annual meeting of the National Council of States, San Diego, California. ED 362499.

Devers, K. L., & Frankel, i t M. *(2000).* Study design in qualitative research - *2:* Sampling and Data Collection Strategies. *Education for Health,* 13, 263-271.

Dzurec, L. C., & Abraham, J. L. (1993). The nature of inquiry: Linking quantitative and qualitative research. *Advances in Nursing Science,* 16, 73-79.

Fetter, D. M. (1987), *A* rainbow of qualitative approaches and concerns. *Education and Urban Society, 20 (1),* 4-8.

Flybjerg, B. (2006). Five misunderstanding about case study research. Qualitative Inquiry, 12 (2), 219-245.

Gilquin, J.F. (1992), *Definitions, Methodologies and Methods in Qualitative Family Research.* Qualitative Methods in Family Research. Newbury Park, CA: Sage Publications.

Guba, E. G. (1990). The alternative paradigm dialog. In E. g. Guba (Ed). *The paradigm dialog* (pp. 17-27). Newbury Park, CA: Sage

Hathaway, R. S. (1995). Assumptions underlying quantitative and qualitative research: *Implications* for institutional research. *Research in Higher Education, 36 (5), 535-562.*

Hoshman, L. T. (1989). Alternate research paradigms: A review and teaching proposal. *Counseling Psychologist, 17 (1), 3-79,*

Jackson, C. L., & Taylor, G. R. (2007). Demystifying Research: A Primer for Novice *Researchers.* The Netherlands: Sense Publishers.

Luba, E. G. (1990). The alternative paradigm dialog. In E. G. Cuba (Ed *Ike paradigm dialog* (pp. 17-27. Newbury Park, CA;

Lodge, P., & Dianne, S. (1988). The qualitative dimension. Paper presented Northern Rocky Mountain Education Research

Lofland, J., & Lofland, L. H. (1995). *Analyzing social settings: A Guide to qualitative observation and analysis (3rd ed.).* Redmond, CA: Wadsworth Publishing Company. Marshall, C., & Rossman, G. B. (1989). *Designing Research.* Newbury Park, CA:Sage Publications.

Mertens, D. M. (2009). Transformative Research and Education. New York: The Guilford Press.Miles, M. B., & Huberman, A. M. (1984). *Qualitative data analysis.* Beverly Hills, CA:Sage

Miller, S., I., & Fredericks, M. (1994). Qualitative research methods: Social epistemology and practical inquiry. New York: Peter Long

Morse, J. M., & Field, P. A. *(1995). Qualitative Research Methods for Health Professional.* Thousand *Oaks, CA: Sage Publications.*

Patton, M. Q. (1990). *Qualitative Evaluations and Research Methods.* Newbury Park, CA: Sage Publications.

Pounder, D. G. (1993). *Rigor in Traditional Quantitative Methods.* Paper presented at the annual meeting of the American Educational Research Association. Atlanta, GA: ED 353975.

Taylor, G. R. *(2000). Integrating quantitative and   qualitative methods in research.* Lanham, MD: University Press of America, Inc.

Taylor, *G. R. (2005). Integrating quantitative and qualitative method in research (2"d ed.).* Lanham, MD: University Press of America, Inc.

Trochim, W., & Donnelly, D. P. (2007). *The research methods knowledge base. (3rd ed.).* Mason, OH: Atmic Dog.

Chapter Eighteen
Introduction Presentation Skills
Marjorie Miles, Ed.D.
George R. Taylor, Ph.D.

As essential part of completing graduate work and research is presentation of one work to others. This is particular true when graduate students are required to give presentations of these, seminars, or other research findings. Presentations may be in several forms such as oral, power point, poster, multimedia presentations.

Preparing for Oral Presentations

In preparing for oral presentation the graduate student or research should organize/select resources and organize material to address the purpose of the presentation. Equally important should be considered the nature and tone of one's voice, body language, and personal appearance. Specific strategies to aid the presenter should include, preparation, delivery, visual aids, multimedia visual aids (http:''lorien,ncl,ac.uk/ming/dept/Tips/present/comms.htm;Anholt, 2006, Kline, 2009).

Preparation

Specific research findings by several authors have indicated that presentations of effective oral presentations should:

1. Choose topics that are familiar with and have competencies in the subject areas.
2. Prepare the structure of the talk carefully and scientifically.
3. Write out a draft presentation and have it reviewed. Make changes as necessary and have a peer to review the final document.
4. Prepare cue cards. Number the cards in case they are dropped. Indicate the visual aid to be used on each card.
5. Practice the presentation individually and in front of a peer. Revise the presentation as recommended (Bovee, 2003; Osborn, 2006; Van Emden & Becker, 2004; Scott & Young, 2001).

Kline (2009) indicated a major challenge in oral presentations is stage fright. In order for presenters to address this issue and to make oral presentations easier the presentation proper preparation will assist in calming the presenters. Everyone is a bit nervous before an oral presentation. The following strategies have been successful in calming presenters:

1. Try standing behind the lectern before anyone else is in the room. Look around, imagine yourself speaking.
2. Chat with members of the audience before your speech.

3. Do practice relaxing exercises such as; sit comfortably, breath in slowly, then held your
    breath for just a few seconds, and exhale slowly.

Analyze the Audience

Analyzing one's situation is often difficult to separate from analyzing the audience.
Audiences participation determine the success of oral presentations. Speaking is successful if the
audiences positively to you. Positive responses of audience depends greatly upon the presenter's
knowledge of the audiences' education and cultural background, and how these factors are infused
in the presentation.

Understand and Articulate your Presentation's Purpose

Oral presentations must be designed around a specific topic with defined objectives for
solving the problem. The purpose must be defined based upon the audiences needs, attitudes,
interests, and background as related to the presentation. An excellent way of getting the attention
of the audiences is to present background information to apprise them of the direction in which the
presentation will follow. It is also desirable to pose questions which will arouse the interests of
the audiences.

Making the Presentation

The fear of public speaking constitutes one of the greatest fears that students and presenters
have. Some research studies have shown that speaking before a group can result in some
psychological and physical discomforts which may influence effective delivery. Several authors
have articulated that these problems can pose a challenge by presenters. Recommended strategies
for reducing fear include some of the following, analyze the audience, articulate the purpose,
choice an appropriate speaking style, practice an effective delivery style, select and use
appropriate visual aids, and keep the message as concise as possible. In concluding, a presentation
leave time for audiences to pose questions. Be prepared to pose questions to the audiences if none
come from them (httpi/www.ruf.edu/-riceowlloral presentations.htm, Kline, 2009; Alley, 2003;
Simons, 2004; Tufte, 2006; Anholt, 2006; Mayer, 2001; and Davis, 2005).

Chose an Appropriate Speaking Style

Choosing an appropriate speaking style is essential to the success of presentations. There may
be effective content, excellent ideas, and accurate supporting statistics. If the style used in
speaking is inappropriate to the audience, the attention of the audiences may be lost. Attempt to
assess what speaking style is appropriate for the audience by determining their educational level
and cultural levels, attitudes, and interests. Style in oral presentations may be improved by using
appropriate non verbal clues (Kline, 2009). Choosing an appropriate speaking style will vary
depending upon the audience. Some recommending strategies are, avoid long and cumbersome
sentences, use language that the audience can understand, and use the active voice as much as
possible. Generally, a presenter should choose a natural style that include short sentences, and
known language pattern of the audience (http://web/cba/neu.edu/z ewertheim/skills/oral.htm).

Delivery

Style in delivering oral presentations by students and presenters should consider the
importance of non-verbal clues. They can be used to improve or distract from the message. As
indicated the education, training, experience, and cultural values may be considered when
choosing what non-verbal clues to infuse.

Delivery may also be improved by incorporating the following strategies:

1. Speak clearly and avoid long complex sentences and use of language not familiar to the
    audience.

2. Clearly define any use of jargon.
3. Pause at major points and ascent the importance of a particular point.
4. Use the active voice as much as possible.
5. Make presentation interesting to the audience by regulating the speed and voice quality in the message.
6. The use of hands should be minimized in the presentation, too much hand movement may be distracting.
7. Adjust visual aids so that you can position yourself in front or on the side of them so that you are not blocking them.
8. Keep the presentation to 20 minutes or less which is usually enforced by moderators.
9. Be aware of the audience reactions and adjust the presentation accordingly.
10. Consult a media specialist if needed to operate technological devices.
11. Articulate clearly and enunciate words distinctly.
    (http:/web.cba.neu.edu/z ewerthei M/shills/oral.htm).

Regardless of the type of presentation being made, success is largely determined by how well your credibility is established. The use of the listed guidelines are recommended in establishing your credibility, along with practice which will build your confidence in presenting the presentations.

Visual Aids

The proper use of visual aids can enhance any oral presentation providing that they are relevant to the message. Some commonly used visual aids include the following:

1. Overhead projection transparencies (OHPs).
2. 35mm slides.
3. Compute projection (Power Point, applications such as Excel, etc.).
4. Video, and film.
5. Real objects – either handled from the speaker's bench or passed around.
6. Flip-chart or blackboard may be used as a scratch pad to accent a point (http/lorein.ncl.ac.uk/Ming/dept/Tios/present/comms.htm).

Power Point Presentations

Students frequently use power point presentations in defending their oral thesis. There are advantages in using power point presentations.

Advantages

Some advantages include that they are:

1. Flexible to use.
2. Easy to modify content.
3. Slides and materials cannot be misplaced or lost.
4. Used in small or large auditoriums.
5. Used to present computer graphics and animations.
6. Not expensive.
7. Easily prepared.
8. Designed to be used repeatedly, and
9. Designed to be manipulated by the student or presenter to focus attention on certain aspects.

Major advantages of power point presentations are that they can present complex computer graphics and animations, summarize large amount of information, addressing large audiences, used for training purpose, and use as a teaching devise.

Disadvantages

Many power point presentations are poorly constructed. Paradi (2003, 2005) listed 10 top annoying features of power point presentations:

1. Speaker read the test presented on the slides.
2. Text too small to read.
3. Slides hard to read because of color.
4. Full sentences are used instead of bullet points.
5. Moving/flying text or graphics.
6. Annoying use of sound.
7. Overly complex diagrams or charts.
8. No flow or ideas, jumped around too much.
9. No clear purpose of the presentation.
10. Too many fonts used

Paradi (2003, 2005) summed up the disadvantages of using power point presentations is that presenters spend too much time working on the power point presentation than thinking about the substance. He also stated that presenters make too many power point slides and that many presenters need technical assistance in developing professional power point presentations.

If you are not familiar with the technological devices, consult a technician to operate them or to assist you. Practice their use before the presentation. Carefully check and edit slides for errors and font and layout. If a slide is used more than once, make as many copies as needed. Do not place too much information on a slide, minimum information to advance your point should be recorded.

The use of computer graphics, power point, and excel combined with color printers and slide project can greatly enhance the presentation. The use of technology can enable the presenter to show web images on a screen.

Research has clearly demonstrated that oral presentations can be effectively improved through the use of visual aids by making them more interesting, more factual, more effective, and more professional. Visual aids also significantly contribute to the audience's understanding and keeping abreast with the presentation.

Multi-Media Visual Aids

Frequently, several visual aids may be required to use in presentations depending upon the nature, scope, and complexity of the problem. The presenter may use drawings, posters, blackboards, charts, pictures, photographs, map, graph, and any other media to project the presentation. As much as possible keep all visual aids simple, easy to read, avoid too many colors, and limit the fonts (Kline, 2009).

Summary

Successfully, oral presentations depends greatly upon effective speaking and organizational skills, preparation, appropriate audio visual resources and materials, practice, and timing. Students should reframe from developing complex visual aids, due to the fact that might distract the audience from the presentation. Students and presenters should be prepared to pass out handouts if technological devise fail. Detail practice is highly recommended to reduce anxiety, other psychological problems, fright, and nervous conditions.

Research Exercise

Use the research design or thesis you have developed and plan an oral presentation to be presented to an audience, choose one of the following:

1. Power Point
2. Poster
3. Multi-Media
4. Document Readers

Develop an instrument for the audience to critique and evaluate the Presentation. Evaluate the results and prepare a written report.

References

Alley, M. (2003). *The craft of scientific presentations: Critical steps to succeed and critical error to avoid.* New York: Springer.

Anholt, Robert, H. (2006). *Dazzel 'em with style: The art of oral scientific presentation.* (2nd. ed.). *Amsterdam*: Elsevier.

Bovee, Courtland L. (2003). *Contemporary public speaking* (2nd ed.).San Diego: Collegiate Press.

Davis, M. (2005). *Scientific papers and presentations* (2nd ed.). New York: Academic Press.

Department of Chemical and Process Engineering. (1999). University of Newcastle Upon Tyne Newcastle Upon Tyne, NE! 7RU, UK. http://lorien.ncl.ac.uk/ming/dept/Tips/present/comms.htm. http:/www.ruf.rice.edu/-riceowl/oral-presentations.htm. http://web.cba.neu-edu/-ewertheim

Kline, R. B. (2009). *Becoming a behavioral science researcher: A guide to producing research that matters.* New York: The Guilford Press.

Mayer, R. E. (2004). *Multimedia learning.* New York: Cambridge University Press.

Osborn, Michael, & Osborn, Suzanne. (2006). *Public speaking* (7th ed.). Boston: Houghton Mifflin.

Paradi, D. (2003). *Summary of annoying PowerPoint Survey.* From http://www.communicateus technology.com /PPresults.htm

Paradi, D. (2005). *What annoys audiences about PowerPoint Presentations?* From http://www. thinkoutsidetheslide.com/PPresults2005.htm

Simons, T. (2004). *Does PowerPoint make you stupid?* From www.Presentations.com/msg /search/article-display.sp? Vnu-content-id=1000482464.

Tuft, E. R. (2006). *The cognitive style of PowerPoint: Pitching and concepts within* (2nd ed.). Cheshire, CT: Graphic Press.

VanEmden, Joan, & Becker, Lucinda. (2004). Presentation skills for students. Basingstoke: Palgrave Macmillan.

Chapter Nineteen
The Final Stage: Some Points to Ponder
George R. Taylor, Ph.D.

INTRODUCTION

We have emphasized throughout this text, but especially in Chapters 16 and 18 how research designs and paradigms may be employed in completing a research project. The final project may be a scholarly paper, or it may be a dissertation which may be quantitatively or qualitatively developed. Implementing the strategies outlined will assist the researcher in developing a quality project. In addition to implementing strategies articulated in the text, the following guidelines for the researcher to consider.

General Guidelines

Guideline 1. An accurate statement of the problem and hypothesis should be clearly stated.

The researcher should clearly describe his/her problem so that misunderstanding can be minimized. It is highly recommended that the research review similar studies to determine how the problems were standardized and solved. The solution of the problem should be proposed before the data are analyzed. The researcher does everything possible to provide his/her readers with procedures for following and understanding the study.

Guideline 2. Description of the method employed in the study must fit the problem under investigation and include a detailed discussion of the research method or methods to be employed.

A description of the steps taken to solve the problem should be systematically delineated. Sub- problems must add up to the totality of the statement of the problem. Each sub-problem should be a researchable unit. The researcher should tell where the sources of information were found and how they were selected. He/she should identify the type of data which were gathered and the ways in which they were analyzed and classified. Additionally, the researcher should be knowledgeable about both quantitative and qualitative research methods. They should indicate in detail just how they went about the job of testing his/her hypothesis and why they think the method followed was effective by addressing the following questions (1) Was a pilot study conducted in order to address and validate issues of sampling?, (2) Was validation and reliability of instruments established?, (3) Were standardizing procedures to be used?, and (4) How were the risk of Type I and II errors in testing hypotheses reduced.

Guideline 3. Definition of terms should be clearly defined and documented.
In some instances, the researcher may find it necessary to explain in detail, the meaning of certain words and phrases being used in the study. When special terms are employed, they should ordinarily be defined and documented at the time they first appear in the paper. A technical term which may be interpreted in more than one way should always be defined and documented so that there can be no question of the exact sense in which it is being used.

Guideline 4. The body of the paper should not only provide evidence, but limitations and interpretation of the data as well should be reported.
Only when the researcher interprets as well as presents the evidence, can readers weigh it an follow his reasoning through to the conclusion. The main body of the paper may be divided into sections in which the various arguments are advanced. The length of sections will depend upon the relative strength of each argument and the amount of evidence which has been uncovered to support it. Every section should be self-sufficient. It should have an introductory statement which tells what the section deals with a limitation, which overviews imposed limitations, and it should have a summarizing statement at the end which reviews the argument and reminds the reader of what the evidence has demonstrated.

Guideline 5. A summary of the research should not contain new information but rather should give a brief and concise summary of the project, be systematically organized, critically analyze the current status of the literature, and include multiple data sources to support the topic.
It should be possible from reading the summary to learn just what the study has achieved and how, without any of the details or documentation, results were generated. The summary restates the entire research showing how the hypothesis has been or not been validated while emphasizing the main points, rather than the details. The total study is reduced to a brief description and the length of the summary depends upon the length of the total study. The summary should be as concise as possible *(Taylor2002, 2005).*

Guideline 6. If the researcher involves using human subjects or animals, the researcher must ensure their welfare and safety by designing studies in accordance with an Institutional Review Board (IRB).
Federal and state laws require that all institutions involved in research activities with humans and animals have an operational board (IRB) to review studies and approve or disapprove them based upon published standards and guidelines. Each institution is required to have an IRB Handbook, which delineates these standards and guidelines.

Guideline 7. The research method chosen should be appropriate to the type of scholarly research conducted.

In Chapters 5 and 6 we have given comprehensive reviews for both quantitative and qualitative research methods. The researcher should choose a paradigm based upon his/her competencies and interests. Types of research activities may include, experimental, naturalistics, phenomenological, laboratory-based, or other approved methods.

> *Guideline 8. The research should make an original or significant contribution to knowledge.*
>
> > Completed research should demonstrate to the professionals in the field your competencies in conducting both quantitative and qualitative research, through the application of sound and proven methods in the two research paradigms.

Specific Guidelines

1. > *Use clear, simple, and non-sexist language.* The researcher should be able to support every statement made, i.e., direct factual statements, assumptions, sources from expert opinions, or assumptions based upon his/her beliefs or philosophy (Frank & Treichler, 1989, Cummings, 2000).

In stating a known fact, the researcher must be sure to state how he/she knows it to be a fact. Ordinarily, this is accomplished by describing the way he/she observed this fact or by indicating the source of his/her information. Sources, if they are books, may be described in footnotes. Other sources such as interviews, manuscripts, or experimental projects, may be described in the body of the paper. A factual statement which the researcher knows to be true, must verify its truth, and usually the quickest and best method of doing this is to identify the source of the information. The researcher must document that what he/she states as fact is not mere opinion. Principles and facts discovered by someone else in the course of careful, scientific research may be stated as demonstrated truths.

In the discovery of truth, opinions carry little weight as compared with factual data. Nevertheless, there may be instances in which no evidence can be found except expert opinion. Although an expert opinion may be in error, there is a better chance that an opinion will be valid if the person giving it is an expert than if the person were chosen at random.

Opinion cannot ever achieve the force of actual fact. When an expert's opinion is quoted, the researcher should introduce it by a phrase such as "In Taylor's opinion..." In essence, the reader should be informed that the statement given is an opinion and not a statement of fact.

2. *Get to the point.* It is recommended that the researcher go directly to the point. If the researcher will dismiss all to make an impression upon his/her readers and try to make the paper not as long as possible but covering relevant issues, the researcher should refrain from adding comments which have nothing at all to do with the study.

> A great many writers waste too much time and space writing useless remarks that they never seem to arrive at the main issue, a description of what was accomplished in the study.

3. *Crystallize writing skills by recording thoughts and ideas on paper.* Employ appropriate writing aids and manuals such as the APA. Choose an appropriate time of

day and place to reflect and write. Save all draft copies to refer to an improve later revisions.

4.   *Systematically organize information on the subject selected.* Some systematical plan should be evident for bringing order to the study. Probably the researchers' best way of accomplishing this is to ask himself what arguments he has developed in favor of the hypothesis which he believes to be the right one. If each favorable argument is set down in turn, together with the evidence proving it, an almost perfect structure for the research report will result.

5.   *The researcher will find it helpful to construct a written outline of his/her project.* This will serve the purpose both of clarifying the scope of the study in the researchers' mind and of helping him plan and write the report.

An outline represents the skeleton of the entire study. It demonstrates how the data have been organized into effective segments and how these segments lead logically to the conclusion reached. The researcher who cannot outline the main points of the study and gather his data into a pattern may find that he/she simply does not have a mind set on a firm and clear picture of the study on which he has been working. Additionally, the outline is a mechanical aid in organizing and presenting data effectively.

As each segment of the study is developed, the outline assists the researcher in maintaining a consciousness of the relationship among all the parts and of the cohesiveness of the whole.

6.   *Keep in mind the reader of the research.* The researcher when writing a report of a study should constantly keep in mind the reader for whom he is writing. It may assist to consider briefly what the critical reader looks for when he reads a scholarly paper.

First of all, the researcher should remember that the reader will not be the average person, but an especially well-trained and critical professional who is probably an expert in the field. This reader is expected to be objective, to read the paper with unusual care, to be skeptical of its assertions unless they are proved by real evidence, and to make certain efforts to assess the accuracy of the scholar's materials. That person may look up the references given in the footnotes to determine whether (1) the footnotes themselves are absolutely correct, and (2) to determine if the researcher has interpreted his sources correctly.

In the case of experimental study, the reader may request additional information on the experiment. In addition to the above, various questions will be raised in the critical reader's mind that must be answered satisfactorily if the report is to be regarded as valid. Is the title an accurately descriptive one, brief and not misleading? Is the problem properly defined and the scope of the study delimited, so that no misunderstanding can develop regarding just what was studied?

7.   *Choose appropriate descriptive data to facilitate understanding of the* data. Illustrations that stimulate personal interests may be extremely effective in a popular book or article, but they have no place in the scholarly paper. The purpose of graphic

presentations in writing up the results of research is not entertainment but provide clarity for the study.

Before attempting to produce graphic information or photographs as part of the paper, the researcher would be well advised to avail himself of the practical suggestions offered in a good book on graphic presentation. If, however, a researcher finds that he has no ability whatsoever, there is no violation of scholarly ethics in hiring a person with artistic training to do this portion of the work for him from the data which the researcher supplies. A photograph made by an expert photographer will prove more satisfactory for illustrative purposes than one bungled by an inexperienced amateur. An artist will know more than the average scholarly investigator about the materials and techniques for an effective chart or graph.

8.   *Choose appropriate descriptive or inferential statistics to facilitate understanding of the data.* The choice of choosing an appropriate statistic can be a critical one. In choosing descriptive statistics, the task is not as complex as in choosing inferential statistics. Descriptive statistics such as graphs, charts, and measures of central tendency, may be used with either quantitative or qualitative measures. Inferential statistics is usually reserved for quantitative measures and must meet the following criteria:

1.   Data must be on the interval level;
2.   Sufficient sample (N= at least 30) should be randomly selected;
3.   Similar studies in the professional literature support the use of the statistic selected (Taylor, 2000, 2005).

When these conditions have been satisfied, inferential statistics may be employed. If the listed assumptions or conditions have not been met, non-parametric statistics must be applied. Refer to Chapter 15 for non-parametric statistical tools commonly in use for the social sciences.

In essence, the appropriate statistics to use depends upon whether or not quantitative or qualitative methods are used. We have summarized in Chapter 1 strategies for choosing appropriate statistics for the two research paradigms.

Summary

The scholarly research report is the means by which the researcher informs others about his/her work. Denzin (1978b) and Mertens (2009) has added clarity to the concept by categorizing triangulation into the following types of data sources, the use of a variety of data, the use of several different researchers in the research, the use of multiple perspective to interpret a single set of data, the use of multiple methods to study a single problem or program. It is not ordinarily written until after the successful completion of the study is conducted. Studies may be both quantitative or qualitative. A scholarly research report is written to inform rather than to entertain or impress. The writer should avoid oratory types of representations and go directly to the point. Prerequisite to writing, the researcher should carefully organize and outline the whole report, which may be quantitative or qualitative in nature. While the research report cannot be said to have any fixed pattern, there is normally an introductory section that describes the problem and the method of study and state the research question and the hypothesis, together with all the evidence in support of these arguments. At the end of the paper, it is customary to summarize briefly the entire study.

The researcher should use clear and simple, but concise, English in writing. He/she should give the source of factual statements and should separate and identify basic assumptions or mere opinions. He/she should keep in mind what the critical and intelligent reader will be looking for when reading the report. The tried and proved methods of graphic and statistical presentation should be studied and used whenever they may help in clarifying the data. Graphs, charts, tables, and other statistical illustrations and arrays must be understandable, accurate, and self-contained. They should not however, take the place of a full verbal and narrative explanation of the data used in qualitative research.

References

Cumming, J. (2000). *Language power and pedagory. Bilingual Children in the crossfire.* Buffalo, New York: Multilingual Matters.

Denzin, N. K. (1978b). *The research act: A theoretical introduction to sociological methods (2nd ed.). New York: McGraw-Hill

Frank, F. W., & Treichler, P. A. (1989). *Language, gender, and professional writing: Theoretical approaches and guidelines for non-sexist usage.* New York: Modern Language Association Publications.

Mertens, D. M. (2009). *Transformative research and evaluation.* New York: The Guilford Press.

Taylor, G. R. (2000). *Integrating quantitative and qualitative methods in research.* Lanham, MD: University Press of America.

Taylor, G. R. (2005). *Integrating quantitative and qualitative methods in research* (2nd ed.). Lanham, MD: University Press of America.

Chapter Twenty
Summary and Conclusion
George R. Taylor, Ph.D.

The researcher must be careful to avoid some common pitfalls in research. First he/she should select the samples without bias and makes sure that they are representative of the population for which he/she wishes to generalize. Second, he/she makes his/her measurements and observations with accuracy, not allowing distortions or prejudices to creep into the data. Third, he/she processes his/her data conscientiously and analyzes it without concealing, discarding, or doctoring the evidence. And fourth, he/she interprets and reports his/her findings fairly, regardless of his/per personal point of view, stating all relevant facts and circumstances, revealing the reliability and validity of his criteria, and defining the limits of probability for his/her conclusions. These points have been well illustrated throughout the text and strategies have been developed to minimize the pitfalls.

In Chapter 1 we have provided a historical overview of the research process. Through this chapter we have attempted to combine research methods with statistics, both quantitative and qualitative methods. In our view, the processes are inseparable; we view the processes as one continuum. This continuum has been outlined and discussed in our Conceptual Framework. In Chapter 4, we indicated that the "Review of the Literature" formed the basis for the Conceptual Framework. Without a comprehensive review, the framework is practically useless. The researcher must be able to identify, read critically, and analyze research findings as reported in the professional literature. Knowledge of library resources and electronic databases will aid the researcher in reviewing the professional research. (Refer to Chapters 2 and 3 for additional details.)

The conceptual model and the scientific method suggest that a series of systematic steps must be evident to successfully complete the research process. These steps are essentially the same for quantitative and qualitative research. Each step follows a hierarchical order and is infused and integrated with each proceeding step. Complete mastery of the lower step is necessary for achievement of the next step. The steps are basic and fundamental are needed to conduct any research.

As indicated in Chapter 4, analysis and findings are the last steps to employ in the research process. These steps involve the use of statistics: descriptive or inferential. Data may be reported in many forms i.e., tables, figures, and graphs. Numerical data may also be used to perform statistical operations. Much of the information on statistical analysis has been adequately addressed throughout this text. We have emphasized the importance of collecting valid data. Conclusions are reached based upon what the data reveal, therefore, data must carefully and systematically collected. Researchers must constantly guard against the potentiality of having subjectivity enter into collecting both quantitative and qualitative data.

Chapter 8 was designed to demonstrate to researchers how to bring order and meaning to group data by using frequency distribution tables and measures of central tendency.

Inferential statistics may be employed when the researcher wishes or is interested in drawing general conclusions for data collected from a large sample. Measurement must be interval or ratio scaled. Data which are not interval/ratio cannot be used with inferential statistics. The type of Central Tendency to employ with interval/ratio data is the mean. The variability is the standard deviation. The Pearson Product Moment Correlation is frequently used to show relationship between variables. Chapter 13 lists several types of inferential statistics to use.

We have presented a sample of parametric and non-parametric statistical tests with practical applications for using them. We have given a rationale for the selection and use of each major type of statistical test. For example, non-parametric tests were suggested when the assumptions underlying the use of parametric tests were not met. Assumptions underlying the use of parametric statistics were also outlined. Details are provided in Chapters 14 and 15. Using parametric and non-parametric statistics can be involved and time-consuming when they are done by traditional means. The use of computers in data analyses are valuable sources to use in analyzing parametric and non-parametric statistics. There are several software packages available to assist the researcher. We have summarized some of them in Chapter 7.

We have stressed throughout the text that there are no absolutes in selecting appropriate statistical tools. We strongly emphasize the use of the review of the literature to aid in the selection. Additionally, we cannot overemphasize that any statistical procedure used in research must be appropriate to the experimental conditions and correlated with the stated hypotheses. Specific strategies have been summarized in Chapters 5 and 6 to provide a blue print for researchers to follow. In conducting both quantitative and qualitative research methods. The case study is a new method added to this edition. It may be used in both the research method, specific procedures have been addressed in Chapter 10.

The value o fusing computerized packages in analyzing quantitative data is articulated in Chapter 8. We have recognized the importance of meta-analysis in research. Because of this importance we have added a new Chapter 9 to the revised addition. Specific techniques have been listed for conducting meta-analysis.

Statistics may be classified into two general sections, descriptive and inferential. Descriptive statistics describe data sources. These statistics are commonly used in constructing graphs, measures of central tendency, variability, and relationships. Data used in descriptive statistics may be presented in nominal, ordinal, interval, or ratio scales. Interval scales may be changed to ranked data and used with the Spearman-Rho Rank Correlation statistics. The type of Central Tendency to use with nominal data is the mode; with ordinal data is the median. Variability may be represented in nominal data by the number of categories used or reported. The range and quartile deviation may be represented with ordinal data sources. Relationship or nominal data is frequently shown by using Cramer's Coefficient of Relationship. Relationship or ordinal data may be shown by using the Spearman-Rho Rank Correlation statistic. Refer to Chapter 13 for additional details.

Many research projects hypothesis have not been achieved due to poor sampling methods. Chapter 11 is new for this edition and was designed to minimized poor sampling in research. The importance and selecting the appropriate types of sampling techniques are discussed.

In Chapter 16 we drew data from Chapters 5 and 6 to construct a "Research Design/Paradigm" for conducting quantitative and qualitative research. A unified research design was introduced showing common elements between the two research methods. It was indicated that both types of research designs begin with observations and concluded with presenting findings and summarizing and drawing conclusions. We supported the view that quantitative research is not superior to qualitative research or vice versa, rather the method chosen should best address the issues or problem under investigation.

In order to guide the researcher in selecting an appropriate method to choose, we outlined major similarities and differences between the two approaches in Chapter 17. We compiled Figure 15.1 to compare these similarities and differences. In our opinion, data from Figure 15.1 will enable the researcher to choose the method which will achieve the objectives of his/her study. In addition to the comparative data in Figure 15.1, we recommend that the researcher assess his/her own abilities to conduct research regardless of the method chosen. Factors such as training and experiences, how an individual views reality, psychological attributes, nature of the problem, and the profile of study participants, impact upon the outcome of the study. We recommend that the researcher carefully compare his abilities with the aforementioned factors and select an approach which will best address his/her concerns. In many instances, the researcher may wish to combine the two approaches.

In Chapter 18, we have provided a model for the researcher to combine the two approaches. We have given examples on how this can be accomplished. The researcher may select from these approaches to combine approaches: (1) the *Two-Phase design*, (2) *Dominant/Less-Dominant Design,* (3) *the Mixed-Methodology Design* to use as an example. This design infuses most of the steps in both designs.

Chapter 18 addressed how this requirement can be successfully demonstrated. Research, if it is to serve the major purpose for which it was designed, must be published and circulated to the attended audience. We have attempted to demonstrate how this process may be achieved in Chapter 19. We are cognizant of the fact that most graduates of Ph.D. programs do not publish their research. This chapter was designed to indicate ways in which research can be published, and reinforce the position that if strategies outlined in this text are followed, they can readily become published authors.

Most graduate students and researchers are required to orally defend their research. There are several avenues used to accomplish this requirement.

Chapter 20 summarized and concluded how all of the chapters and strategies may be achieved in becoming successful researchers.

Elements of Informed Consent
For Competent Adults or Adolescents
From: Guidelines to the Use of Human Subjects in Psychosocial Research.
University of Pittsburgh 1983-1985.

Description:

- *Be brief and non-technical.* The first two sentences should give a brief explanation of the study and identify why a particular subject or patient has been asked to be in the study. Example: *the purpose of this research is to determine if people of various ages and with different types of illnesses have different problem-solving skills. Because you have diabetes, you are asked to participate in this study.* The remainder of the description should include:

a. Aims;
b. Approximate number of subjects/patients (sex and age range);
c. Duration of participation;
d. Tests or diagnostic procedures and/or questionnaires;
e. Volume of blood to be drawn, in terms of tablespoons or ounces (tablespoons=15 ml.; maximum allowable amount=450 ml. during eight weeks.

- *Risks and Benefits.* Include all reasonable foreseeable risks and discomforts. Such risks could be physical, psychosocial, or legal. Also mention any special precautions taken to avoid such hazards. If blood is to be drawn, then if appropriate, mention in the consent form the possibility of a *bruise or soreness at the site of arterial/venipuncture, or a spasm with loss of blood flow at the site of the puncture.* Include any benefits to the subject/patient or to scientific knowledge.

- *Alternative Treatments. This* is applicable to research in which there is a choice of therapeutic interventions.

- *New Information.* If applicable, the form should include the statement, *"..new information gained during the time the research is in progress and which is relevant to participation will be provided"* Note: Such new information and any change in the project should also be sent to the IRB for review and approval.

- *Costs and Payments.* Include any cost(s) or payment(s) to the subject/patient or reimbursement for related expenses. If appropriate, include a statement such as *"...all costs not related to the research will be charged to me just as though I were not part of this study."*
Confidentiality. Some assurance of protection of confidentiality must be included. Please describe your plans, then include appropriate sections of the following statement: I understand that any information about me obtained from this research, including answers to questionnaires, history, laboratory data, findings on physical examination, or audio or videotapes will be kept strictly confidential. Such information which will carry personal identifying material will be kept in locked files. I do understand that my research records, just like hospital records, may be subpoenaed by court order. It has been explained to me that my identity will not be revealed in any description or publication of this research. Therefore, I consent to such publication for scientific purposes.

- *Right to Refuse or to End Participation.* The following is a suggested paragraph which should be adapted to your protocol:

> I understand that 1 am free to refuse to participate in
> this study or to end my participation at any time and
> that my decision will not adversely affect my care at
> this institution or cause a loss of benefits to which I

might be otherwise entitled. *Note:* Use asterisks (**)
to separate the section using "you" from that using
"I."

- *No Compensation for Physical Injury or Illness..* The following paragraph must be
  included in all research which carries a significant risk to the subject/patient:
  > I understand that in the event of a physical injury or
  > illness resulting from the research procedure, no
  > monetary compensation will be made. Emergency
  > medical treatment which may be necessary will be made
  > available to me without charge.

- *Voluntary Consent. This* paragraph should be on the same page as the signature:
  > I certify that I have read the preceding or it has been read to me and that I
  > understand its contents. Any questions I have pertaining to the research
  > have been and will be answered _____. A copy of this consent
  > form will be given to me. My signature below means that I have freely
  > agreed to participate in this experimental study.

_____	_____
Date	Subject/Patient Signature

_____	_____
Date	Witness Signature

- *Acknowledgment of f Parent or Gordian.* If minors (13-18 years of age) will
  be part of the study, please add the following: I, _____, have
  also read the preceding and agree to the participation of my child.

_____	_____
Date	Signature of Parent/Guardian

_____	_____
Date	Signature of Witness

- *Investigator's Certification.* The researcher/qualified investigator
  should   read   and   sign   the   statement   below: I,
  _____, certify that I have explained to the above
  individual the nature and purpose, the potential benefits, and
  possible risks associated with participating in this research study,
  have answered any questions that have been raised, and have
  witnessed the above signature.

_____	_____
Date	Signature *of* Investigator

_____	_____
Date	Signature of Witness

Elements of Informed Consent For Subjects Representative
No psychosocial research shall be performed without the informed consent of the
subject/patient except where (1) the subject/patient is incompetent or unable to
comprehend the information and (2) an appropriate representative of the subject/patient has
given information consent. *

Appendix A (continued)

With regard to the participation of minor subjects/patients:

1. If the minor is between the ages of 13 and 17 (inclusive), the parent or guardian and the child must give informed consent.

2. If a minor is below the age of 13, the informed consent of the parent or guardian must be obtained and the child given an explanation of the research. This may entail the use of a consent form especially prepared to facilitate understanding by a minor of such age (see below):

    When incompetent adults are sought as subjects/patients for psychosocial research, the spouse or legal guardian must give informed consent. The consent form should be similar to that for competent adults with appropriate blanks for insertion of the subjects/patients name and for indicating the relationship of the subjects representative to the subject.

Modification of this basic rule /nay be made in the case of deception studies and other extraordinary circumstances.

Child's Consent Form

There is a moral obligation on the part of the investigator and the parents (or guardian) to assist the child to understand his/her role in the project. Therefore, under most circumstances, we require that a simplified consent form be read and explained to children 6 to 12 years of age. He/she should be asked to sign. Thirteen through seventeen-year-olds should *sign* a regular consent form which is then countersigned by a parent. Should the investigator believe that the use of a child' consent form is inapplicable or contraindicated in a particular project, the investigator should include a statement explaining his/her view in the protocol. Elements of the child' consent form are:

1. Simple familiar English, not slang.

2. Explain the following:

    a. Reason for asking the child to be in the study.

    b. Purpose of the study.

    c. Procedure.

    d. Risks or discomforts-physical or psychosocial.

    e. Benefits, if any.

    f. Right to refuse or withdraw.

    g. Investigator's willingness to answer questions.

Federal Policy Concerning Informed Consent Introduction.

Informed consent is one of the primary ethical requirements underpinning research with human subjects; it reflects the basic principle *of respect for persons.* It is too often forgotten that informed consent is an ongoing process, not a piece of paper or a discrete moment in time. Informed consent assures that prospective human subjects will understand the nature of the research and can knowledgeable *and voluntarily* decide whether or not to participate. This assurance protects all parties B both the subject, whose *autonomy* is respected, and the investigator, who otherwise faces legal hazards. The "proxy consent" f someone other than the subject is not the same as the subject' own consent, although it may be an acceptable substitute when a subject is unable to give informed consent. [See Guidebook Chapter 6, *"Special Classes of Subjects."*]. Federal Policy consent requirements are provided in ".116 and .117; FDA consent requirements are provided in 21 CFR.20-27 and 21 CFR 56.109.

Overview

The *Nuremberg Code,* developed by the International Military Tribunal that tried Nazi physicians for the "experiments" they performed on non-consenting inmates of concentration camps, was the first widely recognized document to deal explicitly with the issue of informed consent and experimentation on human subjects. The first principle of the code states:

> *The voluntary consent of the human subject is absolutely essential. This means that the person involved should have legal capacity to give consent; should be so situated as to be able to exercise free power of choice without the intervention of any element of force, fraud, deceit, duress, over-reaching, or other ulterior form of constraint or coercion; and should have sufficient knowledge and comprehension of the elements of the subject matter involved as to enable him to make an understanding and enlightened decision. This latter element requires that before the acceptance of an affirmative decision by the experimental subject there should be made known to him the nature, duration and purpose of the experiment; the method and means by which it is to be conducted; all inconveniences and hazards reasonable to be expected;;and the effects upon his health or person which may possible come from his participation in the experiment.*

All subsequent codes and regulations, insofar as they pertain to competent, adult subjects, follow these principles closely.

Although the elements of informed consent (i.e., full disclosure, adequate comprehension, voluntary choice) are easy to enumerate, recent empirical studies suggest they are not so easy to achieve. Even the best intentions do not ensure against failures of communication B information may be poorly conveyed or subjects may forget (if indeed they ever understood) that they are involved in a research project. Enhancing the likelihood that informed consent will take place is a challenge to which IRBs should respond with imagination and good judgment. When the proposed research will involve vulnerable subjects or the research design involves incomplete disclosure or deception, the challenges to the IRB are even greater. Certain populations (e.g., children or mentally retarded individuals) may not be able to understand the required information, whereas other populations (e.g., *prisoners* or *institutionalized* individuals) are so situated that the voluntariness of their consent may be in doubt. Hospitalized patients, particularly those who are seriously ill or undergoing emergency treatment, may also need special protection. Problems raised by the involvement of some vulnerable populations are discussed in other sections of this Guidebook. *[See* Chapter 6, "Special Classes of Subjects."]

IRB Considerations

The issued discussed in this section are general IRB considerations regarding informed consent, and they apply generally to the review of research that involves human subjects. Problems surrounding the use of deception or incomplete disclosure are discussed near the end of this section under the headings *Exceptions, Deception* and *Incomplete Disclosure, Placebos, Randomization,* and *Double-Mixed Clinical Trials.*

The Regulations.

The federal regulations require that certain information must be provided to each subject [Federal Policy § 116(a)]:

1. A statement that the study involves research, an explanation of the purposes of the research. and the expected duration of the subject's participation, a description of the procedures to be followed, and identification of any procedures which are experimental;

2. A description of any reasonable foreseeable risks or discomforts to the subject(s);

3. A description of any benefits to the subject(s) or to others which may reasonably be expected from the research;

4. A disclosure of appropriate alternative procedures or courses of treatment, if any, that might be advantageous to the subject;

5. A statement describing the extent, if any, to which confidentiality of records identifying the subject will be maintained;

6. For research involving more than minimal risk, an explanation as to whether any compensation and an explanation as to whether any medical treatments are available if injury occurs and, if so, what they consist of, or where further information may be obtained;

7. An explanation of whom to contact for answers to pertinent questions about the research and research subjects' rights, and whom to contact in the event of a research related injury to the subject; and

8. A statement that participation is voluntary, refusal to participate will involve no penalty or loss of benefits to which the subject is otherwise entitled, and the subject may discontinue participation at any time without penalty or loss of benefits to *which* the subject is otherwise entitled.

The regulations further provide that the following additional information be provided to subjects, where appropriate [Federal Policy §116(b)]:

1. A statement that the particular treatment or procedure may involve risks to the subject (or to the embryo or fetus, if the subject is or may become pregnant) which are currently unforeseeable;

2. Anticipated circumstances under which the subject's participation may be terminated by the investigator without regard to the subject's consent;

3. Any additional costs to the subject that may result from participation in the research;

Appendix B (continued)

4.   The consequences of a subject's decision to withdraw from the research and procedures for orderly termination of participation by the subject.

5.   A statement that significant new findings developed during the course of the research which may relate to the subject's willingness to continue participation will be provided to the subject; and

6.   The appropriate number of subjects involved in the study.

Investigators may seek consent only under circumstances that provide the prospective subject or his/her representative sufficient opportunity to consider whether or not to participate, and that minimize the possibility of coercion or undue influence. Furthermore, the information must be written in language that is understandable to the subject or representative. The consent process may not involve the use of exculpatory language through which the subject or representative is made to waive or appear to waive any of the subject's legal rights, or releases or appears to release the investigator, sponsor, institution, or agents from liability for negligence [Federal Policy §116].

Adequacy of the Content

One of the IRB's most important activities is evaluating the information to be provided to potential subjects in light of the risks and benefits of the proposed research procedures. Each IRB member brings a different perspective to this review. Certain consent documents provided by the investigators. Other members may add their reactions to the way information is provided or question the adequacy of the information. Whether or not the information is deemed "adequate" depends partly on the impression being conveyed (e.g., whether it is clear that a procedure is to be done for research purposes).

In making a judgment concerning what information should be disclosed in the informed consent process, the IRB should attempt to view the matter from the subject's perspective by asking what facts the subjects might want to know before deciding whether or not to participate in the research. Information could be deemed "material" if it might influence *the* decision of any reasonable person. For example, the risk of death from cardiac catherization might be statistically small, and, therefore, seem unimportant to an investigator, but the risk may loom large for people invited to undergo the procedure for the benefit of others. Research in sensitive areas such as child abuse, illegal activities such as drug or alcohol abuse, or reportable communicable diseases such as HIV, also may pose risks to subjects about which they should be informed. Where the potential for the need to report such information to authorities exists, subjects should be so informed before agreeing to participate in the study. Depending on the circumstances, potential subjects may also feel it is "material" to be informed about additional costs that might arise during the course of the research, the identity of the research sponsor, any circumstances that would make it difficult or dangerous to withdraw from the research, or the amount or kind of inconvenience involved.

Expression

IRB's must ensure that information will be presented to prospective subjects in language they can understand. How well subjects understand that information will vary according to the population from which subjects will be drawn. For example, if all the subjects will be registered nurses, they will probable understand most medical terms, but if the population consists of college students, an intermediate level of understanding can be anticipated. If English is not the subject population's primary language, the explanations and the forms should be translated into the subjects' native language.

The medical teams and complex sentences in oral presentations and consent forms often need to be presented in simpler terms B even for the educated layperson. If the prospective subjects include children, persons whose primary language is not English, or populations with the average of a sixth grade education, the IRB should take special care to ensure that both oral presentations and consent forms are comprehensible to all subjects. In these cases, ordinary language should replace technical terms (e.g., upper extremities are better referred to as arms, hematoma as a bruise, veni puncture as taking blood from your arm with a needle, etc.).

Some IRB's find that their lay members are particularly helpful in suggesting necessary modifications. Others ask members of the proposed subject population (e.g., children, clinic patients) to review consent forms and indicate what parts they do not understand.

In addition, *the informed consent may not contain any exculpatory language.* Subjects may not be asked to waive (or appear to waive) any of their legal rights, nor may they be asked to release the investigator, sponsor, or institution (or its agents) from liability for negligence.

Process

It is essential that IRB members think of informed consent not as a form that must be signed, but as an educational process that takes place between the investigator and the prospective subject. No one can guarantee that another person has understood the information presented; one can only inform prospective subjects as clearly as possible. No one can guarantee that another's choice is voluntary; one can only attempt to remove obvious impediments to free choice by being alert to coercive aspects of the consent procedure. In cases where there is reason for special concern about pressure (e.g., when patients are invited to participate in research conducted by their physician, or when students, military personnel, employees, etc., are asked to participate in research conducted by their supervisors), the IRB may require some form of monitoring (such as the presence of an impartial observer). If the research presents significant risk, or if subjects are likely to have difficulty understanding the information to be provided, the IRB may suggest that investigators employ devices such as audiovisual aids, tests of the information presented, or consent advisors.

Because obtaining informed consent is an educational process, the IRB should do what it can to enhance the prospective subject's comprehension of the information presented. It should consider the nature of the proposed subject population, the type of information to be conveyed, and the circumstances under which the consent process will take place (e.g., manner, timing, place, personnel involved). After answering these questions, the IRB may want to suggest changes in the timing or location of an investigator's first contact with potential subjects, or changes in how others will contact subjects during or following the study. For example, some investigators may plan to release their data to a "data broker" who will in turn make the data available to other researchers. IRB's should review the appropriateness of making the data available in this way, and should ensure that subjects will be informed about who will have access to the data and who might contact them.

Sometimes the information to be imparted to prospective subjects is so complex or possible disturbing that it may require some time for it to be absorbed and appreciated. In these circumstances, the IRB might suggest that the investigator either present the information and discuss the issues with prospective subjects on more than one occasion, or that a period of time elapse between imparting the information and requesting a signature on the consent form. During this waiting period, prospective subjects might be encouraged to discuss their possible participation with family members, close friends, or trusted advisors. Other approaches to communicating complex information include the use of audio-visual materials and brochures.

Documentation

In most cases, the federal regulations require that informed consent be documented [Federal Policy §.117; FDA regulations 21 CFR 50.27], but they also provide for some important exceptions. Documentation usually involves the use of a written consent form containing all the information to be disclosed and signed by the subject or the subject's legal representative. It should be reiterated, however, that these documents are not substitutes for discussion. The person who signed the consent form must be given a copy as a reference and reminder of the information conveyed. A "short form" may sometimes be used [Federal Policy '.117(b)(2); FDA regulations 21 CFR 50.27(b)(2). The use of a short form means that the information is presented without benefit of a written version of the consent document. Before a short form can be used, the IRB must first review and approve a written summary of what will be presented. Each oral presentation must be witnessed by a third person, who must sign both the consent form and a copy of the written summary of the presentation. A copy of the summary must be provided to those who sign the consent form so that they have the information available for future reference [Federal Policy '.117(b)(2)].

The IRB may waive the regulatory requirement for written documentation of consent in cases where: (1) the principal risks are those associated with a breach of *confidentiality* concerning the subject's participation in the research (e.g., studies on sensitive topics such as drug abuse or sexual deviance); and (2) the consent document is the only record linking the subject with the research [Federal Policy '.1 1 7(c)(1)]. Written documentation of consent may also be waived when the research presents no more than *minimal risk* and involves procedures that do not require written consent when they are performed outside of a research setting [Federal Policy '.117(c)(2); FDA regulations on IRB review, 21 CFR 56.109(c)]. [See Guidebook Chapter 3, Section A, "Risk/Benefit Analysis. "]

At institutions that require IRB review of all research involving human subjects (including research exempt from the federal regulations), the IRB may decide to waive consent documentation requirements for research that would be exempt from the federal regulations (e.g., most survey and observational research). IRB's taking such an approach should be careful, however, to make sure that the subjects will be provided adequate information about the research. The IRB may decide that, in some cases, subjects should be provided written copies of the information conveyed despite the fact that they are not asked to sign a consent form.

Exceptions

Federal regulations on informed consent specify the information that must be disclosed to prospective subjects [Federal Policy §.116; FDA regulations on consent, 21 CFR 50.25]. The regulations do permit modifications in the consent procedure, and, under certain circumstances, informed consent may be waived entirely if the research meets certain conditions [Federal Policy §,116(c)-(d)]. Such modifications and waivers are not allowed under FDA regulations. [See 21 CFR 50.23, which sets out conditions under which the obtaining of informed consent for use of a test article can be deemed infeasible]. Situations in which modification or waiver of consent may be indicated call for careful consideration by the IRB. Decisions to waive informed consent or documentation of informed consent should be clearly documented in the IRB's minutes. [See Guidebook Chapter 6, Section F, "Traumatized and Comatose Patients."]

The IRB may approve a waiver of some or all of the consent requirements provided that: (1) the research involves no more than *minimal risk* to subjects [see Guidebook Chapter 3, Section A, "Risk/Benefit Analysis"]; (2) the waiver or alteration will not adversely affect the rights and welfare of the subjects; (3) the research could not practicably be carried out without the waiver or alteration; and (4) whenever appropriate, the subjects will be provided with additional pertinent information after they have participated in the study [Federal Policy §. 116(d)]. Most commentators suggest that the IRB also determine whether the knowledge being sought is important enough to justify whatever invasion of privacy may be required either to obtain information about non-consenting (or unaware) subjects or to involve them in research under false pretenses. [See Guidebook Chapter 3, Section D, "Privacy and Confidentiality."]

Appendix B (continued)

Under the Federal Policy (but not FDA regulations), if the research is designed to evaluate or demonstrate possible changes in (or alternatives to) provision of benefits or services provided for under federal, state, or local programs, an IRB may approve alteration or waiver of the consent requirements [Federal Policy '.116(c)]. If the research could not practicably be carried out without the waiver or alteration of the consent requirements, the IRB may approve such a waiver. Both the *National Commission for the Protection of Human Subjects and the President's Commission for the Study of Ethical Problems in Medicine and Biomedical and Behavioral Research* recommended that such waivers be granted only if subjects will not be denied benefits or services to which they are otherwise legally entitled.

Record Reviews

Sometimes, especially in epidemiological studies, scientists need to review thousands of records to identify appropriate subjects for their study. (Consent is not an issue for record reviews of deceased individuals because federal regulations apply only to research involving living human subjects [Federal Policy §.102(f)]. It is often difficult, if not impossible, to obtain the permission of everyone whose records are contained in the files. For this preliminary part of the research, IRB's will generally waive the consent requirement if: (1) they are satisfied that the information contained in the files is not particularly sensitive; (2) the investigator has devised procedures to protect the confidentiality of the information to be collected; and (3) the study could not practicably be carried out if consent were required. Some university hospitals notify all incoming patients that their records may be reviewed for research purposes; others provide an opportunity to consent (or refuse to consent) to such use.

Contacting potential subjects to obtain further information is a more sensitive phase of the research. IRB's should consider how the investigator proposes to make the initial contact with potential subjects (e.g., through employer, physician, institution having custody of the records, or directly by the investigator) and what information will be conveyed at that time. *[See Guidebook Chapter 3, Section D, "Privacy and Confidentiality," and Chapter 4, Section E, "Epidemiologic Studies."]*

In making decisions regarding record reviews and plans for contacting individuals thus identified, IRB's should consider the importance of the research, the extent to which privacy will be invaded, the sensitivity of the information to which the investigators will have access, plans for further contact of the subjects, and the feasibility of obtaining consent from all prospective subjects. For further discussion of records research, including consent issues, *see* Guidebook Chapter 4, Section E, "Epidemiologic Studies."

Observation in which Subject's Identity will be Recorded

Behavioral scientists sometimes need to observe the behavior of people who either are not aware that they are being observed or who are unaware that their behavior is being recorded for research purposes.

Because subjects might behave differently if they knew they were being observed, researchers may request that the consent requirements be waived (if subjects must be unaware of their involvement, they will not have the opportunity to consent or refuse to participate in the research). Videotaping of the responses of passersby to staged emergencies (e.g., heart attacks or criminal assaults), observing the interaction between patients and staff in mental hospitals, and studying homosexual activities in public restrooms are three examples of this kind of study.

In the first case, the subjects have no knowledge of (and therefore have not consented to) the presence of an observer or recording equipment.. When the behavior observed may be embarrassing, or when the staged conditions are stressful, this kind of study poses ethical problems for the investigator and the IRB. In the second example, although the patients and staff of the mental hospital may be aware that someone is observing their behavior, they may not be aware of why they are being observed. In the study, "On Being Sane in Insane Places," social scientists disguised themselves as mental patients and made important observations of the behavior patterns of both patients and staff in mental hospitals. This kind of research presents ethical problems, because the subjects might not consent to the pseudo-patient's presence if they were aware of the real purpose.

In the "Tea Room Trade" study, a social scientist adopted the role of "watch queen" (i.e., lookout) for homosexuals engaged in sexual acts in public restrooms. Although his subjects obviously knew of his presence, they did not know (at least until after publication of his results) that they were being studied. The unwitting subjects also did not know that the investigator recorded their license plate numbers and searched motor vehicle registration files for their names and addresses. A year later, he disguised his appearance and interviewed these subjects, purportedly for a different kind of study, thus obtaining information about their family and social life. Commentators have suggested that the subjects would neither have consented to the researcher's presence in the restroom nor responded to his later survey questionnaire had they known his real purpose.

The "Tea Room Trade" study raises many of the same ethical questions as the other two examples, but the problems are compounded because the investigator identified the subjects, and through further deception, obtained possibly private information about their family and social life. (Identifying the subjects placed them at risk of serious legal, social, and economic harm since the behavior being studied was illegal.)

The last two studies illustrate another sensitive problem IRB's must consider when reviewing research involving covert observation. Although consent requirements can be waived if the IRB determines that the knowledge to be gained is important, this decision can easily be influenced by the extent to which IRB members approve of either the subject matter or what they expect may be the findings of the research. IRB members should guard against the inclination to approve or disapprove research based upon their personal feelings about the possible outcome of a research proposal. Drawing the line between judgments about the social or scientific value of a particular study and personal attitudes towards the subject matter of that study is admittedly difficult. IRB members should try to distinguish between qualms they may have about the subject matter (e.g., homosexuality or drug abuse) and qualms they may have about the research methods (e.g., covert observations, staged events, and so forth).

Deception and Incomplete Disclosure

Sometimes, particularly in behavioral research, investigators plan to withhold information about the real purpose of the research or even to give subjects false information about some aspect of the research. This means that the subject's consent may not be fully informed. For example, to discover whether certain kinds of background music are more distracting than others in a learning situation, an investigator might recruit subjects and explain that certain aspects of learning and memory are being studied. If the research is to be conducted, some of the consent requirements must be waived. Subjects would be told that they would be required to learn sets of words and then be tested on how well they remember those words, but they would be deceived about the purpose of the research and certain elements of the study design.

A contrasting example, much discussed in the literature, is the Milgam study of obedience. Subjects of this study were told that, as part of a learning study, they were to give electric shocks each time a "student" made an error in learning. Although they consented to participate in a study of learning, they were unwittingly involved in a study of their own obedience and willingness to inflict pain. Subjects were told about the true nature and purpose of the research after they had participated. This research has been criticized for the emotional stress it caused and the "inflicted insight" provide to the subjects about their own behavior (neither of which they had consented to). Although Milgram's follow-up studies indicated that few if any subjects reported that they had misgivings about participating in the research, many

element of deception. Most commentators now believe that if subjects are told they may receive a placebo, and if the design of the clinical trial is explained to them, no deception is involved.

When the particular therapy a subject receives will be assigned on a scientifically *random* basis, this selection process must be explained to prospective subjects in language they can understand. Merely telling them that the assignment to treatment will be done randomly, mathematically, or by lottery may not be sufficient. Instead, more of an explanation should be given. In a two-arm trial, for example, subjects should be told that there is a 50% chance of receiving one of two treatments thought to be beneficial for patients with their particular kind of disease; that one is the standard treatment and the other is the experimental treatment; that the experimental treatment is thought to be at least as good as the standard treatment; and that their physician will not be the person who decides which treatment they receive. If the study involves the use of placebos, subjects should be told the chances of receiving the various possible treatments, including the chance of receiving a placebo.

It is important that prospective subjects understand that a *double-masked* design means that neither they, their physicians, nor the investigators treating and evaluating them will know which treatment they have received. If it is important to the research design that neither the investigators nor the subjects know about developing trends in the data, the fact that such developments will not affect their assignment during the course of the study should be communicated to prospective subjects prior to enrollment. [*See* Guidebook Chapter 4, "Considerations of Research Design."]

Subjects should understand that although they may withdraw from the study at any time, they will not be given any information about which treatment(s) seem to be better or worse until the study is completed. The significance of developing trends in the data has played an important role in placebo trials involving experimental AIDS drugs. When sufficient data showed the drug AZT to be effective in slowing the progress of the disease, the status of subjects receiving the placebos was revealed, and they were offered the drug. Continued provision of placebos once the experimental drug was shown to be effective was considered unethical: IRB's should consider the relevance of developing trends in the data to continued consent.

In double-masked clinical trials, there should be a mechanism for someone other than the investigator to break the code to discover which treatment a particular subject has been given in case the subject experiences a worsening of his or her condition or an adverse affect that requires medical intervention. This procedural safeguard should also be explained to prospective subjects.

Consent as a Continuing Process

Consent is not a single event; rather, it is a process. Since subjects always retain the right to withdraw from a research project, their continuing consent is important. IRB's should be aware that subjects often seem to forget they are involved in research or have difficulty distinguishing research interventions from diagnostic and therapeutic interventions. When a research proposal is first approved, the IRB should determine whether consent should be renegotiated as a formal matter during the course of the research. If renegotiation is required, the frequency and/or events that will trigger this process should be decided upon and made clear to the investigators.

Federal policy also requires that investigators inform subjects of any important new information that might affect their willingness to continue participating in the research [Federal Policy §.116]. For instance, a totally independent study might find an unanticipated adverse

Appendix B (continued)

effect (e.g., birth defects or carcinogenicity) in a drug or substance being used in research. IRBs should determine whether any new findings or reports of adverse effects (in the present study or other studies) should be communicated to subjects. The IRB should also receive copies of any such information conveyed to the subjects.

When the proposed subjects are seriously ill, or for some other reason, might not be able to make decisions about continuing in the research (e.g., children or cognitively impaired individuals), the IRB may suggest that family members be_ closely involved with the research to evaluate its impact on the subject and to request that the subject be withdrawn from the study if conditions warrant.

Points to Consider

1. Do the investigators plan to involve a particularly vulnerable subject population?

2. Do the proposed explanations of the research provide an accurate assessment of its risks and anticipated benefits? Is the possibility (or improbability) of direct benefit to the subjects fairly and clearly described?

3. Is the language and presentation of the information to be conveyed appropriate to the subject population? (Consider the level of complexity and the need for translation into a language other than English.)

4. Are the timing of an setting for the explanation of the research conducive to good decision making? Can anything more be done to enhance the prospective subjects' comprehension of the information and their ability to make a choice?

5. Who will be explaining the research -to potential subjects? Should someone, in addition to, or other than the investigator be present?

6. Should subjects be reeducated and their consent required periodically?

7. Should the IRB monitor incoming data to determine whether new information should be conveyed to participating subjects? How often should this occur? Who is responsible for bringing new information to the attention of the IRB between scheduled reviews?

8. If a waiver of some or all of the consent requirements is requested, does the importance of the research justify such a waiver? Is more than minimal risk involved? Can the research design be modified to eliminate the need for deception or incomplete disclosure? Will subjects be given more information after completing their participation? Would the information to be withheld be something prospective subjects might reasonable want to know in making their decision about participation?

Applicable Laws and Regulations

- Federal Policy for the protection of human subjects.
- Federal Policy §.116 [General requirements for informed consent]
- Federal Policy §. 117 [Documentation of informed consent]
- 21 CFR 50 [FDA: Informed consent]

Appendix B (continued)

- 21 CFR 50.20 [FDA: General requirements for informed consent]
- 21 CFR 50.23 [FDA: Exception from general requirement]
- 21 CFR 50.25 [FDA: Elements of informed consent]
- 21 CFR 50.27 [FDA: Documentation of informed consent]
- 21 CFR 56 [FDA: IRB review and approval]

Local Laws

Federal requirements for informed consent do not necessarily meet all the requirements of local laws. Therefore, IRB's should be aware of any state and local requirements regarding informed consent.

Appendix C

Internet Services

. Net Library http://www.netlibrary.com/
. E-Barry http://corp.ebrary.com/
. History E-Book Project www.historybook.org

Electronic Journal Tracing Services
Searches all of our journal holdings (print and electronic) so you can find out which databases index a particular journal and if it is available full-text.

. Ebsco's A-Z http://atoz.ebsco.com/welcome/defacult.asp
. Serial Solutions http://www./serialsolutions.com/Home.asp

Environmental/Science Database
. Environmental Sciences and Pollution Management (CSA) http://www.csa.com/csa/factsheet/envclust.shtml
. Lexis Nexis Environmental http://www.lexisnexis.com/academic/ environmental/Environment Abstract.asp

Humanities
. MLA Bibliography http://www.ovid.com/site/catalog/DataBase/ 121.jsp?top=2&mid=3& bottom=7&subsection=
10

Psychological Tests
. HAPI http://www.ovid.com/site/catalog/DataBase/866. Jsp?top=2&mind=3&bottom=7&sub section=10
. Fiction Catalog http://www.hwwilson.com/Databases/fictioncat _e.htm
. Children's Catalog http://www.hwwilson.com/Databases/childscat_ e.htm

The Library of Congress World Wide Web Site http://www.loc.gov/

The Library of Congress' web site provides continuously updated information on all aspects of the Library's services and collections. Major components of the Library's resources available via the Internet are described below.

American Memory http://memory.loc.gov/
Select digitzed collections from the National Digital Library Program, including photographs, maps, sound recordings, manuscripts, early motion pictures, and other primary source materials. (Note: very few books are available full-text at this site.) The Learning Page for educators, K-12 audiences, and life-long learners provides activities and lesson plans for using the American Memory collections. The Library also offers a web site for children and families at http://www.americaslibrary.gov./ Library of Congress Online Catalog http://www.loc.gov/catalog/

The web-based Library of Congress Online Catalog has approximately 12 million bibliographic records representing books, serials, computer files, manuscripts, cartographic materials, music, sound recordings, and visual materials. A Z39.50 interface for the catalog also is available.

Appendix C (continued)

THOMAS http://thomas.loc.gov/
This site provides Congressional information including full-text legislation and the Congressional Record back to the 101st Congress, bill summary and status back to the 93rd Congress, committee information, text of select historical documents, and links to other government online information.

Electronic Exhibits http:///www.loc.gov/exhibits/
Online versions of current and former Library of Congress exhibitions including American Treasures of the Library of Congress. Also features information on recent acquisitions of note.

Copyright http://www.loc.gov/copyright/
Information on how to register for Copyright protection, downloadable forms, searching Copyright, and new developments in copyright law.

Critical Values of r for the Pearson Correlation Coefficient

Leedy adopted a list of questions by Beck (1990) that students and colleagues should address before they publish their work. This checklist can assist you to clearly and successfully develop your research proposal.

Checklist: Criteria for Critiquing a Research Report

Step 1. The Problem

    Is the problem clearly and concisely stated?

    Is the problem adequately narrowed down into researchable problem?

    Is the problem significant [enough to warrant a formal research effort]?

    Is the relationship of the identified problem and previous research clearly described?

Step 2. Literature Review

    Is the literature review logically organized?

    Does the review provide a critique of the relevant studies?

    Are gaps in knowledge about the research problem identified?

    Are important relevant references included?

Step 3. Theoretical or Conceptual Framework

    Is the theoretical framework easily linked with the problem (or does it seemed forced)?

    If a conceptual framework is used, are the concepts adequately defined, and are the relationships among the concepts clearly identified?

Step 4. Research Values

    Are the independent and dependent variables operationally defined?

    Are any confounding variables present? If so, are they identified?

Step 5. Hypotheses

    Are the hypotheses clear, testable, and specific?

Appendix D (continued)

Does each hypothesis describe a predicted relationship between two or more variables included in each hypothesis?

Do the hypotheses logically flow from the theoretical or conceptual framework?

Step 6. Sampling

Is the sample size adequate?

Is the sample representative of the defined population?

Is the method for selection of the sample appropriate?

Is any sampling basis in the chosen method acknowledged?

Are the criteria for selecting the sample clearly defined?

Step 7. Research Design

Is the research design adequately described?

Is the design appropriate for the research problem?

Does the research design address issues related to the internal and external validity of the study?

Step 8. Data Collection Method

Are the data collection methods appropriate for the study?

Are the data collection instruments described adequately?

Do the measurement tools have reasonable validity and reliability?

Step 9. Data Analysis

Is the results section clearly and logically organized?

Is the type of analysis appropriate for the level of measurement for each variable?

Are the tables and figures clear and understandable?

Step 10. Interpretation and Discussion of Findings

Does the investigator clearly distinguish between actual findings and interpretations?

Are the interpretations based on the data obtained?

Appendix D (continued)

Are the findings discussed in relation to previous research and to the conceptual/theoretically framework?

Are all generalizations warranted and defended?

Are the limitations of the results discussed?

Are the implications of the results discussed?

Are recommendations for future research identified?

Are the conclusions justified?

References

Beck, C. T. (1990, January-February). The research critique: General for Evaluating a research project. Journal of Gynecology and Neonatal Nursing, 19, 18-22.

Leedy, 2005, p. 298-300).

GLOSSARY

Case studies
: The researcher explores a single entity or phenomenon ("the case") bounded by time and activity (e.g., a program, event, process, institution, or social group) and collects detailed information through a variety of data collection procedures over a sustained period of time.

Ethnographic studies
: The researcher studies an intact cultural group in a natural setting over a specific period of time; a cultural group can be any group of individuals who share a common social experience, location, or other social characteristic of interest.

Experimental studies
: Characterized by random assignment of subjects to experimental conditions and the use of experimental controls.

Phenomenological Studies
: Human experiences are examined through the detailed description of the people being studies – the goal is to understand the "live experience" of the individuals being studied; involves studying a small group of people intensively over a long period of time.

Qualitative Research
: A process of inquiry with the goal of understanding a social or human problem from multiple perspectives; conducted in a natural setting with a goal of building a complex and holistic picture of the phenomenon of interest.

Quantitative Research
: An inquiry into an identified problem, based on testing a theory composed of variables, measured with numbers, and analyzed using

statistical techniques; the goal is to determine whether the predictive generalizations of a theory hold true.

Quasi-Experimental Studies

Share almost all the features of experimental designs except that they involve non-randomized assignment of subjects to experimental conditions.

Random Assignment

All subjects have an equal chance of being Assigned to a given experimental condition; a procedure used to ensure that experimental conditions do not differ significantly from each other.

Survey

Questionnaires or interviews for data collection with the intent of generalizing from a sample population to a larger population of interest.

Bibliography

Agar, M. (1986). Speaking of ethnography. *Qualitative Research Methods Series,* Vol. 2. Beverly Hills, CA: Sage.

Ary, D., Jacobs, L.C., & Asghar, R. (1990). *Introduction to Research in Education.* New York: Holt, Rinehart, and Winston, Inc.

Best, J. W. (1959). *Research in education.* Englewood Cliffs, NJ: Prentice-Hall, Inc.

Biddle, B. J., & Anderson, D. S. (1986). Theory, methods, knowledge, and research on teaching. In M. C. Wittrock (Ed.). *Handbook on research no teaching* (3rd ed.). New York: MacMillan.

Blaisdell, E. A. (1993). *Statistics in practice.* New York: Sanders College Publishing Company.

Bogdan, R. C., & Biklen, S. K. (1992). *Qualitative research for education: An introduction to theory and methods.* Boston: Allyn & Bacon.

Borg, W. R., & Gall, M. D. (1989). *Educational research* (5th ed.). New York: Longman Publishing Company.

Borg, W. R., & Gall, J. P., Gall, G., & Gail, M. D. (1993). *Applying education research,* New York: Longman Publishing Company.

Brase, C. H., & Brase, C. P. (1991). *Understandable Statistics: Concepts and Methods* (4th ed.). MA: D. C. Heath and Company.

Bruning, J. L., & Kintz, B. L. (1987). *Computational Handbook of Statistics* (3rd ed.). Glenview, IL: Scott Foresman.

Bruyn, S. R. (1966). *The human perspective in sociology.* Englewood Cliffs, NJ: Prentice-Hall.

Buttlar, L. J. (1989). Education: *A guide to reference and information sources.* Englewood, CO:\ Libraries Unlimited.

Campbell, D. T., & Stanley, J. C. l(1963). *Experimental and quasi-experimental designs for\research.* Chicago: Rand McNally.

Cary, R. (1988). *A general survey of qualitative research methodology.* ERIC Publication ED 30448.

Charles, C. M. (1988). *Introduction to educational research.* New York: Longman Publishing Company.

Clark, M. (1994). *Phenomenology research methods.* Thousand Oaks, CA: Sage.

Cochran, W. G., & Cox, G. (1957). *Experimental designs.* New York: John Wiley & Sons, Inc.

Cole, A. (1994). *Doing life history and in practice.* Paper prepared for the Annual Meeting of the American Educational Research Association, New Orleans, LA.

Cook, T. D., & Campbell, D. T. (1979). *Quasi-experimentation.* Chicago: Rand McNally.

Cook, T. D. (1995). *Evaluation Lessons Learned.* Plenary keynote address of the International Evaluation Conference. Vancouver, British Columbia.

Cooper, H. M. (1989). *Integrating research: A guide for literature review* (2nd ed.). Newburg Park, CA: Sage Publications.

Cooper, P. W. (1993). *Field relations and the problem of authenticity in researching participants perceptions of teaching and learning in classrooms.* British Educational Research Journal, 19, 4, 323-338.

Creswell, J. W. (1994). *Qualitative and Quantitative Approaches.* Thousand Oaks, CA: Sage Publications.

Creswell, J. W. (1998). *Research Design: Qualitative Inquiry and Research Design: Choosing Among Five Traditions.* Thousand Oaks, CA: Sage Publications.

Dennis, M. L. (1994). *Integrating qualitative and quantitative methods in substance abuse research.* ERIC Ej 500515.

Denzin, N. K. (1978b). *The research act: A theoretical introduction to sociological methods* (2nd ed.). New York: McGraw-Hill.

Denzin, N. K. (1989a). Interpretive Biography. Newburg Park, CA: Sage Publications.

Denzin, N. K., & Lincoln, Y. (1994). *Handbook on qualitative research.* Thousand Oaks, CA: Sage Publications.

Dereshiwsky, M. I., & Packard, R. D. (1992). *When words are worth more than a thousand number: The power of qualitative research procedures in evaluating the impact of educational programs and practices.* Paper presented at the annual meeting of the National Council of States, San Diego, CA: ED 362499.

Devore, J. & Peck, R. (1986). *The Exploration and Analysis of Data.* St. Paul, MN: West Publishing Company.

Douglas, B. G., & Moustakas, C. (1985). *Heuristic Inquiry: The internal search to know. Journal of Humanistic Psychology, 25,* (3).

Dowdy, S., & Wearden, S. (1991). *Statistics for research.* New York: John Wiley and Sons.

Drew, C. J. (1980). *Introduction to Designing and Conducting Research.* St. Louis: The C.V.Mosby

Durkin, T. (1997). *Using computers in strategic qualitative research.* In Miller and Dingwall (Eds.). Content and method in qualitative research. Thousand Oaks, CA: Sage Publications.

Elmore, P. B., & Woehlke, P. L. (1997). Basic statistics. New York: Longman.

Evans, J. D. (1996). *Straight forward statistics.* Pacific Grove, CA: Brooks Cole Publishing Company.

Feagin, J., Orum, A., & Sjoberg, G. (Eds.). (1994). *A case for case study.* Chapel Hills, NC: University of North Carolina Press.

Fetter, D. M. (1987). A rainbow of qualitative approaches and concerns. *Education and Urban Society, 20,* (1), 4-8.

Fielding, N. G. and Lee, R. M. (1991). *Using Computers in Qualitative Research.* Newbury Park, CA: Sage Publishing Company.

Fielding, N. G. and Lee, R. M. (1998). *Computer analysis and qualitative research.* Thousand Oaks, CA: Sage Publications.

Francisco, B. (1992). Doctoral dissertation. *The effects of whole language versus phonics on students with significant autistic-like behaviors in a level 5 program in the Baltimore City Public Schools.* Baltimore, Maryland.

Frank, F. W., & Triechler, P. A. (1989). *Language, gender, and professional writing: Theoretical approaches and guidelines for non-sexiest usage.* New York: Modern Language Association Publications.

Gall, M. D., Borg, R. W., & Gall, M. P. (1996). *Educational research* (6th ed.). White Plains, NY: Longman Publishers.

Geiger, S. N. G. (1986). Women's life histories: Methods and content signs. *Journal of women in culture and society,* 11, 334-351.

Gilgun, J. (1999). Finger nails painted red: A feminist semiotic analysis of a hot text. *Qualitative Inquiry,* 5 (2), 181-206.

Gilquin, J. F. (1992). *Definitions, Methodologies and Methods in Qualitative Family Research.* Qualitative Methods in Family Research. Newbury Park, CA: Sage Publications.

Giorgi, A. (Ed.) (1985). *Phenomenology and psychological research.* Pittsburg, PA: Duquesne University Press.

Glaser, B. G., & Straus, A. L. (1967). *The discovery of ground theory: Strategies for qualitative research.* Hawthorne, NY: Aldine.

Glaser, B. G. (1978). *Theoretical sensitivity: Advances in the methodology of ground theory.* Mill Valley, CA: Sociology Press.

Glaser, B. G. (1992). *Emergence versus Forcing: Basics of Grounded Theory Analysis.* Mill Valley, CA: The Sociology Press.

Glass, G. V. & Hopkins, K. D. (1996). *Statistical methods in education and psychology* (3rd ed.). Boston: Allyn and Bacon.

Glassford, R. G. (1987). Methodological reconsideration: The shifting paradigms. *Quest, 39,* 295 312.

Gravetter, F. J.. & Wallnau, L. B. (1996). *Statistics for the behavioral sciences.* New York: West Publishing Company.

Gronlund, N. E., & Lunn, R. L. (1990). *Measurement and evaluation in teaching* (6th ed.). New York: MacMillan Publishing Company.

Guba, E. G. (1981). Criteria for assessing the trustworthiness of naturalistic inquiries. *Educational Communication and Technology Journal, 29,* 75-91, as cited in Owens (1982). Methodological perspective: Methodological rigor in naturalistic inquiry : Some issues and answers.*Educational Administrative Quarterly, 18* (2), 1-21.

Guilford, J. P. (1965). *Fundamental Statistics in Psychology and Education.* New York: McGraw Hill Book Company.

Hahn, H., & Stout, R. (1994).*The internet complete reference.* Berkeley, CA: Osborne McGraw-Hill.

Harris, M. (1968). *The rise of anthropological theory.* New York: Cromwell.

Harris, M. B. (1995). *Basic statistics for behavioral science research.* Needhamd Height, MA: Allyn & Bacon.

Hathaway, R. S. (1995). Assumptions underlying quantitative and qualitative research: Implications for institutional research. *Research in Higher Education, 36* (5), 535-562.

Hays, W. L. (1994). *Statistics* (5th ed.). New York: Harcourt-Brace College Publishers.

Heise, D. R. (1988). *Computer Analysis of Cultural Structures.* Social Science Computer Review. 6, 183-197.

Henkel, R. E. (1975). Part-whole correlations and the treatment of ordinal and quasi-interval data as interval data. *Pacific Soc. Review,* 18, 3-26.

Hinkle, D. L. Wiersma, W., & Jurs, S. G. (1994). *Applied statistics for the behavioral sciences* (3rd ed.). Boston: Houghton-Mifflin Company.

Hoshman, L. T. (1989). Alternate research paradigms: A review and teaching proposal. *ounseling Psychologist, 17,* (1), 1-79.

Huch, S., W., & Cormier, W. H. (1996). *Reading statistics and research* (2nd ed.). New York: Harper Collins College Publishers.

Jacob, E. (1987). Qualitative research traditions: A review. Review of *Educational Research,* 57, 1-50.

Jacob, E. (1998). Clarifying qualitative research: A focus on traditions. *Education Research,* 17 (1), January-February, 16-24.

Jaeger, R. M. (1984). Sampling in education and the social sciences.

Jensen, R. E. (1985). *Ethical issues in clinical psychology.* Lanham, MD: University Press of America.

Jensen, R. E. (1992). *Standards and ethics in clinical psychology.* Lanham, MD: University Press of America.

Jick, T. D. (1979). Mixing qualitative and quantitative methods: Triangulation in action. *Administrative Science Quarterly, 24,* 602-611.

Kerlinger, F. N. (1979). *Behavioral research.* New York: Holt, Rinehart, & Winston.

Kimmel, A. J. (1996). *Ethical issues in behavioral research.* Cambridge, MA: Blackwell Publishers.

Kirk, J., & Miller, M. L. (1968). *Reliability and validity in qualitative research.* Beverly Hills, CA: Sage.

Kirk, R. E. (1990). *Statistics: An introduction* (3rd ed.). New York: Rinehart & Winston.

Kirk, R. E. (1995). *Experimental design: Procedures for the behavioral sciences* (3rd ed.). Pacific Grove, CA: Brooks/Cole.

Kitao, K. S. (1991). *Principles of quantitative research.* RIEN.ED 333755, pp. 1.22.

Kneller, G. F. (1984). *Movement of thought in modern education.* New York: John Wiley.

Kurtines, M. (1992). *The role of values in psychology and human development.* New York: MacMillan Publishers.

Lecompte, M. D. & Schensal, J. (1999). Designing and conducting ethnographic research. *Ethnographer's Tool Kit,* Vol. 1. Walnut Creek, CA: Altalyira.

Leedy, P. (1996). *Practical research: Planning and design.* New York: MacMillan Publishing Company.

Leedy, P. D., Newby, T., & Ertmer, P. A. (2001). *Practical research: Planning and design* (7th ed.). New York: Prentice Hall.

Lincoln, Y. S., & Guba, E. G. (2000). Paradigmatic controversies, contradictions, and emerging influences. *In Handbook of Qualitative Research* (2nd ed.). pp. 163-188, edited by Norma K. Denzin and Yvonna S. Lincoln. Thousand Oaks, CA: Sage.

Litwin, M. (1995). *How to measure survey reliability and validity.* Thousand Oaks, CA: Sage Publications.

Lodge, P., & Dianne, S. (1988). *The qualitative dimension.* Paper presented at Northern Rocky Mountain Education Research Association. ED301118.

Lofland, J., & Lofland, L. H. (1995). *Analyzing social settings: A guide to qualitative observation and analysis* (3rd ed.). Belmont, CA: Wadsworth Publishing Company.

Marshall, C., & Rossman, G. B. (1989). *Designing qualitative research.* Newbury Park, CA: Sage.

McKay, J. A. (1992). Professional development through action research. *Journal of Staff Development,* 13, (1), 18-21.

McMillan, J. H. (1996). *Educational Research: Fundamentals for the Consumer* (2nd ed.). New York: Harper Collins College Publishers.

McNamara, J. F. (1994). *Survey and experiments in educational research.* Lancaster, PA: Technomic Publishing.

Merriam, J. E., & Makower, J. (1988). *Trend watching: How the media create trends and how to be the first to uncover them.* New York: Tilden Press, American Management Association (AMACOM).

Miles, M. B., & Huberman, A. M. (1984). *Qualitative data analysis.* Beverly Hills, CA: Sage.

Miller, S. I., & Fredericks, M. (1994). Qualitative research methods: Social epistemology and practical inquiry. New York: Peter Long.

Minimum, E. W. et al. (1993)*Statistical Reasoning in Psychology and Education.* New York: John Wiley & Sons.

Minitab, Inc. MINITAB Reference Manual (1991). Release 8, P.C. Version. State College, PA: Minitab Inc.

Morse, J. M., & Field, P. A. (1995). Qualitative research methods for health professional. Thousand Oaks, CA: Sage.

Moustakas, C. (1994). *Phenomenological Research Methods.* Thousand Oaks, CA: Sage Publications.

Moustakas, C. (1996). *Heuristic Research: Design, Methodology, and Applications.* Newbury Park: Sage Publications.

Natanson, M. (1973). *Phenomenology and the social sciences.* Evanston, IL: North Western University Press.

Nunnally, J. C. (1967). *Psychometric theory.* New York: McGraw-Hill.

O'Mery, A. (1983). *Phenomenology: A Method for Nursing Research .* Advances in Nursing Science. 5, 49-63.

Patton, M. Q. (1987). *How to use qualitative methods in evaluation.* Newbury Park, CA: Sage.

Patton, M. Q. (1990). *Qualitative Evaluations and Research Methods.* Newbury Park, CA: Sage.

Patton, M. Q. (2002). *Qualitative research and evaluation methods (3rd ed.).* Newbury Park, CA: Sage.

Pickett, W., & Burrill, D. F. (1994). The use of quantitative evidence in research: A comparative study of two literatures. *Educational Research, 23* (6), 18-21.

Polkinghorne, D. E. (1989). *Phenomenological Research Methods.* In R.S. Valle and S. Halling (Eds.) *Existential Phenomenological Perspectives in Psychology.* New York: Plenum.

Pounder, D. G. (1993). *Rigor in Traditional Quantitative Methods.* Paper presented at the annual meeting of the American Educational Research Association. Atlanta, GA: ED 363975.

Plummer, K. (1983). *Documents of Life: An Introduction to Problems and Literature of a Humanistic Method.* Thousand Oaks, CA: Sage Publications.

Ray, M. A. (1994). *The Richness of Phenomenology: Philosophic, theoretic and methodological concerns.* In J.M. Morse (Ed.) *Critical Issues in Qualitative Research Methods.* Thousand Oaks, CA: Sage Publications.

Reisman, C. K. (1993). *Narrative analysis.* Newsbury Park, CA: Sage Publications.

Robinson, D. N. (1992). *Social discourse and moral judgement.* San Diego, CA: Academic Press.

Runyon, R. P. (1977). *Non-parametric statistics.* Reading, MA: Addison-Wesley Publishing Company.

Ryan, G. W., & Bernard, H. R. (2000). *Data management and analysis methods.* In Denzin and Lincoln (Eds.). Handbook of qualitative research (2nd ed.). Thousand Oaks, CA: Sage Publications.

Schwandt, T. A. (1997a). *Qualitative inquiry: A dictionary of terms.* Thousand Oaks, CA: Sage Publications.

Schwandt, T. A. (2001). *Dictionary of qualitative inquiry* (2nd ed.). Thousand Oaks, CA: Sage Publications.

Shank, G. (1993). *Qualitative research? Quantitative research? What's the problem? Resolving dilemma via a post constructivist approach approach.* Presented at the Association for Educational Communication and Technology Convention. ED 362202.

Shaw, M. E. & Wright, J. M. (1967). *Scales for the measurement of attitudes.* New York: McGraw-Hill.

Slavin, R. E. (1986). Best-evidence synthesis: An alternative to metaanalytic and traditional reviews. *Educational Researcher, 15* (9), 5-11.

Siegel, S. (1956). *Non-Parametric Statistics for the Behavioral Sciences.* New York: McGraw-Hill Book Company.

Smith, L. M. (1994). *Biographical Methods* in N. K. Denzin & Y. S. Lincoln (Eds.) *Handbook on Qualitative Research.* Thousand Oaks, CA: Sage Publications.

Snedecor, G. W., & Cochran, W. G. (1956). *Statistical methods* (6th ed.). Ames, IO: Iowa State University Press.

Spradley, J. P. (1980). Participant observation. New York: Holt, Rinehardt & Wilson.

Stake, r. (1995). The art of case study research. Thousand Oaks, CA: Sage Publications.

Steckler, A. (1992). Toward integrating qualitative and quantitative methods: An introduction. *Health Education Quarterly,* 19, 1-8.

Stern, P. N. (1994). Enroding grounded theory. In J. M. Morse (Ed.) *Critical Issues in Qualitative Methods.* Thousand Oaks, CA: Sage Publication.

Steward, D. and Mickunas, A. (1990). Exploring Phenomenology: A guide to the field and its literature (2nd ed.). Athens, OH: Ohio University Press.

Stoynoff, S. J. (1990). English language proficiency and study strategies as determinants of academic success for international studies in U.S. universities. *Dissertation Abstracts International, 52* (1), 97A.

Strauss, A. and Corbin, J. (1990). *Basics of Qualitative Research.* Newbury Park, CA: Sage Publications.

Stringer, E. T. (1996). *Action Research: A Handbook for Practitioners.*

Swanson, S. (1992). *Mixed-method triangulation: Theory and practice compared.* Paper present at the Annual Meeting of the American Educational Research Association, San Francisco.

Taylor, G. R. (2000). *Integrating quantitative and qualitative methods in research.* Lanham, MD: University Press of America.

Tesch, R. (1990). *Qualitative Research: Analysis, types, and software tools.* Bristol, PA: Falmer.

Thorndike, R. M., Dinnel, D. L. (2001). *Basic stqtistics for the behavioral sciences.* Upper Saddle River, NJ: Prentice Hall, Inc.

Van Manen, M. (1990). *Researching lived experience: Human Science for an Action Pedagogy.* London, Ontario: Althouse.

Weber, R. P. (1990). Basic content analysis. Newbury Park, CA: Sage Publications.

Wolcott, H. F. (1988). Ethnographic research in eduction. In R. M. Jaeger (Ed.), *Complimentary methods for research in education* (pp. 187-210). Washington, DC: American Educational Research Association.

Wolcott, H. F. (1994). *Transforming qualitative data: Descriptions, analysis, and interpretation.* Thousand Oaks, CA: Sage Publications.

Wolf, R. M. (1982). Validity of tests. In H. E. Mitzel (Ed.), *Encyclopedia of Educational Research* (5th ed.), 4, pp. 1991-1998. New York: Free Press.

Yin, R. K. (1989). Case study Research: Design and Method. Newbury Park, CA: Sage Publications.

Contributors

George R. Taylor, Ph.D. Is professor of Special Education and Chair Emeritus, Department of Special Education at Coppin State University, Baltimore, Maryland, and Core Faculty, the Union Institute and University, Cincinnati, Ohio. His knowledge and expertise in education is both locally and nationally renown. He has made significant contributions through research and publications in the fields of Special Education and Research Methods. He has published 22 textbooks and over 20 professional articles. Additionally, Dr. Taylor has directed several federal grants and conducted numerous workshops and seminars for teachers at the local, state, and national levels. Dr. Taylor's education includes an earned Doctorate degree in Special Education and Educational Psychology from the Catholic University of America.

Anthony R. Curtis, Ph.D. Is professor at Tembrook Community College. His academic experiences in the use of computers and electronic data searches cover a span of years from 1967 to present. These experiences include teaching and directing information centers at several academic institutions. Other positions include president and publisher, editor, and manager of a broadcast station. He has made significant contributions to the field through numerous publications.

Theresa L. Harris, Ph.D., is an Associate Professor in the Department of Adult and General Education since 1989. She held the position of Chairperson for one year. Dr. Harris has more than two decades of varied experiences in education, counseling, and criminal justice. She has been assisting State of Maryland departments including departments of education and criminal justice, local education, private sector organizations, and working with individual schools in formulating strategies and practices for implementing successful changes in the academic outcomes of student performance. Dr. Harris' education includes an earned Doctorate degree in Social Psychology/Sociology from Howard University, as well as continuing credits from Johns Hopkins School of Medicine, Social Work.

Dr. Thomas M. James is the Director, Education Technology Center at Coppin State University. His experience encompasses a variety of positions in education and industry. He is an experienced educator having filled positions at Hampton University, and University of Maryland at College Park. In his present position he is responsible for involving the Faculty, Staff, and Students of the School of Education in the effective use of technology. His current assignment focuses on empowering them with strategies and proficiencies to apply 21st century technology skills and dispositions in teacher education training at Coppin State University and in their future careers as educators. To superior to qualitative research or vice versa, rather the method chosen should best address the issues or problem under investigation.

Dr. Marjorie E. Miles is an Assistant Professor at Coppin State University. For 25 years, Dr. Miles was a servant leader in public education. Dr. Miles' career path in the BCPSS has included leadership as a classroom teacher, a Curriculum Specialist, an Assistant Principal, Principal, Director of Compensatory and Funded Programs and Executive Assistant to an Assistant Superintendent. She is also an ABD of a Ph.D. in Organizational Leadership at the University of Maryland. Her collaborative efforts have allowed her to continue to work with public schools in various capacities. Some of Dr. Miles' most recent accomplishments include working with several community organizations and Connection Academy to pilot a virtual program at Matthew Henson Elementary School. Dr. Miles currently serves as secretary on the Board for the Coppin Heights Development Corporation; and on various occasions, Dr. Miles provided services to Rosemont Elementary Middle School and Coppin Academy High School.

During her tenure at Coppin State University she has managed to write and be awarded a competitive research mini grant which supports her research and publishing efforts. She has also received a mini grant from the Abel Foundation to support the Matthew Henson Virtual Summer Learning Pilot Program (2009). More recent, she has been identified at the Coordinator of the Urban Education Corridor Grant funded by Congressional Earmark monies to the University.

As junior faculty, Dr. Miles is researching, writing, and collaborating to creating new programming for the School of Education (M.Ed. in Contemporary Educational Leadership) and is working on several grants with her colleagues (PRAXIS II in collaboration with Arts and Science and the Urban Education Corridor).

Michael Trumbull, Ph.D. is presently chair of the Department of Psychology at Pikes Peak Community College. His training is in qualitative research focusing on qualitative research methods. His limited licensed psychologist and provides psychotherapy to outpatients. He is a nationally certified alcohol and drug abuse counselor and is an Adjunct Faculty Member of the Union Institute where he has conducted numerous research seminars.

Dr. Kriesta L. Watson's background includes over fourteen years of administrative experience with ten years concentrated in the area of institutional research and assessment within both public and private higher educational institutions. Currently, she is the Assistant Professor of Education and Director of Institutional Research and Assessment at Shenandoah University spearheading the re-engineering of the registration, records, research, reporting, and assessment functions. As the former Director of Assessment at Coppin State University (CSU), she strengthened institutional assessment practices. Dr. Watson has presented at numerous local and national conferences. Dr. Watson's research interests include studying retention efforts concentrated on minority achievement and student learning assessment within private and public colleges and universities to examine teaching and learning experiences. Dr. Watson holds a Doctorate of Education from Morgan State University. Additionally, she received her Master of Education from Harvard University in Cambridge, Massachusetts and Bachelor of Arts from the University of Michigan in Ann Arbor.

Dr. Charity Welch is an associate professor in the Graduate School of Education at Coppin State University. With an emphasis on preparing high quality teachers, she directs the university's partnership program with nearby school districts. Dr. Welch has also worked as a national technical assistance provider, assistant to the superintendent, a senior research analyst and in private industry. She serves on two editorial boards and was selected for the United States Department of Education's Standing Panels. She has authored several research, evaluation, and technical documents and presented research findings at national and international conferences. Dr. Welch earned her Ph.D. at the University of Virginia, Curry School of Education.

Dr. Jacqueline H. Williams is an Assistant Professor and Chairperson, Department of Adult and General Education Graduate Program at Coppin State University. She previous as the Associate Director of Admissions at Coppin State University from 1988 – 2005. She received her Ed.D in Higher Education from Morgan State University in 2006, and an M.S. degree in Adult and General Education from Coppin State University in 1993. Dr. Williams have made numerous publications. She also have affiliations with Kappa Delta Phi, International Honor Society in Education, Maryland Higher Education Commission, STAC Committee, Maryland Association of Teacher Education (MAYE), Morgan State University National Alumni Association, Inc., Delta Sigma Theta Sorority, Inc., 100 Black Women, Capital City Chapter.

Breinigsville, PA USA
25 September 2010
245984BV00004B/1/P